THE MENDELSSOHNS ON HONEYMOON

The Mendelssohns on Honeymoon

The 1837 Diary of Felix and
Cécile Mendelssohn Bartholdy
Together with Letters to their Families

EDITED AND TRANSLATED BY
Peter Ward Jones

CLARENDON PRESS · OXFORD
1997

Oxford University Press, Great Clarendon Street, Oxford OX2 6DP

Oxford New York
Athens Auckland Bangkok Bogota Bombay
Buenos Aires Calcutta Cape Town Dar es Salaam Delhi
Florence Hong Kong Istanbul Karachi
Kuala Lumpur Madras Madrid Melbourne
Mexico City Nairobi Paris Singapore
Taipei Tokyo Toronto Warsaw
and associated companies in
Berlin Ibadan

Oxford is a trade mark of Oxford University Press

Published in the United States
by Oxford University Press Inc., New York

British Library Cataloguing in Publication Data
Data available

Library of Congress Cataloging in Publication Data
Mendelssohn–Bartholdy, Felix, 1809–1847.
The Mendelssohns on honeymoon : the 1837 diary of Felix and Cécile
Mendelssohn Bartholdy together with letters to their families /
edited and translated by Peter Ward Jones.
p. cm.
Includes bibliographical references and index.
1. Mendelssohn–Bartholdy, Felix, 1809–1847—Diaries.
2. Mendelssohn–Bartholdy, Cécile, 1817–1853—Diaries. 3. Composers—
Germany—Diaries. 4. Mendelssohn–Bartholdy, Felix, 1809–1847—
Correspondence. 5. Mendelssohn–Bartholdy, Cécile, 1817–1853—
Correspondence. I. Jones, Peter Ward. II. Title.
ML410.M5A3 1997 780'.92'2—dc21 [B] 97–5419
ISBN 0–19–816597–8

1 3 5 7 9 10 8 6 4 2

Typeset by Graphicraft Typesetters Ltd., Hong Kong
Printed in Great Britain
on acid-free paper by
Bookcraft Ltd.
Midsomer Norton, Somerset

Acknowledgements

OVER 300 individuals appear within the pages of the diary and letters and it has proved possible to identify a surprisingly large percentage of them. This and the solving of the many topographical and other problems could not have been achieved without the assistance of a great many individuals and institutions. My greatest debt is owed to Rudolf Elvers. It was he who first prompted me to tackle this edition, and his knowledge of all things Mendelssohnian has been a constant source of enlightenment. Town archives and libraries have taken a great interest in the project, and thanks are due to Jeannine Schools (Stadsarchief, Antwerp), Frau Maria Gaglin (Stadtarchiv, Bad Homburg), Dr A. Fink-Madera (Stadtverwaltung, Bad Kreuznach), Dr Hans-Günter Klein (Staatsbibliothek zu Berlin Preußischer Kulturbesitz), Herr Kossmann and Frau Klaedtke (Stadtarchiv, Bingen), Maria Twist (Central Library, Birmingham), Charlotte A. Kolczynski (Boston Public Library), I. Condette (Bibliothèque municipale, Boulogne-sur-Mer), Peter Meadows (Cambridge University Library), Dr Groten (Historisches Archiv, Cologne), Dr Götz Czymmek (Wallraf-Richartz-Museum, Cologne), Dr Oswald Bill (Hessische Landes- und Hochschulbibliothek, Darmstadt), Dr Elisabeth Scheeben (Stadtarchiv, Düsseldorf), Dr Matthias Wendt (Robert Schumann-Forschungsstelle, Düsseldorf), Dr F. Schadek (Stadtarchiv, Freiburg im Breisgau), Franz Flach (Stadtarchiv, Groß-Gerau), Frau Monika Rademacher (Stadtarchiv, Hanau), Dr Klaus Häfner (Badische Landesbibliothek, Karlsruhe), Dr Christoph Hellmundt and Dr Ralf Wehner (Sächsische Akademie der Wissenschaften zu Leipzig), Herr Schmidt (Stadtarchiv, Koblenz), Christine Banks (British Library, London), Peter Horton (Royal College of Music, London), Joseph Wisdom (St Paul's Cathedral, London), Dr Dobras (Stadtarchiv, Mainz), Dr Pia Müller-Tamm (Städtische Kunsthalle, Mannheim), Friedrich Teutsch (Stadtarchiv, Mannheim), Frau Brigitte Höft (Stadtbücherei, Mannheim), Dr Gisela Scheffler (Staatliche Graphische Sammlung, Munich), P. von Wijngaanden (Archiefdienst, Rotterdam), Rolf Göttert (Stadtarchiv, Rüdesheim), Dr Harthausen (Pfälzische Landesbibliothek, Speyer), Frau Eva Haupt (Museum auf Burg Rheinfels, St Goar), J.-Y. Mariotte (Archives municipales, Strasbourg), Michel Martinez (Bibliothèque nationale et universitaire, Strasbourg), A. Weber (Gemeindearchiv, Trebur), Frau Adelheid Arefi (Hessische Landesbibliothek, Wiesbaden), Dr Fritz Reuter (Stadtarchiv, Worms), and Richard Green (York City Art Gallery).

In Frankfurt a special debt is owed to Dr Ann Kertsing and Dr Werner Wenzel of the Stadt-und

Universitätsbibliothek, Dr Roman Fischer, Tobias Picard, and Frau Silvia Stenger of the Institut für Stadtgeschichte, and Dr Hans-Joachim Ziemke of the Städelsches Kunstinstitut for so patiently dealing with my many questions concerning that city. A chance meeting in Heidelberg with Dipl.-Ing. Johannes Esser at the Heiliggeistkirche led to his investigating the problems of the Heidelberg pages of the diary with a thoroughness which surpassed all expectations. In Lörrach Walter Jung has taken a lively interest in the southernmost part of the Mendelssohns' journey and clarified several points. Other individuals to whom grateful thanks are due are Revd Canon Thaddeus Birchard (London), Frau Renate Hahn (Speyer), Mrs Ruth Halliwell (St Andrews), Renate Hellwig-Unruh (Berlin), Ruthard Hirschner (Ettenheim), Madame Geneviève Honegger (Strasbourg), Prof. Dr Hans Musch (Freiburg), Dr Bärbel Pelker (Mannheim), Herr B. Schätzle (Lenzkirch), Prof. Guenther Roth (New York), Dr Ritchie Robertson (Oxford), and John Wittich (London).

Various people have offered valuable assistance on checking details of the transcription and translation, including Dr Michael Cooper, Dr Bettina Wagner, and Bill and Stephanie Clennell. A particular debt is owed to Dr Thomas Christian Schmidt of Heidelberg, whose bilingual abilities and general knowledge on Mendelssohn have improved the texts substantially. In the Bodleian Library Map Room Betty Fathers and her successor Nick Millea have furnished me with numerous maps and help on topographical matters. I am also most grateful to the Trustees of the Barbara Pym Award for a grant in 1991, which enabled me to make an invaluable visit to Germany in order to retrace the honeymoon journey. For permission to reproduce items from their collections thanks are due to the Bodleian Library, the Staatsbibliothek zu Berlin Preußischer Kulturbesitz, the Music Division of the New York Public Library for the Performing Arts, the Stadtarchiv, Mainz, and the Stadtarchiv and the Historisches Museum, Frankfurt. At Oxford University Press my warmest thanks are due to Bruce Phillips and Helen Foster for their encouragement and efficiency in seeing the work onto the printed page, while a special word of praise is reserved for my copy-editor, Heather Watson, who did a meticulous job and helped sort out the typographical problems caused by a jointly written diary. Finally, I have to praise the forbearance of my colleagues in the Bodleian Music Section and my own family, who have so patiently borne the cluttering up of their respective working and living areas with so many additional books and papers during the past six years.

P.W.J.

Contents

List of Plates

(between pp. 126 and 127)

Abbreviations

THE following are frequently cited abbreviations in the footnotes.

Bodleian Library, MS MDM	Bodleian Library, Oxford, M. Deneke Mendelssohn manuscript collection.
GB	Bodleian Library 'Green Books' of Mendelssohn's incoming correspondence (MSS MDM b. 4 and d. 28–53). Letters are cited by volume and item number within the set.
Klingemann, *Briefwechsel*	Karl Klingemann [jr.] (ed.), *Felix Mendelssohn-Bartholdys Briefwechsel mit Legationsrat Karl Klingemann in London* (Essen, 1909).
NYPL	New York Public Library Mendelssohn family letters.

Introduction

In the summer of 1836, the 27-year-old Felix Mendelssohn Bartholdy, already established as Germany's leading composer of the day, was in need of a wife. His siblings had all preceded him into wedlock. His elder sister Fanny (b. 1805) had been the first when she married the artist Wilhelm Hensel in 1829 after a courtship lasting several years. Then his younger sister Rebecka (b. 1811) married the mathematician Lejeune Dirichlet in 1832, and most recently his brother Paul (b. 1812) had married Albertine Heine in 1835. Felix's sense of isolation was further increased in November of that year by the death of his father, Abraham, an event which prompted him into promising Fanny at Christmas that he would look around for a bride on the Rhine in the course of the summer.[1]

Mendelssohn, possessed of genius, fame, family fortune, and good looks could not be described as other than a highly eligible bachelor. Only his physical stature—he was no more than about 5′6″ in height—might have been seen by some as less than ideal. He had always had an eye for pretty girls, right from a Berlin childhood sweetheart such as Betty Pistor[2] to the daughters of English friends like the Taylor and Horsley families. But these relationships never seemed to have gone beyond flirtatious friendship at most. A deeper attachment was formed with the 16-year-old pianist Delphine von Schauroth, whom he encountered in Munich in 1830 on his way to Italy. It was for Delphine that Mendelssohn wrote his G minor Piano Concerto, and on his return to Munich in 1831 there were suggestions of marriage in the air, but both Mendelssohn and his parents seem to have decided it was premature. Delphine soon married an Englishman, Hill Handley, though there are indications that Mendelssohn regretted having let the opportunity pass. Writing to the Munich clarinettist Heinrich Bärmann in 1834, he asks about Bärmann's reaction to the news of Delphine's marriage, and says his own was 'Donnerwetter' (Damn it).[3] His father once said to Felix's friend Eduard Devrient, commenting on his failure to find a suitable opera libretto, that 'I am afraid that Felix's fastidiousness will prevent his getting a wife as

---

[1] Sebastian Hensel, *The Mendelssohn Family* (London, 1881), ii. 1.

[2] See 'From the Memoirs of Ernst Rudorff', trans. and annotated by Nancy B. Reich, in R. Larry Todd (ed.), *Mendelssohn and his World* (Princeton, 1991), 259–71.

[3] Letter of 7 July 1834, printed in [Ludwig Nohl (ed.)], *Letters of Distinguished Musicians*, trans. Lady Wallace (London, 1867), 422–6.

well as a libretto'.[4] His two years as music director in Düsseldorf from 1833 to 1835 brought a wife no nearer, although there does appear to have been a brief involvement with a widowed lady of the town.[5] The move to Leipzig, to become conductor of the Gewandhaus orchestra in the autumn of 1835, brought him a great sense of musical fulfilment, but no obvious brides-in-waiting.

Mendelssohn's contract obliged him to be in Leipzig only for the six months of the Gewandhaus season, which lasted from October to March, so he was free for the remainder of the year to do as he wished. In the summer of 1836 he had to fulfil the all-important task of conducting the première of *St Paul* at the Lower Rhine Music Festival, which was being held in May in his former haunt of Düsseldorf. He was then planning to travel to his beloved Switzerland and on to Genoa for some sea-bathing. But as early as February a plea had come from the Cäcilienverein in Frankfurt am Main for Mendelssohn to direct the choir for six weeks in the summer, as its regular conductor, Johann Nepomuk Schelble, was suffering from an illness which was ultimately to prove fatal. Schelble (1789–1837) had founded the choir himself in 1818, and a high proportion of its members were drawn from the upper echelons of Frankfurt society. With it Schelble particularly cultivated the music of the old masters, Palestrina, Bach, and Handel—he gave a performance of the *St Matthew Passion* in 1829, the same year as Mendelssohn's famous revival of the work in Berlin—and Mendelssohn had known him and admired his work since his first visit to Frankfurt as a boy in 1822. *St Paul* itself was originally intended for the Cäcilienverein, and only Schelble's failing health had caused its première to be moved to the Lower Rhine Music Festival. In the circumstances Mendelssohn readily agreed to come to Frankfurt to help out his friend, and forwent his other travel plans.

On Sunday 1 May Mendelssohn left Leipzig for Düsseldorf, travelling by way of Frankfurt, where he arrived on 4 May in order to make final arrangements for his future stay.[6] That same day he was also to set eyes for the first time on his future bride. He left Frankfurt on 6 May, continuing on to Düsseldorf, where, after lengthy rehearsals, *St Paul* was given a highly successful première on 22 May, attended by his brother Paul and his wife, and by Fanny, who sang in the chorus. While in Düsseldorf he agreed to accompany his friend Wilhelm Schadow, director of

[4] Eduard Devrient, *My Recollections of Felix Mendelssohn-Bartholdy* (London, 1869), 193 (translation modified).

[5] Eric Werner, *Mendelssohn: A New Image of the Composer and his Age* (New York, 1963), 247.

[6] Mendelssohn's engagement diaries for 1836 and 1837 are preserved (Bodleian Library, MSS MDM f. 4 and 5), and provide many of the details of his movements and activities cited here up to the time of his marriage.

the Kunstakademie, to the Dutch seaside resort of Scheveningen in August to take the sea-bath treatment available there and to give Schadow's son Rudolph help with his Latin. Returning to Frankfurt on 7 June, he first directed the Cäcilienverein on the day after his arrival. Amongst works studied that summer were parts of Handel's *Samson* and Bach's B minor Mass, together with the latter's cantata *Gottes Zeit ist die allerbeste Zeit*. He lived in Schelble's house overlooking the Main, for the Schelbles had gone to their property in Baden for the duration of Mendelssohn's stay.

Living on the Pfarreisen was his good friend, the composer, pianist, and teacher Ferdinand Hiller, of whom Mendelssohn saw a great deal, and who was to be his closest confidant over the following weeks. Through Hiller Mendelssohn met Rossini, who was visiting Frankfurt to attend a Rothschild family wedding, and a dinner was held in his honour at the well-known Mainlust inn. Though not caring for Rossini's music, Mendelssohn was charmed by the man himself. He also often saw his aunt Dorothea von Schlegel. The eldest sister of Abraham, she was for some time rather disapproved of by Mendelssohn's mother, Lea, and her circle for the irregular life she had led by Mendelssohn family standards. First married to the banker Simon Veit, she had left him for the writer Friedrich von Schlegel, while her spiritual pilgrimage had led from her native Judaism through a Protestant period to a mystical brand of Catholicism. She was now living in Frankfurt as a 73-year-old widow at the home of her younger son, Philipp Veit, director of the Städelsches Kunstinstitut. Whatever the rest of the family thought, Felix much enjoyed her company, for she was still in possession of a very lively mind.

Mendelssohn's chief preoccupation, however, soon centred on a certain house by the Fahrtor on the banks of the Main. Here in her parents' house lived Elisabeth Jeanrenaud, the widow of the former French Reformed Church pastor, together with her two attractive daughters. The pastor, Auguste Jeanrenaud (1788–1819), came of Swiss Reformed stock from the Neuchâtel area. Having been consecrated in 1808, he was appointed assistant to Jean Daniel Souchay at the French Church in Frankfurt in 1810, succeeding him when Souchay died the following year. Three years later he married his predecessor's granddaughter, Elisabeth Souchay. Her father, Cornelius Carl Souchay (1768–1838), had become a very prosperous merchant, head of the family firm of C. C. Souchay, and a partner in Schunck, Souchay & Co. His fortune was founded initially mainly on overseas trading in textiles and food, and latterly on merchant banking business. Links with England were particularly strong, with branches in London and Manchester, in which relatives were closely involved. He had married Helene Elisabeth Schunck (1774–1851), a member of another prominent family from nearby Hanau.[7] They lived in a mansion built round a courtyard, close to the Fahrtor (an ancient gatehouse just south of the Römer) with a splendid view of the busy river. Their house itself was known within the family simply as the Fahrtor, although its proper name was 'Zur alten Scheuer'. The site is now occupied by a modern building belonging to the St Paul's Lutheran congregation.

Auguste and Elisabeth Jeanrenaud's first two children, Carl and Julie, were born in Frankfurt, but Auguste's increasingly poor health then forced a temporary move to Lyons, where a second daughter Cécile Sophie Charlotte was born on 10 October 1817. The family returned to Frankfurt in 1818, but Auguste died on 16 April 1819, leaving his wife expecting a fourth child, Augustine, who was born shortly afterwards. Following Auguste's death Elisabeth moved from the apartment the family had occupied above the church to the second floor of her parents' house, which was to remain her home for most of the rest of her life. Jacques Petitpierre, himself related to the Jeanrenauds, has provided a very full background history of the Jeanrenaud/Souchay clan in the book *Le Mariage de Mendelssohn*,[8] which includes many portraits of its members. One splendid portrait unknown to Petitpierre, however, was that of Mme Jeanrenaud and her children, painted by Bernhard Schlösser in 1835. It is now in the Historisches Museum in Frankfurt and is reproduced as Plate 1. Petitpierre's work has to be used with caution, since he is often inaccurate on matters of detail, and it is not always apparent where he is relying on the many documentary sources he had access to, and where on his powers of imagination.

Cornelius Carl Souchay was often away from Frankfurt on business, and the Fahrtor household was very much dominated by old Mme Souchay, of whom everyone seemed to be in awe, and who proved increasingly tiresome with age. Here Elisabeth Jeanrenaud brought up her children, although the youngest, Augustine, did not survive childhood, and died in 1832. By 1836 Carl Jeanrenaud was destined for the legal profession, while Julie and Cécile were 20 and 18 respectively at the time of their first meeting with Mendelssohn. Despite the family's Reformed Protestant religious adherence, the Jeanrenauds certainly led no killjoy existence, but participated fully in the patrician social life of Frankfurt, attending balls and going to the theatre, where the Souchays had a private box.

[7] Useful background on the family and business relationships of the Souchays, Schuncks, Beneckes, and other members of the Frankfurt mercantile circle is to be found in Guenther Roth, 'Weber the would-be Englishman: Anglophilia and Family History', in Hartmut Lehmann and Guenther Roth (edd.), *Weber's Protestant Ethic* (Washington, DC, and Cambridge, 1993), 83–121, and in Hertha Marquardt (ed.), *Henry Crabb Robinson und seine deutschen Freunde* (Göttingen, 1964–7).

[8] (Lausanne, 1937); Eng. trans. as *The Romance of the Mendelssohns* (London, 1947). References are to the English edition.

Mendelssohn's first encounter with the Jeanrenauds was not an accidental one. A cousin of theirs, Fritz Schlemmer, who had trained as a lawyer but was also a very keen amateur musician, spent much time in Leipzig during Mendelssohn's first winter there, whilst he was acting as tutor to one of the Rothschilds. Very much an elegant 'man of the world', he became a good friend of Mendelssohn, and was also known to Lea. In a letter of 2 May 1836 from Cécile to her cousin Cornelie Schunck in Leipzig we read: 'We recently had a letter from Fritz announcing the visit of M. Mendelssohn. I am delighted, but one has heard so much about him, that I rather fear I may have too exalted an idea of his charm. Tell Fritz I shall write to him about Mendelssohn's stay, and of the effect that he made. On second thoughts, don't say anything to him, do you understand?'[9] That the Jeanrenauds wasted no time in becoming acquainted with him can be gathered from Mendelssohn's engagement diary, when on the day of his arrival from Leipzig, 4 May, we read: 'Evening Cäcilienverein . . . Visit to the Souchays'. Confirmation is offered by the letter of Mendelssohn to his friend Karl Klingemann in London a year later when he notes: 'on the 4th [May] I will celebrate with Cécile the anniversary of our meeting'.[10] He visited them again the following day.

Once he had returned to Frankfurt from Düsseldorf Mendelssohn became a frequent visitor to the Fahrtor. Cécile was not particularly musical, although she sang soprano in the Cäcilienverein and had at least rudimentary abilities on the piano.[11] Her real talent lay in drawing—she was still taking lessons from a local artist Anton Rad'l—and it was their common enthusiasm for the pictorial arts that seems to have provided Felix with the perfect pretext for his courtship. Significantly Cécile is shown with a drawing book and pencil in the Schlösser family portrait. They were soon spending time drawing together, and one of Felix's drawing books contains a fine view of the river with the Fahrtor and its neighbouring Rententurm ('Revenue Tower') as seen from the windows of Cécile's house, which was executed on 24 July (see Plate 3).[12] The Fahrtor was replaced in 1840, but the Rententurm is still there today, albeit rebuilt after destruction in 1944. The book itself was evidently a present from Cécile, for on 9 July he notes in his engagement diary: 'Drawing book from Cécile', and the first drawing in it is dated 12 July.

That Felix was soon in love with Cécile became clear from the way he spent his evenings on

[9] MS MDM d. 21, fo. 138.

[10] 30 Apr. 1837, printed in Karl Klingemann [jr.] (ed.), *Felix Mendelssohn-Bartholdys Briefwechsel mit Legationsrat Karl Klingemann in London* (Essen, 1909), 215.

[11] See Cécile's letter to Cornelie Schunck of 26 July 1836 (MS MDM d. 21, fos. 143–4), where she says she would not dare to play to Mendelssohn as Cornelie does.

[12] MS MDM d. 11, fo. 2.

Hiller's sofa constantly talking 'about the loveliness, charm and beauty of the chosen one'.[13] But at least in the beginning he appears to have been rather reticent in her presence. According to Hiller again, Cécile told him later that because of Felix's hesitant manner towards her on his first visits to the Jeanrenaud household, she thought that Felix was interested in her mother (then aged just 40 and still very good looking).[14] Felix in fact was not able to enjoy Cécile's company for the whole of his six-and-a-half-week stay in Frankfurt, for on 16 June she left to spend about two weeks with relatives in Heidelberg. It is interesting to note that in neither of Cécile's two letters to her mother that she wrote while away does she mention Felix, although regards are sent to others, including Fritz Schlemmer, who by then was also back in Frankfurt.[15] Local Frankfurt society, however, was soon beginning to speculate on the relationship. The first indications that Felix gave to his own family that something was stirring came in a letter to his mother of 14 June 1836, when he mentions knowing 'a nice Souchay family (relatives of the Schuncks) with two wonderfully pretty daughters'.[16] In his letter of 13 July to Lea and Fanny it has become 'a very beautiful girl',[17] and on 24 July to Rebecka he confesses 'I am so dreadfully in love, as never before in my life',[18] although he is still uncertain as to how far it is reciprocated, and does not yet mention Cécile by name.

On 26 July, however, it was time to leave Frankfurt for the Dutch seaside, and Schadow himself came down to Frankfurt to join him before they set off. Two days earlier a grateful Cäcilienverein had given him a parting gift of a travelling dressing-case inscribed prophetically 'FMB und Caecilia'.[19] Travelling by boat from Mainz, Mendelssohn and Schadow stopped off at Horchheim near Koblenz to visit Felix's banker uncle, Joseph Mendelssohn, who had an estate with a vineyard there. They continued on to Cologne and Düsseldorf, before starting the final steamer journey to Holland on 31 July with the additional company of Schadow's son and another artist friend of Mendelssohn, Johann Wilhelm Schirmer, who was heading for Rotterdam. Accommodation at Scheveningen itself proved impossible to find, so they had to live at The Hague and commute daily for their sea-bath treatment, of which a minimum of twenty-one sessions was decreed efficacious. Schadow failed to last the course and departed on 15 August, leaving Felix alone, but the latter completed the full twenty-one treatments before setting out on the return journey to Frankfurt on 22 August. Apart from giving Rudolph Schadow the promised Latin instruction, Felix passed his time in sketching and writing letters. Doubtless he wrote to

---

[13] Ferdinand Hiller, *Mendelssohn: Letters and Recollections* (London, 1874), 60 (translation modified).
[14] Ibid. 60.   [15] MS MDM d. 18, fos. 49–52, letters of 16/17 and 23 June 1836.   [16] NYPL, No. 270.
[17] NYPL, No. 269.   [18] NYPL, No. 271.   [19] It is now in the Mendelssohn-Archiv, Staatsbibliothek zu Berlin.

Cécile—letters that are not extant—though he also wrote several letters to Elisabeth Jeanrenaud, which are so full of compliments that in other circumstances it might well have been thought that it was the mother who was the object of his attentions.[20] In addition he wrote to his own family, who had been eagerly speculating on his amorous involvement. Rebecka indeed had already written to him talking about his 'fiancée'.[21] Felix wrote back on 6 August saying this was premature, but in response to Rebecka's questioning he at last revealed some information about her:

And now I will answer your letter point by point. What does she look like? Very nice indeed. Speaks? German and a good deal of French, for she is the daughter of the French pastor Jeanrenaud (a niece of Mme Schunck and many other acquaintances) and has Cécile as forename. Walks? Like a somewhat spoilt child. Is she musical? No, not in the least. That is the funniest thing of all. But she can draw. But I don't take that into consideration.[22]

In her letter of 29 July[23] Lea had already virtually given her blessing on whatever decision Felix might make, for which Felix thanks her on 9 August, while again stressing that all was as yet undecided. Cécile's presence, however, 'had afforded me very happy days in Frankfurt, just at a time when I had great need but little expectation of them'. He was most concerned that none of these thoughts should reach their Frankfurt acquaintances, and that neither Rebecka nor Paul should go there in the meantime, as they were considering doing.[24] Cécile herself, if she was hopeful of developments, appears to have kept her thoughts to herself. In a letter to Cornelie Schunck of 26 July, just after Felix's departure, the most she would admit to was that 'We have enjoyed each other's company very much when drawing the view from our window'.[25] One recent biographer, Wilfrid Blunt, developing a hint in Petitpierre, implies that later on in this letter there is mention of a bet between Cécile and her mother concerning Cécile's prospects of gaining Felix. Proper reading of the letter, however, makes it apparent that the bet was between Felix and Cécile as to whether or not he would have a boring time in Holland.[26]

Some of Mendelssohn's biographers have viewed Felix's trip to Holland as having been undertaken chiefly to test out his true feelings about Cécile, and Blunt consequently deemed it symptomatic of a rather conventional bourgeois attitude, rather than the action of a man passionately in love. But, as we have seen, the Dutch holiday with Schadow was planned back at the time of

---

[20] Letters of 13 and 20 Aug., MS MDM d. 18, fos. 6–9. Felix's original drafts of these letters are also in the same volume (fos. 1–4).

[21] Letter of 28 July 1836. Bodleian Library 'Green Books' of Mendelssohn's incoming correspondence (MSS MDM b. 4, d. 28–53), GB V 110.

[22] NYPL, No. 273.   [23] GB V 111.   [24] NYPL, No. 274.   [25] MS MDM d. 21, fos. 143–4.

[26] Wilfrid Blunt, *On Wings of Song* (London, 1974), 188; Petitpierre, *Romance of the Mendelssohns*, 130–1.

the *St Paul* première, and Felix would have regarded it as a promise that had to be kept. That he went unwillingly we know from the same letter of Cécile to Cornelie Schunck, and that he became bored there and longed to be back in Frankfurt is evident from letters to Ferdinand David and Hiller,[27] but apart from any consideration of absence making the heart grow fonder, the sea air was a useful and necessary restorative for Felix, as he admitted to Fanny the following year, when he was encouraging her to take a similar course of action.[28]

From 26 to 31 August Felix stopped off at Horchheim again on his way south, and while there had to have leeches applied to a foot he had injured at the baths, and which was still giving trouble. Once back in Frankfurt a decision was not long in coming. On 9 September a family expedition was made to the tiny spa of Krontal (now part of Kronberg) in the Taunus hills north of Frankfurt, and there Felix and Cécile became engaged. The news was communicated by Felix to Lea the same day, but at the Jeanrenauds' request it was decided to keep the engagement a secret from the world at large for the time being. Etiquette in their social circle demanded that a newly engaged couple pay courtesy calls on all their acquaintances. With Felix having to head back to Leipzig, it was decided to postpone a public announcement until nearer Christmas, when Felix planned to be back in Frankfurt, and the social obligations could be fulfilled.[29] Inevitably, however, the engagement became common knowledge within a very short time.

What can be added to the description of his future bride that Felix offered to Rebecka? First, there can be no doubt of her physical beauty. Elise Polko, whose reminiscences of Mendelssohn often carry hero-worship to a point of absurdity, seems fairly accurate in her depiction of Cécile: 'Her figure was slight, of middle height, and rather drooping, like a flower heavy with dew, her luxuriant golden-brown hair fell in rich curls on her shoulders, her complexion was of transparent delicacy, her smile charming, and she had the most bewitching deep blue eyes I ever beheld, with dark eyelashes and eyebrows'.[30] This is confirmed by her portraits, especially the best-known one, painted by Eduard Magnus in 1845. Her manner was always quiet and reserved, perhaps too much so, and this could give strangers an impression of coldness—according to Polko, Leipzigers referred to her as 'the fair Mimosa'. But although she had little to say in company, she was otherwise a skilled social hostess with a love of fashionable clothes, which, however, never

---

[27] Letter to David of 11 Aug. 1836, printed in part in Julius Eckardt, *Ferdinand David und die Familie Mendelssohn* (Leipzig, 1888), 82–4, and in full in *Felix Mendelssohn Bartholdy, Briefe aus Leipziger Archiven*, ed. Hans-Joachim Rothe and Reinhard Szeskus (Leipzig, 1972), 131–3; letter to Hiller of 7 Aug. 1836 in Hiller, *Mendelssohn: Letters and Recollections*, 62.

[28] Letter of 24 June 1837 (p. 169).   [29] Letter of Felix to Lea, 18 Sept. 1836, NYPL, No. 280.

[30] Elise Polko, *Erinnerungen an Felix Mendelssohn-Bartholdy* (Leipzig, 1868), 60; Eng. trans., *Reminiscences of Felix Mendelssohn-Bartholdy*, trans. Lady Wallace (London, 1869), 60.

led her into putting on airs. She freely acknowledged that her intellectual skills were no match for those of her husband, and was happy to profess the conventional opinions and attitudes typical of girls of her social class. She may have been not at all musical by Felix's standards, but he was later to praise the soundness of her musical judgement. To classify her as 'rather exhaustingly pious' as Wilfrid Blunt did,[31] is hardly justified by the evidence. Although she was certainly a regular worshipper, there is no hint of excessive piety in her diary or letters. She was to prove excellent at domestic arrangements, and for the moody, almost hyperactive Felix, she was a born homemaker and ideal companion. Accusations by Eric Werner and others that she encouraged the more bourgeois elements in Mendelssohn's music, and could therefore be held responsible for perceived weaknesses in his compositional output after his marriage, do not bear close examination, as Marian Wilson has recently pointed out.[32] After Felix's death, her correspondence reveals an astute mind when it came to dealing with matters of Felix's musical estate.

Attention has been drawn by Werner and others to the similarities between the Mendelssohn and Souchay/Jeanrenaud families regarding their essentially clannish nature, stemming in part from the distinctness of their respective Jewish and Huguenot roots. At least on a subconscious level Felix seems to have sought out a bride from a family which brought back memories of the security of his own home background. As Felix expressed it in a letter of 13 September 1836 to Rebecka just after his engagement: 'By the way, when dusk is approaching I sit myself down next to two sisters on the sofa here in front of me, and we talk about all the good and bad times of our past and future life, and are glad that we enjoy doing so, and I sit in the middle between the two, and tell them that it is now the second time that I am able to sit chatting thus between two sisters . . .'.[33]

On 19 September Felix set off back to Leipzig to prepare for the new Gewandhaus season, with the marriage probably already arranged for the end of the following March, once his commitments in Leipzig were over. Petitpierre, incidentally, is wrong in suggesting that Cécile also went to visit her aunt there that autumn.[34] Despite the lack of an official announcement, news of the engagement was soon circulating in Leipzig as well as Frankfurt. At the final concert before Christmas on 12 December the programme included the finale from *Fidelio* with the words 'wer ein holdes Weib errungen' ('he who has gained a lovely wife') and at the end of the concert Felix improvised

[31] Blunt, *On Wings of Song*, 188.
[32] Marian Wilson, 'Mendelssohn's Wife: Love, Art and Romantic Biography', *Nineteenth-Century Studies*, 6 (1992), 1–18.
[33] NYPL, No. 278. He also wrote in a very similar vein to Lea and Fanny on 18 Sept. (NYPL, No. 280).
[34] Petitpierre, *Romance of the Mendelssohns*, 137.

on that theme much to the delight of the Leipzigers.[35] The next day he set off for Frankfurt, arriving on the 15th. Thereupon the postponed round of visits to acquaintances began—no fewer than 170 were made in the three days of 20–2 December.[36] As a Christmas present for his fiancée Felix had prepared something very special—an album containing musical and literary autographs, including amongst others short compositions of Bach, Haydn, Mozart, and Beethoven, a Goethe drawing and poem, and songs of Fanny which she had copied out at Felix's request and which her husband had then decorated.[37] Rebecka provided a special protective cover, which unfortunately no longer exists. Contributions of family, friends, and fellow musicians continued to be added to it over the years. Presents to Felix included a portrait of Cécile by Joseph Binder, an artist from Vienna then teaching at the Städelsches Kunstinstitut; Felix found it a very poor likeness.

Felix left Frankfurt again on 28 December, returning to Leipzig on the 30th, but this time expecting Cécile and her mother to pay a visit there shortly. After much uncertainty they finally arrived on 30 Janaury, Felix having gone to meet them in Weimar. Apart from seeing Felix and her relatives, the Schuncks, part of Elisabeth Jeanrenaud's intention seems to have been to investigate a possible home for the couple, but in the event this was left unresolved. Lea Mendelssohn had been suggesting that she should herself pay a visit to Leipzig while the Jeanrenauds were there. Felix was at first very much against the idea, partly because of the strain of the journey on the ageing Lea in the harsh winter conditions—she was never a keen traveller—and partly out of apprehension that a meeting of the two families when both were on unfamiliar territory might not be for the best. He proposed it should wait until they could make a summer journey to Berlin as a married couple, when there could be a grand family reunion.[38] Lea remained keen, however, and so in his next letter Felix promised to suggest to the Jeanrenauds that they travel to Berlin for a couple of days.[39] Elisabeth Jeanrenaud apparently took some persuading, but eventually agreed, only for her to go down with influenza on 17 February, the evening before they were due to set out.[40] On eventually recovering, Mme Jeanrenaud was anxious to return with

[35] Letter of Felix to Rebecka Dirichlet, 13 Dec. 1836, NYPL, No. 303. Max Müller's memoirs wrongly associate this improvisation with a performance of Beethoven's Ninth Symphony (where the same words occur), but this did not take place that season until 13 Mar. 1837 (see 'From the memoirs of F. Max Müller', in R. Larry Todd (ed.), *Mendelssohn and his World*, 256).

[36] Letter of Felix to Karl Klingemann, 19 Jan. 1837 (Klingemann, *Briefwechsel*, 210), and engagement diary.

[37] MS MDM c. 21. The Bach manuscript (4 chorale preludes from the *Orgelbüchlein*) has in recent years been shown not to be autograph. Fanny's songs were subsequently moved to a new album given by Felix to Cécile at Christmas 1844 (MS MDM b. 4).

[38] Letter to Lea, 14 Jan. 1837, NYPL, No. 307.   [39] Letter to Lea, 28 Jan. 1837, NYPL, No. 308.

[40] Werner, *Mendelssohn: A New Image*, 304, is wrong in suggesting that Elisabeth Jeanrenaud feigned illness three times to avoid the journey; illness is only mentioned once in the letters, and it was perfectly genuine.

Cécile to Frankfurt, and on 4 March the packing was done, only for her to change her mind and decide to stay, when she heard that Lea was planning to come to Leipzig after all to hear Felix conduct *St Paul* on 16 March. The opportunity to meet Felix's mother proved too strong a temptation for Elisabeth Jeanrenaud, despite her own mother wanting her back in Frankfurt. In contrast to his earlier reluctance for a meeting in Leipzig, Felix on 4 March wrote to Lea urging her to come as soon as possible in case Mme Jeanrenaud should change her mind yet again.[41] Lea duly arrived on 8 March, and so the two mothers met. We do not know what their mutual initial impressions were, and they were only to encounter each other in person on two further occasions, in Leipzig in 1839 and Berlin in 1841, but they maintained a correspondence.

After the successful performance of *St Paul* Lea left for Berlin the following day, while Felix, Cécile, and her mother left together on 19 March, arriving in Frankfurt two days later, just one week before the wedding was due to take place. It was indeed a strange turn of events; having been initially rather uncertain as to whether they would make the journey at all, the Jeanrenauds ended up spending over six weeks in Leipzig, returning with the wedding imminent. The ceremony was set for Tuesday 28 March, two days after Easter that year. Felix had last-minute problems with his papers, despite having obtained what he thought were the necessary documents from Berlin through Lea some weeks previously. His lawyer and friend in Leipzig, Konrad Schleinitz, was finally able to send the required missing declaration in time, and the wedding took place in the French Reformed Church, conducted by Paul Appia, Auguste Jeanrenaud's successor as pastor. The official entry in the city's marriage register is reproduced as Plate 4. The church was in what is now the Goetheplatz, but no longer exists, having been destroyed in the 1944 air raids on the town. Petitpierre reproduces photographs of both its exterior and interior, and also reprints part of the address which Appia gave, which was based on Psalm 92.[42] Although Cécile's relatives and Frankfurt high society were naturally there in force, the only person from Felix's family present was his old aunt, Dorothea von Schlegel. The absence of his mother and siblings has led biographers to much misleading conjecture. Did they disapprove of the alliance? Was Felix deliberately trying to keep them at a distance until it was all settled? The truth is more mundane and practical. Lea, in her 60th year, was in indifferent health as well as being a poor traveller. The previous year Felix had had to dissuade her from undertaking the journey to Düsseldorf to hear the première of *St Paul*. A wintry journey from Berlin to Frankfurt

---

[41] NYPL, No. 315.

[42] Petitpierre, *Romance of the Mendelssohns*, 145–6. A manuscript copy of the whole address is to be found in the Bodleian Library, MS MDM c. 29, fos. 73–4.

would have been considered quite impossible for her. As for his sisters, both Fanny and Rebecka were at that time pregnant, which naturally precluded their travelling so far. Fanny in fact was to suffer a miscarriage just about the time of the wedding.[43] In a letter to Cécile of 23 December 1836 she had foreseen that she would not get to Frankfurt, when she referred in jest to the possibility of them marrying in Leipzig: 'Certain reasons, which modesty prevents my mentioning, make me think this a very good plan'.[44] His brother Paul had already explained in a letter to Cécile as far back as 11 November 1836 that business commitments would oblige him and Albertine to be in Hamburg at the time of the marriage, and that regretfully 'everyone must put his career first'.[45] He had been in the family bank since 1833, and was involved at this time in taking over a Hamburg banking house, which in 1837 became the firm of 'Paul Mendelssohn Bartholdy'.

Accounts of the wedding are surprisingly sparse. Felix himself did not bother to describe the event in his next letter to Berlin, since he was sure that Elisabeth Jeanrenaud or Dorothea von Schlegel would have already written to them about it, but unfortunately no such letters have survived. We know that the wedding breakfast was held at the grandparents' Fahrtor house, and that there a group of ladies under Hiller's direction sang a wedding song composed specially by Hiller himself to greet the couple on their arrival.[46] Petitpierre does offer some further details: magnificent floral decorations in the church, a work of Felix's played on the organ, the carriages carrying the elegant guests to and from the church, chains being put across the road by the church to keep the noisy crowd at a distance, and a long list of guests' family names. But his source for this information remains a mystery. It may possibly be based on a 'diary' of Eduard Souchay, Cécile's uncle and a Frankfurt senator, from which Petitpierre quotes elsewhere in his book.[47]

At half past five the same evening the couple left Frankfurt for Mainz on the first stage of their honeymoon in a new blue and brown carriage which Felix had purchased, arriving there at

---

[43] See letter of Felix and Cécile to Elisabeth Jeanrenaud, 15 Apr. 1837 (p. 141).

[44] Hensel, *The Mendelssohn Family*, ii. 27.   [45] MS MDM d. 21, fo. 68.

[46] Hiller, *Mendelssohn: Letters and Recollections*, 91. The singers were not, as is often said, part of the Cäcilienverein, which Hiller was indeed then conducting, but were 'the ladies belonging to a select small choral society which I had conducted every week during the winter at the E.'s house'.

[47] This diary is not to be found amongst the Eduard Souchay *Nachlaß* in the Stadtarchiv, Frankfurt, and is not identical with a substantial manuscript autobiography owned by his descendants, photocopies of which are held by the Stadtarchiv, and in which Mendelssohn curiously is not mentioned at all. A non-autograph copy of Souchay's recollections of Felix and Cécile, however, is to be found in Bodleian Library, MS MDM c. 29, fos. 65–9, which tallies with Petitpierre's quotations; it contains no description of the wedding day.

nine. Felix had reserved the Mainz accommodation, at the Rheinischer Hof, during the previous week, but for the rest of their honeymoon they drove from place to place without advance planning. Their general intention was to head south up the Rhine to Freiburg im Breisgau and possibly into Switzerland, and then to return to Frankfurt by way of Heidelberg, but their progress was to be determined by the weather. Spring was late in coming that year, and the couple had to endure much rain and even snow, although they also enjoyed fine days, and succeeded in travelling by way of Worms and Speyer to Strasbourg, and then on to Freiburg, where they spent three weeks before heading north again via Rastatt to Heidelberg. Here they spent six days in the company of Cécile's relatives, and then returned to Frankfurt and the Fahrtor house on 13 May.

The Mendelssohn collection in the Bodleian Library, Oxford, has a wealth of material relating to the Mendelssohns' personal life—letters, diaries, drawing books, account books, honorary diplomas, hair, even Felix's medical prescriptions—the couple and their descendants rarely threw anything significant away. It also includes much informative correspondence from Cécile's side of the family. Amongst the most attractive items in the whole collection is the volume commonly referred to as the 'Honeymoon Diary', although it covers a longer period than the honeymoon proper.[48] Measuring 22×14 cm. it is bound modestly in Mendelssohn's favourite style of green paper-covered boards. Its 160 pages provide the only substantial record of the couple's daily life together, and one all the more valuable since all Felix's letters to Cécile were burnt on her death at her request—only one escaped, and that too is preserved in the Bodleian Library.[49] Petitpierre reproduces a number of the diary's illustrations, but it is clear that he had only a limited opportunity to look at the text, as his summary of it is highly inaccurate, especially as regards the later parts of their journey.

The diary's entries start the day after the wedding and continue for the first six months of their marriage. The volume itself, however, was not actually bought until over two weeks later, when they were in Freiburg. On 16 April the diary itself records: 'Walk to Welz's shop to order this book'. The diary is first mentioned in correspondence when Felix wrote to Elisabeth Jeanrenaud on 27 April. So the details of their journey southward were written up during some of the rainy days they had to endure in Freiburg. The diary's text while the couple are together is written largely in Cécile's own very untidy and idiosyncratic hand, with occasional interjections by

<hr />

[48] MS MDM e. 6.
[49] MS MDM c. 42, fos. 131–2. Cécile's letters to Felix are fortunately still largely preserved, since Felix had most of them bound with his other incoming correspondence in the 'Green Books'.

Felix. The three dozen or so pen-and-ink drawings with which the text is illustrated appear to be mostly the work of Felix, although a few are certainly Cécile's, and sometimes they worked on them jointly. As the diary text itself is full of privately shared jokes, not all of which are now comprehensible to outsiders, so too the drawings often contain elements of fantasy or are a humorous commentary on the text. They are not always intended to be accurate topographical depictions of the places they visited.

The diary contains many references to one or other of the newly-weds spending time drawing. Fourteen of Felix's drawing books are known to exist,[50] but unfortunately there is no extant book from 1837, though a few individual sketches survive, which appear to have been taken from such a book.[51] It is possible that the missing book or books are still in existence somewhere, and may yet emerge. Although some of the drawings were entered directly into the diary, most of those of a topographical nature would certainly have been based on pencil sketches done *in situ*.

Once the honeymoon proper was over, the couple settled down in the Fahrtor house in Frankfurt to spend some time with Cécile's family as Mme Jeanrenaud had requested. During the honeymoon Elisabeth Jeanrenaud had shown all the signs of being an archetypal specimen of mother-in-law. She was clearly 'highly strung' by nature, and apprehensive at handing over her younger daughter into the clutches of a man, even if he were Germany's most eminent musician. One incident illustrates this particularly well. In their Freiburg letter of 15 April to Cécile's mother (p. 142) the couple mention having been for a long walk to the Loretto Chapel. Unfortunately Mme Jeanrenaud had received word from an acquaintance in Strasbourg that Cécile had been unwell during their stay there. Clearly alarmed by this and by the exertion implied in their Freiburg letter, she sent a letter to Cécile, accusing the pair of irresponsibility, of not loving her, and suggesting that Felix did not know how to take good care of her daughter. This `letter is not extant, but its contents are obvious from the two conciliatory letters that Felix and Cécile hastened to send her in return (pp. 142–6), assuring her that Cécile was quite well, that the walk was not at all strenuous, and that they both loved her dearly! Felix was to prove a superb diplomat in dealing with Mme Jeanrenaud, and also, as we glean from the diary entry of 1 June, with the formidable Mme Souchay.

---

[50] 11 in the Bodleian Library, 2 in the Staatsbibliothek zu Berlin, and 1 in Yale University Library.

[51] A drawing book of Cécile's, which she had been using since about 1836, is in the Bodleian Library (MS MDM c. 6). In it were kept loose 6 pencil drawings by Felix and Cécile done during the honeymoon, and evidently taken from a smaller size sketchbook. They are now secured in place. How far Cécile actually used her own book during the honeymoon is unclear. There are two incomplete sketches of Heidelberg, which may belong to the honeymoon period. On the other hand, immediately following these are sketches of Anweiler and Trifels, which the couple certainly did not visit in 1837.

As early as January Mendelssohn had received an invitation to go to England to conduct *St Paul* at the Birmingham Musical Festival in September, an invitation he was keen to take up. The circumstances of his wedding led him to delay a firm decision until April, when he accepted. He naturally intended to take Cécile with him, and even started to give her English lessons in preparation. Four pages of the exercises he devised have been preserved, demonstrating the formal manner of his tuition[52] (see Plate 5). But not long after their arrival back in Frankfurt it emerged that Cécile was pregnant,[53] and on the firm advice of the family doctor, not to mention her mother's insistence, it was reluctantly agreed that she would not be able to travel to England, particularly in view of the rapid return journey that would be necessary in order that Felix could be back in Leipzig for the start of the Gewandhaus season. The combination of the stay in Frankfurt to please Mme Jeanrenaud and the commitment to Birmingham meant that a promised visit to Berlin that summer could no longer be fitted in. This was to prove a cause of some annoyance to Felix's sisters in particular, and the long delay before they had an opportunity to become acquainted with Cécile made for an uneasy start to their relationship.

The couple spent seven weeks in Frankfurt, which included a few excursions into the neighbourhood, and during this time Felix was able to make progress on the D minor Piano Concerto he intended to play in Birmingham. Then, together with Cécile's mother and her sister Julie, they set out for a summer holiday on 4 July. This journey took them first to Bingen for a month, then northwards down the Rhine to Koblenz, where they visited, but did not stay with, Felix's uncle and aunt at Horchheim, and on to Bonn, Cologne, and Düsseldorf. It was here, after a few days in the company of Felix's old acquaintances, that the time for separation came on 24 August. Felix left on the steamer for a journey that would take him to London, while Cécile and her family set off back to Frankfurt to await his return. Before they parted the couple had clearly agreed to keep the diary going, for Cécile continued to write entries at the top of each page, leaving room below for Felix to add in an account of his own activities on the corresponding days at a later date. In fact it was to be two years before he actually did so,[54] relying on notes he had made in a pocket diary he took with him,[55] his prodigious memory, and perhaps also the letters he had sent Cécile from England.

Felix's account of his activities in England constitutes some of the most interesting pages of

---

[52] MS MDM c. 29, fos. 1–4.   [53] Felix gave the news to his mother in the letter of 8 June 1837 (see p. 164).
[54] In a letter to Karl Klingemann of 1 Aug. 1839 Mendelssohn describes the writing up of the diary (Klingemann, *Briefwechsel*, 239).
[55] MS MDM g. 4.

the diary from the musical point of view. He records his various sessions of organ-playing in London, including the well-known incident in St Paul's Cathedral when the organ-blower went off, leaving him stranded in the middle of Bach's A minor Fugue. There is also the poignant account of the sudden illness and death of his friend Friedrich Rosen, Professor of Oriental Languages at London University. Mendelssohn's impressions of the Birmingham Musical Festival are also highly revealing. The festival had been started in 1786, organized by and in support of the General Hospital. It became a triennial event producing huge profits for its charitable purposes, and entered its most important era with the opening of the new Town Hall in 1834 with its enormous Hill organ. The hall clearly delighted Mendelssohn, as did the instrument, but certain aspects of the festival he viewed less favourably. He was horrified to discover that the whole of the festival's four days of music had to manage with a single day's general rehearsal, so that much of the programme was actually performed without any rehearsal—a consequence of so many of the singers and players having to come from London and other towns. Until he put his foot down it looked as if even his new piano concerto would have to be given without any rehearsal. He was not alone in considering this a highly unsatisfactory state of affairs. The *Morning Chronicle*'s critic on Wednesday 20 September devoted much space to this problem, which was not of course confined to Birmingham, but afflicted all the provincial festivals. Another cause for dissatisfaction was the Committee's decision to shorten *St Paul* by omitting a few numbers towards the end, just so that some miscellaneous items could be included after it. One feature of the performances of *St Paul*, both in Birmingham, and in London the previous week (which Mendelssohn had attended), strikes us now as very strange in an oratorio. Not only were individual numbers applauded, they were even encored. But despite his reservations about its organization, Mendelssohn returned for the 1840 festival, when he conducted the first English performance of the *Lobgesang* (Hymn of Praise), and again in 1846, when he conducted the première of *Elijah*.

On this occasion, Mendelssohn, although gratified by his customary enthusiastic reception from English audiences, constantly missed Cécile, as we know not only from the diary—which being written up so much later, and for Cécile's eyes, could be considered a slanted record—but also from his letter to Lea on 4 October shortly after his return to Leipzig. Cécile for her part spent the time of separation pining for Felix, visiting friends and preparing to leave Frankfurt. As soon as he had played the organ for the last time at the start of the Friday morning concert in Birmingham, Felix set off on the return journey. Travelling by coach to London and then on overnight to Dover, he had the misfortune to suffer a stormy crossing which landed him in Boulogne rather than Calais. After enduring rattling coaches across to the Rhine at Cologne, he boarded a steamer southwards, only to be halted by fog near Koblenz, and had to take another coach to Mainz, and finally to Frankfurt. The diary concludes on an appropriate romantic note at half past two in the afternoon of 27 September at the moment of the Mendelssohns' reunion. No attempt was made to continue it further, despite the presence of many blank pages in the volume.

The couple had to leave Frankfurt the very next day, and arrived in Leipzig on Sunday 1 October, just in time for Felix to conduct the first Gewandhaus concert that same evening. Finding suitable accommodation had not proved easy, as there was a distinct shortage in Leipzig at that time. The problem being unresolved before their marriage, Felix had left it to his friend Ferdinand David, leader of the orchestra, and his new aunt Julie Schunck to fix something up for them.[56] After at least one further disappointment, an apartment in a new block still under construction was finally secured at the beginning of July.[57] Known as Lurgensteins Garten, it overlooked the Thomaskirche and Thomasschule near the eastern town gates. But it was not ready for occupation until the beginning of December,[58] so Frau Schunck had found them temporary accommodation in a flat below their own, and next door to their new one.[59] The Mendelssohns thus settled down in Leipzig, with Cécile expecting their first child, Carl Wolfgang Paul, who was born on 7 February 1838. Fanny finally got to see her new sister-in-law in October 1837 when the Hensels paid a fortnight's visit to Leipzig, and she afterwards communicated her approval to Klingemann:

She is amiable, childlike, fresh, bright, and even-tempered, and I consider Felix most fortunate; for though inexpressibly fond of him, she does not spoil him, but when he is capricious treats him with an equanimity which will in course of time most likely cure his fits of irritability altogether. Her presence produces the effect of a fresh breeze, so light and bright and natural is she.[60]

Felix's brother, Paul, and his wife came to Carl's baptism in Leipzig in March (Paul was his godfather), but Rebecka had to wait until Felix and Cécile visited Berlin in April before she set eyes on Cécile. Thereafter any initial strains in the relationship between Felix's siblings and Cécile

---

[56] Letter of Mendelssohn to David, 2 June 1837 (*Felix Mendelssohn Bartholdy, Briefe aus Leipziger Archiven*, 137).

[57] Letter of Mendelssohn to Konrad Schleinitz, 3 July 1837, printed in *Die Tonhalle*, i (1868), 525.

[58] Letter of Mendelssohn to Ignaz Moscheles, 12 Dec. 1837, printed in *Letters of Felix Mendelssohn to Ignaz and Charlotte Moscheles*, trans. and ed. Felix Moscheles (London, 1888), 158.

[59] Letter of Mendelssohn to Klingemann, 5 Oct. 1837 (Klingemann *Briefwechsel*, 222).

[60] Hensel, *The Mendelssohn Family*, ii. 37. The Hensels left Leipzig on 28 Oct. (cf. letter of Cécile to Elisabeth Jeanrenaud of 25–8 Oct., MS MDM d. 18, fos. 60–1).

appear to have healed. If, as Werner points out, the women did not always see eye to eye in the early 1840s, when Felix and his family were living in Berlin at the Mendelssohn family home together with Lea, Paul and Albertine, and the Hensels, this would hardly be an unusual state of affairs in such circumstances.[61]

Cécile does not feature prominently in Mendelssohn biographies after the year of their marriage. She settled happily into the role of housewife and mother of their five children. She did accompany Felix on what was to be her sole visit to England in 1842, but otherwise, when mentioned at all, it is almost solely within a domestic context, in which she was apparently entirely content. In contrast to Clara Schumann or Fanny, there were no underlying conflicts of domestic duty and artistic ambition. She did, however, continue to develop her interest in drawing and painting, particularly after Felix's death in 1847, when it would seem to have provided a source of consolation. How accomplished she became can be seen in a number of oil paintings—a medium never tackled by Felix—done a year or so before her own death in 1853 at an even younger age (35) than Felix himself. Three are reproduced by Petitpierre.

What is the nature of the diary the Mendelssohns kept? Cécile's style is very concise, almost telegraphic at times. This is no literary travelogue written with an eye to publication, but with its little shared jokes and illustrations it is nevertheless far more than just the *aide-mémoire* that it sometimes approaches. Because this is not the confidential private diary of a single individual, but something that was seen by the other party, it clearly is not a vehicle for all the innermost thoughts of the one concerning the other. There is, however, no reason to doubt the mutual joy that each found in the other, and their marriage appears to have been an entirely happy one to the end. Of their more intimate moments the diary contains no more than gentle hints, as when commenting on the discomfort of their inn at Worms, Cécile adds: 'One agreeable thing, there was, however, which I will refrain from mentioning!' One shared activity that is prominently mentioned, but not hitherto associated with Felix, is his habit of reading aloud to his wife (and sometimes others) in the evenings. His love of good literature, inculcated since early childhood, was obviously something he wished to share with his bride. When it came to taste in architecture, the Mendelssohns were clearly of their time. With the exception of the church at St Blasien, no baroque building, however grand, earned favourable comment, and most were passed over in silence. Instead, in keeping with the Romantic spirit, their enthusiasm was reserved for the Romanesque and medieval cathedrals of the Rhine, and the ruined castles along its bank.

---

[61] Werner, *Mendelssohn: A New Image*, 380.

Cécile's handwriting is quite individual, and, as she herself confessed, often difficult to decipher, and although bilingual, neither her German nor French was faultless when it came to grammar and spelling. It should not be forgotten that she was still under 20 at the time, and to expect the observations and reflections of a mature woman would be unreasonable. A few years later when Robert and Clara Schumann married in 1840, they too kept a joint diary which, unlike the Mendelssohns, they maintained for several years. The Schumanns knew of the existence of the Mendelssohns' diary, and Robert refers to it in their own.[62]

Attention has already been drawn to the fact that the Honeymoon Diary was actually started a couple of weeks into the journey, and there are indications that subsequent entries were sometimes written up a few days in arrears, rather than it being faithfully completed each day. This is most obvious, when, as in the entry for 13 July, an event is recorded, only to be crossed out and transferred to another day. All the illustrations are in pen and ink, and were probably for the most part worked up from pencil sketches in lost drawing books. A few individual leaves from these books have survived, having been placed loose in one of Cécile's drawing books.[63] The division of labour between the couple in the illustrations is hard to assess. The fact that the illustration is numbered or lettered clearly in the hand of one or the other does not necessarily mean that it was the unaided work of that individual, as they themselves admit to working on drawings jointly. But the lion's share of the illustration seems to have fallen to Felix.

Three compositions appear within the diary's pages. The first is an Allegretto for piano composed for Cécile at Freiburg, the second a song, 'Die Freundinn', written in Bingen for the birthday of Cécile's friend Marie Bernus, and the last a canon composed in the coach on the return journey from England. They are presented here both in facsimile, and in transcription in the Appendix. Mendelssohn published none of them in his lifetime. Apart from these, the diary charts the process of various works that Mendelssohn was working on over these six months—the organ preludes of the Preludes and Fugues, Op. 37, two of the Op. 44 string quartets, the setting of Psalm 42, and the D minor Piano Concerto, Op. 40. Other works, such as the psalm setting *Laudate pueri*, Op. 39 No. 2, and the Capriccio in E major for piano, Op. 118, also date from this time, making it one of the composer's most productive periods.

A retracing of the journey undertaken during preparation of this edition proved very instructive when comparisons were made between the description and illustrations in the diary and the

---

[62] *Robert Schumann Tagebücher*, ed. Gerd Nauhaus (Leipizg, 1971–87), ii. 155; the joint marriage diary is published in English as *The Marriage Diaries of Robert & Clara Schumann*, ed. Gerd Nauhaus, trans. Peter Ostwald (London, 1994).

[63] See above, n. 51.

present-day scene. All the topographical depictions can still be traced, although it is noticeable that, contrary to expectations suggested by present-day anxieties of destruction of the forests, there are actually many more trees in evidence today than in the same scenes in the diary. No doubt the demand for wood as a fuel and as building material would help account for this situation, particularly in the vicinity of towns. A few of the inns visited are still in existence, although almost without exception they have been completely rebuilt since the Mendelssohns' time.

If the diary provides the most detailed picture of Felix and Cécile's day-to-day life for their first six months together, it is not the only source of such information. It is most importantly complemented by the letters which were regularly sent to members of their immediate family, and which have been preserved almost intact in the collections of the Staatsbibliothek zu Berlin, the Bodleian Library, and the New York Public Library. It has been decided to include these alongside the diary, and the great majority of them are being published for the first time. All the extant letters for this period to Cécile's mother and sister, and to Felix's mother and sisters have been included. Only those addressed to his brother Paul will not be found here—they contain relatively uninteresting material on financial matters (Paul took care of Felix's banking arrangements) or information which is also to be found in letters to other members of the family; occasional use, however, has been made of them in the notes. Apart from incidental detail that these family letters are able to add to what is in the diary—often helping to elucidate some of its more obscure references—they provide a fascinating picture of the tensions and anxieties which arose in Felix and Cécile's relationships with their families at a time when they were all adjusting to the new situation. Firm assurance that marriage would not affect the love of either party for their own parents and siblings is a constant theme. Felix in particular in the later letters had to make peace with his own family over his new travel plans, which meant that he would not be able to bring Cécile to Berlin in the summer as originally envisaged. It is important, however, to bear in mind that these letters are not an isolated group, for they of course form just a small part of the very regular correspondence with relations of both families which extended throughout their lives.

Notes on the Edition and Translation

IN the edition of both the diary and the letters, Felix's words are printed in italic and Cécile's in roman type. The German original of the diary is written largely in the present tense, but in translation it has seemed more natural to replace this by the past tense. The often telegraphic style of the original has been generally retained; only very occasionally have sentences been joined up for the sake of better comprehension. Place-names are given in their modern form; personal names are as in the original, although minor variations of spelling of the same name have been eliminated. Cécile in particular, however, was often writing down names which she had only heard spoken and these sometimes turn out to be incorrect—for example 'Schwerer' for 'Schwörer' or 'Belzig' for 'Besselich'. In such cases the original form has been left in the text, with the correction indicated in the notes. Where names are only indicated by initials, they have been expanded to their full form where positive identification is possible, as is usually the case. Felix most commonly writes and refers to his sister Rebecka as Beckchen. Since 'Becky' is such a close English equivalent, it has been chosen in preference to leaving the German diminutive as it stands. Dates at the head of the original diary entries often give only the day of the week or the date of the month. For convenience of reference they have all been standardized to a full form. The place and date of a letter have been uniformly put at the head of the text. The diary and all the letters were written in German, with the exception of Cécile's letters to her mother, which were in French. Where isolated English or French words were used in the original text, these have been put in double quotation marks.

In the latter portion of the diary, when the couple are writing their separate accounts, some editorial reordering of the text has been necessary. Whereas Cécile starts each day with a new entry on a fresh page, Felix often writes a continuous account stretching over two or three days. To keep the respective accounts in step with one another in such situations, Cécile's entries for the days concerned have been placed together before Felix's own rolling narrative. As the letters are intended to be read in conjunction with the relevant portions of the diary, only supplementary notes are provided for them, and so the diary notes may also need to be consulted for information on people and events. Cross-references to earlier notes are only given where they are to be found in parts of the diary not contemporaneous with the letter in question. A German edition of this work is currently being published by Atlantis-Verlag, Zurich and Mainz.

The Diary

Mainz,[1] Wednesday, 29 March 1837

Rose at ten in the morning and went for a stroll to the Citadel, from where Felix did a sketch of the town.[2] After dinner Felix was unwell, and remained so until three o'clock in the morning. The next day, Thursday 30 March, *in a mood matching the glorious weather*, we walked together to the post office and B. Schott's.[3] Then we left Mainz in the excellent carriage and, with warm rain falling, drove through lovely country along the Rhine past the famous wine-growing villages[4] to Worms. Found a dreadful inn there,[5] with a cold room and no trace of any comforts. There was, however, one agreeable thing which I will refrain from mentioning!

Worms, Friday, 31 March

Walked through the mud and rain to the cathedral.[6] On the way Felix bought me a copy of Hebel's poems.[7] We admired the cathedral for a long time, and Felix fell in love with the

[1] The Mendelssohns stayed at the Rheinischer Hof on the Rheinstrasse—see the entry for 4 July and letters to their families (pp. 124–7, 131). The hotel, complete with their balcony, is seen in Pl. 6.

[2] The Citadel is a baroque fortification on elevated ground on the south side of the town. Although Felix's sketchbook is not extant, a signed pencil drawing by Cécile of the same view and also dated 29 Mar. exists in the Mendelssohn-Archiv of the Staatsbibliothek zu Berlin (see Pl. 7). As only Felix is mentioned as sketching, Cécile may have begun her own drawing later that day, basing it on one Felix did *in situ*. Felix's letter to Elisabeth Jeanrenaud of 30 Mar. notes that Cécile had been drawing the previous day, and Cécile in her contribution to the same letter says that Felix had helped her with her drawing, which, however, was not yet finished. The drawing was intended as a gift for her mother (see p. 128).

[3] Music publishing firm in Mainz, founded by Bernhard Schott in 1780. In 1837 it was run by his sons Johann Andreas (1781–1840) and Johann Joseph (1782–1855).

[4] Felix's letter to his mother of 2 Apr. (p. 131) mentions Laubenheim, Oppenheim, Bodenheim, and Nierstein. We do not know if they stopped at Oppenheim to admire the magnificent Gothic Katherinenkirche, one of the finest churches along the Rhine.

[5] Most likely to have been the Schwan (also known as the Post).

[6] It is not surprising that the Mendelssohns were not over-impressed with the general state of Worms. Murray's *A Hand-Book for Travellers on the Continent* (1836) describes it thus: 'On entering within its gates, large enclosures, some waste, some turned into vineyards and gardens, are seen on either hand; these were once covered with populous streets and fine buildings. Grass now grows even in the existing streets, many houses are untenanted or falling to ruin, and the whole city has a decayed and unanimate aspect; the only commerce left to it is in the corn, rape oil, and wines produced in the neighbourhood.' It had been virtually destroyed by the French under Mélac in 1689.

[7] Johann Peter Hebel (1760–1826), German poet, teacher, and theologian. Best known for his poems in south Swabian dialect, first published as *Alemannische Gedichte* in 1803.

little door *(Fig. a)*.[1] The guide then pointed out to us the church of St Martin, where Luther is portrayed standing before the Diet, a truly sobering experience.[2] Wrote to Mother for the first

(at Worms by the Rhine)—cf. the 'Nibelungenlied'

Fig. a

[1] *zu Wormbse an dem Rine*, 'At Worms on the Rhine', is a recurrent phrase in the medieval epic *Nibelungenlied*, formerly known also as *Der Nibelunge Nôt*. The Burgundian court of the brothers Günther, Gernôt, and Giselher at Worms is one of the principal settings of the poem. Felix in his letter to his mother of 2 Apr. (p. 131) mentions 'the door of Worms Cathedral, where the Nibelungen play', referring to the scene in the story where the two queens, Kriemhild and Brunhild, quarrelled before the cathedral door. This, however, has traditionally been taken to mean the north door, not the south one shown here. The drawing of the Romanesque cathedral is far from correct in its detail. Although the doorway is accurately portrayed, there is no rose window in the south transept (there is, however, one above the west door), the Gothic side chapels to the right of the doorway are wrong, and there should be a central tower shown above the crossing. The cathedral lost its episcopal status in 1803, and became an ordinary parish church.

[2] There is some confusion here. Although there is a Martinskirche in Worms, it is a Catholic church, which naturally would not have had a picture of Luther. The church meant is the Protestant Trinity Church (Dreifaltigkeitskirche), an 18th-cent. Baroque building in the market square just to the east of the cathedral. The church was gutted in an air raid in 1945, and the interior subsequently rebuilt in the 1950s in a modern style. The portrayal of Luther before the Diet by Johann Martin Seekatz was on the west wall above the two galleries; in the new interior a modern mosaic version of the same subject is to be found between the two halves of the organ.

time.[1] Departure from Worms after the table d'hôte dinner, and arrival in Speyer at a nice friendly inn with obliging hosts.[2] Brief hour by the stove and organization of our room. (*Roast beef with prunes! Genius of a waiter!*) *FMB.*

Saturday, 1 April

Walk to the post office and cathedral[3] after breakfast. Inspected it inside and out, and strolled round the garden—the Heidentürmchen[4]—the Roman antiquities[5]—Christ on the Mount of Olives.[6] After dinner climbed up to the gallery, where I felt giddy for the first time in my life. Saw the clock and the bells—startled by the striking of the small bell. Lovely view into the interior of the building, where a service was in progress, and a wonderful one over the surrounding country.

Sunday, 2 April

The combination of being comfortable in our agreeably furnished room, beautiful weather, and the beginning of Felix's "passion" for the waiter, made for an unqualified decision to spend several days here. The afternoon visit of Herr Arendt [sic]*,[7] nearly brought about a change of mind. His stories of the crypt and the baptismal spring, and of the Virgin beneath the towers.

---

[1] The letter from Worms (see p. 124) was started by Felix on 30 Mar., but Cécile's contribution was written a day later, and the Worms postmark is dated 1 Apr.

[2] They stayed at the Post (Wittelsbacher Hof) according to Eduard Souchay's recollections (see Introduction, n. 47).

[3] The magnificent Romanesque cathedral in 1837 differed from its present appearance. Following considerable destruction by the French in 1689, when the whole town was razed, it was rebuilt in the 1770s by Ignaz Neumann with a new baroque west façade, including a cupola but no west towers, and it is in this form that the Mendelssohns saw it (Fig. c). The present neo-Romanesque façade and west towers date from the 1850s, and the whole building underwent thorough restoration from 1957 to 1967, involving further attempts to return it to its original Romanesque form.

[4] 'The little pagan tower' in the cathedral garden is the only surviving part of the medieval town wall.

[5] In 1826 an 'Antikenhalle' in the classical style was built on the northern side of the cathedral garden to house Roman finds from the Palatinate. They were later transferred to the Historisches Museum der Pfalz, and since 1930 the 'Antikenhalle' has been a memorial to the dead of World War I.

[6] A sculpture group dating from the beginning of the 16th cent. It is the only surviving part of the medieval cloisters which were situated on the south side of the cathedral. When the Mendelssohns saw it many of the figures were in a delapidated state, and it underwent restoration in the later 19th cent.

[7] Guillaume Arendt (1808–65), Professor at Louvain University. Born into a Protestant Berlin family, Arendt attended Berlin University, and was well known to the Mendelssohn family. While lecturing at Bonn he converted to Roman Catholicism in 1832, and was appointed a professor at the Catholic University of Louvain in 1834, where he was also chief librarian from 1836 to 1839. His courses there included ones on archaeology and Roman antiquities. He had associations with Speyer from 1832, and it was there he died.

The use of so many authoritative words was quite a new experience for me.[1] The impression he made, however, was dissipated again by the fresh clear air, and especially in the evening!

*('Arend, Senior Librarian and Professor at Louvain University' was printed on his visiting card. O Belgians!)

Monday, 3 April

Stricken with toothache until the evening, when Felix procured a little miracle-worker, Herr Bracht [sic],[2] who brought me relief (with his tooth cement).

Tuesday, 4 April

Already out of doors again, spent a long time drawing my beloved Heidenturm (Fig. b).[3]

Fig. b

Walk along the Speyerbach,[4] with its splendid view of the cathedral and the bridges in the evening light (Fig. c).

---

[1] Much of Arendt's information proved to be highly unreliable (see the letter to Rebecka Dirichlet of 11 Apr. (p. 137)). There have been various statues of the Virgin beneath the crossing; the present one dates from 1930.

[2] Maximilian Brach (1804–64), a Speyer dentist.

[3] The original pencil drawing of this, signed by Cécile, is preserved in the Bodleian Library, MS MDM c. 6, fo. 12a (see Introduction, p. xxiv).

[4] The stream on the north side of the cathedral which flows into the Rhine.

(*The depiction of spring and the sunbeams are the result of imagination*)—*the artist*

Fig. c

In the morning we walked for a good half-mile along the Rhine as far as the river crossing.[1] Misunderstandings on the way. Made plans at the boatman's cottage. Return at three for lunch. In the afternoon Felix played the organ of an atrociously decorated church—a wretched box of whistles.[2] Walk to the cathedral and down into the crypt. Baptismal font,[3] but no spring. The sacristy—the subterranean chapel with its strange pillars[4] (*Fig. C*).

[1] Up to five ferry crossings were situated in the vicinity of Speyer. A German half-mile is about 3.5 km., so that perhaps the import-ant ferry at the village of Rheinhausen (Rheinhäuser Fähre) was meant.

[2] Almost certainly the Protestant Trinity Church, built in 1701–3, with ceiling paintings by Johann Christoph Guthber. The organ was an instrument of 1814 by Johann Georg Geib and his son from Frankenthal.

[3] A Romanesque font without a pedestal is to be found in the crypt.

[4] It is not clear what is meant by the 'underground chapel' as opposed to the crypt, which is the only true underground area of the cathedral. Perhaps the St Emmeram chapel is intended. This is the lower part of a two-storeyed double chapel, only dimly lit by

Fig. C

In the course of the evening and well into the night endured the loathsome company of Rhinelanders who behaved little better than their large dogs.

Thursday, 6 April

(see Fig. d).[1]

Fig. d

Reading aloud of Hebel's poems. Felix's attempt to draw Heiner and Fritz[2] led to the creation of the small picture of Felix and me walking in Speyer's cathedral garden, and the idea of sending it to Mother.

light from above. Its pillars have very distinctive and highly ornate capitals, showing Byzantine influence. They do not, however, really resemble the one shown in Fig. C, which if anything is more like those of the crypt itself.

[1] Like Fig. b, the original pencil drawing, again signed by Cécile, is in MS MDM c. 6, fo. 12b. The significance of the key is unknown.

[2] Probably the brothers Heinrich and Fritz Schlemmer, sons of Georg Wilhelm Maximilian and Wilhelmine Schlemmer, and first cousins once removed of Cécile. Johann Friedrich Philipp (Fritz) (1803–90) matriculated as a student in Heidelberg in 1820, and was a tutor to the Rothschild family for a while, before settling down as a lawyer in Frankfurt. Mendelssohn dedicated his Six Organ Sonatas, Op. 65, to him. See the Introduction (p. xv) for the role he played in the Mendelssohns' courtship. Heinrich (1808–85) was his younger brother.

Visit to Herr Arend. The wind and rain were bad omens for the next day's journey. Nevertheless we packed our things. Lamartine *was read out aloud by Cécile, as he never was in Jerusalem.*[1]

Friday, 7 April

Blinded by the snow on the roofs as soon as we woke up. Two decisions—one difficult, not to travel—the other easy, 'To stay in bed'.

The snowfall persisted for the whole day and right through to

Saturday, 8 April

In spite of this we set off at nine o'clock. Felix parted with reluctance from the waiter, the inn, and from everything in Speyer. Once again I found the carriage very nice and smooth. The snow prevented us from seeing the view, which must have been very fine. (Just as Herr Arend had said the Rhine was on our left side.) Border fortress at Lauterburg. French soldiers with red breeches. Innkeeper with a red cap *(Fig. e)*. Courteous customs officers. A quick lunch and quick driving by the mounted postilion. Magnificent countryside between Lauterburg and Beinheim.

Fig. e

Arrival at the Hôtel de Paris[2] in Strasbourg. Torrent of waiters. Supped entirely à la français and retired to a small and uncomfortably furnished room. *It had a great many shortcomings, and only a small stove, but a good boots.*

[1] Alphonse de Lamartine (1790–1869), French poet and statesman, whose *Méditations poétiques* and *Harmonies poétiques et réligieuses* were being widely read at this time. In 1835 he published his *Souvirs, pensées et paysages, pendant un voyage en Orient, 1832–1833,* which included an account of his visit to the Holy Land.

[2] The Hôtel de la Ville-de-Paris was in the rue de la Mésange near the Place Broglie. Rebuilt in 1848, it became amongst the most fashionable in the later 19th cent., and Wagner and Gounod were among other composers who stayed there. It remained in business until 1991.

Felix went off to the Minster in the morning and returned quite enchanted, and dragged me away from *the dirty laundry, in which I was deeply immersed* (many thanks for the fine compliment)! I walked with him though the old narrow streets until all of a sudden we stood before this miracle *(Fig. f)*.

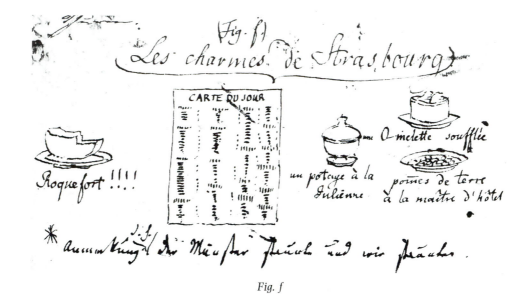

Fig. ƒ

Mutual astonishment.* The three main portals—the St Lorenz portal—the galleries—the windows—gargoyles from which the water runs off (Arend)—the unfinished and the completed tower.[1]

* *Note: i.e. the Minster astonished, and we were astonished.*

Within, the wonderful stained-glass windows—the rosette window above the door—the organ—the pulpit—the unusual choir. After a table d'hôte lunch with rather vulgar company,

[1] Although both the north and south towers of the west façade were completed in the mid-14th cent., only the north tower had a spire added to it (in the first half of the 15th cent.), giving the façade its exceptionally asymmetrical appearance. Neither here nor in Freiburg did they ascend the tower, even though the Strasbourg ascent was a favourite one with visitors. The weather, however, was bitterly cold during their stay (see Felix's letter to Rebecka of 11 Apr. (p. 136)), and Cécile's experience of giddiness in Speyer may also help to account for their remaining on the ground.

another visit to the Minster, where a priest with a trembling, whining voice was preaching: 'Knock and it shall be opened unto you' *(Fig. g)*.[1]

A short spell in front of the stove and then to the Theatre.[2] Vaudeville 'Salvoisy, ou l'amoureux de la reine', and a comic opera 'Cosimo'.[3] We fled after the first act of the opera. Most delightful supper.

Fig. g

[1] The famous pulpit, with its many small statues, was the work of Hans Hammer in 1485. Felix's drawing shows it with a sounding board, which is no longer there. This was made by Vallastre in 1824 in the neo-Gothic style. It was badly damaged when two bombs hit the cathedral in 1944, and was finally removed in 1952.

[2] In the Place Broglie; it was built 1804–21, with a portico of six Ionic columns above which are statues of the Muses. This façade survived a fire of 1870.

[3] The comédie-vaudeville *Salvoisy, ou l'Amoureux de la Reine* by A. E. Scribe, M. N. Balisson de Rougemont, and A. B. B. Decomberousse, and the opéra bouffon *Cosimo* by A. Vilain de Saint-Hilaire and Paul Duport.

Visit to Mme Passavant,[1] the result of which is an invitation to return in the evening, which is accepted by Felix *after it had been declined by Cécile*. Advice from Mr Louis *(le domestique de place)* as to the best shops. At two o'clock organ playing by Herr Wagenthaler[2] and his wife on the Silbermann organ[3] in the Minster, whilst we crept around among the pipes and trunking, it being the first time in my life that I had seen the inside of an organ. Awkward way back down through the tower, which Frau Wagenthaler had to negotiate twice every day. Dinner au Rocher de Cancale.[4] Set out for Mme Passavant's at half past seven. To our amazement we found a large gathering there. Herr and Mme Berg,[5] Monsieur Blaÿ,[6] and many others. They played a $4,5,6,7,8$tet by Mayseder. Felix was then pressed to play on the piano, but he resisted firmly like a lion until supper time. Fortunately we made our escape, with Herr Klimmrath[7] on my arm as far as the courtyard door.

Tuesday, 11 April

In the middle of breakfast, while we were studying our newspapers—Felix the French government *(Crisis, Molé or Guizot[8] or neither of the two)* and I the Meunier affair[9]—Herr Berg arrived

[1] Emma Passavant, youngest of the three daughters of the Strasbourg merchant, Jean J. Klimrath (1760–1835). She married the Frankfurt merchant Christian Passavant (1785–1829), and after his death moved with her children back to Strasbourg in 1835, where she resided in the Cour d'Andlau, 8 rue des Écrivains, a mansion belonging to her brother-in-law, Fritz Ehrmann. The Passavants had been a prominent Basle family since the 16th cent., and in the 17th had established a Frankfurt branch.

[2] Joseph Wagenthaler (1795–1869). He became *maître de chapelle* at Strasbourg Minster in 1819, adding the duties of organist in 1823. His wife was also an organist, and continued to act as an organist at the cathedral after Joseph's death.

[3] Andreas Silbermann (1678–1734), who with his brother Gottfried, constituted the first generation of the famous organ-building family, was a resident of Strasbourg, and responsible for building many organs in the city. For the cathedral he built a new three-manual organ in 1713–16 using the old 15th-cent. case. Alterations were made to it in 1833, shortly before the Mendelssohns' visit. Such radical transformation and destruction of Silbermann's work occurred in unfortunate later rebuilds, that a new organ by Alfred Kern was constructed in 1981, still in the medieval case, incorporating just a few of the surviving Silbermann pipes.

[4] A restaurant in the Place Broglie, known especially for its oysters—Cancale is a Breton village well known for its oyster-catching.

[5] Conrad Mathias Berg (1785–1852), Alsatian pianist, teacher, composer, and writer on music, resident in Strasbourg from 1808. His wife, Flore Elise, née Klimrath, was presumably the sister or daughter of 'Herr Klimmrath'.

[6] Presumably the violinist Bley, who ran a violin class in Strasbourg from 1836 to 1842.

[7] Perhaps J. H. Daniel Klimrath, a lawyer, who lived at 23 rue des Serruriers. He was presumably an uncle or cousin of Emma Passavant.

[8] The French prime minister, Count Louis-Mathieu Molé (1781–1855), had taken office in Sept. 1836, with the ambitious François Guizot (1787–1874) as Minister of Education. A dispute over King Louis-Philippe's demand for a grant for his eldest daughter in Mar. 1837 led to a government crisis, and Molé offered his resignation. In the end Guizot left the government on 15 Apr., and Molé continued in office.

[9] On 27 Dec. 1836 the 22-year-old Pierre-François Meunier fired a pistol into Louis-Philippe's carriage while the king and three of his sons were travelling to the opening of the Chamber of Deputies. Injury was limited to the effects of broken glass. The Court of Peers sentenced Meunier to death, but Louis-Philippe commuted it to exile, and even apparently provided him with money to live on in

Fig. h

(Fig. h). Jeremiah and the ruins of Jerusalem rolled into one. His Lamentations. Visit to the Strasbourg shops. My lovely purchases. Table d'hôte lunch. French fellow-diners. Music! Butchered Strauss waltzes, on hearing which one of the uncouth men said 'J'aime ça, c'est si plaintif.' Then wine was poured out for me, and the men sang and talked in an unseemly manner. Felix teased me that I was born in France. I went up to our room beside myself.

We walked to the Église Neuve[1] where Herr Hepp[2] was sitting in the little room. Herr Wagenthaler played. I went for a walk with his daughter.

It is Rebecka's birthday. On arrival back at the hotel we both wrote to her.[3] At supper we drank her health. My indisposition in the evening caused Felix the next morning

America. The newspapers at this time were reprinting the official report made to the Court regarding the incident and subsequent interrogation of Meunier and other possible accomplices.

[1] The Temple Neuf, a 13th-cent. Dominican church with an organ of 1749 by Johann Andreas and Johann Daniel Silbermann. The church was burnt down in 1870 and rebuilt in the Romanesque style.

[2] Johann Heinrich Hepp (1776–1844). Succeeded his father, Sixtus I. Hepp, as organist of the Temple Neuf in 1806.

[3] See p. 136 for Felix's letter. Cécile's appears not to be extant.

to go to Mme Passavant in order to ask about her doctor. Our encounter in the street. Felix's joy and happiness. We walked to the ramparts where he explained to me how the doctor had reassured him, how he had been to Herr Berg's and played with Madame Berg, how Madame Passavant had once again asked him to come to see her. Table d'hôte lunch, then spent time with her children. Another visit to the Strasbourg shops (Fig. i).

Fig. i

Mme Piqué:[1] 'O madame, faut prendre ce ruban, avec les petits poussons verts, c'est printemnier, c'est charmant.'

Farewell visit to Mme Passavant. Final look at the Minster. Final souper français. Final attempt to summon that which we willingly dispensed with.

---

[1] A Jos. Picquet, 'marchand de soieries', 27 rue du Dôme, is listed in Hoellbeck's *Almanach du commerce . . . de Strasbourg* for 1836.

Departure from Strasbourg at nine. Encountered the old baron who breakfasted with us every morning, *and who had made a great impression on me.* The Citadel[1]—the Rhine bridge[2]—Kehl—customs. Glorious countryside—fine people. For a long time we could still see the Minster. Ichenheim. Midday meal in Kenzingen. Blunt conversation of the doctor, who wanted to alarm us on account of the influenza epidemic. In the afternoon the scenery became ever more beautiful as we approached the mountains. Funny little postilion. *Yes!!! (Fig. k).*

Fig. k

[1] Built in 1682–4 on the east side of the city as part of Vauban's fortifications, it was destroyed in the German bombardment of 1870.
[2] This was a bridge of boats.

The road was immensely busy. People, cattle, and carts alternated ceaselessly. We gathered that it was market day in Freiburg. We caught our first sight of the Minster just before entering the town. Pleasant impression made on us by Freiburg in the sunshine. Arrival at the Zähringer Hof.[1] We turned down the room with the balcony on account of the smoke, and moved into a yellow one decorated with pictures of the story of Psyche.[2] Walk to the cathedral,[3] for which, however, we were too spoilt. Comfortable furnishing of the alcove.

Friday, 14 April

Felix went off to the post office and returned with the disturbing news of Fanny's accident,[4] but also of her recovery, together with an out-of-date letter from Julie and business letters. We then went together to the Schlossberg.[5] Wonderful view of the many mountain ridges and the fertile Freiburg plain. Nicely laid-out path—the crucifix—the inscription. Table d'hôte lunch with only one guest. In the afternoon a stroll to the Loretto Chapel on a hill not far out of Freiburg.[6] Uncertainty as to which has the finer view, the Schlossberg or this. First sight of the Güntherstal[7] and my passion for it. We returned, and first wrote to Fanny before going to bed.

Saturday, 15 April

The morning's post was taken care of, then we had our midday meal with numerous others, amongst whom in particular a man from Basle conversed eagerly with Felix and invited him to

---

[1] This was Freiburg's leading hotel, situated in the Kaiser Strasse (now Kaiser-Joseph Strasse) just round the corner from the Minster, on the site now occupied by the Kaufhof. In 1837 it was run by the widowed Friederike Rehfuss. With the coming of the railway, a new Zähringer Hof was erected in 1862 in the Bahnhofstrasse, which survived until the bombing of the town in 1944.

[2] The tale of Cupid and Psyche (found in the *Golden Ass* of Apuleius) was depicted in a remarkable series of 13 scenes on wallpaper printed from 1,500 plates by the Parisian workshop of Joseph Dufour to designs made by Louis Lafitte in 1814. Unfortunately the paper was badly damaged in the course of removal during a renovation of the building, and remnants which were transferred to the Augustinermuseum perished in the 1944 bombing, as did the original hotel building.

[3] The 13th–16th-cent. Minster, with its famous open-work spire, is one of the finest Gothic buildings in Germany. The windows, despite Cécile's comment that they were 'mostly new' (see entry for 21 Apr.), actually contained quite a mixture of medieval and modern glass.

[4] Fanny had suffered a miscarriage (see Felix and Cécile's letters to Elisabeth Jeanrenaud of 15 Apr. (p. 141)).

[5] The hill overlooking the town on the east contained the ruins of the ancient castle fortress, which was finally blown up on Louis XV's orders in 1745.

[6] The sandstone Loretto hill to the south of the old town is surmounted by a tiny pilgrimage chapel erected in 1657.

[7] The Günterstal, with its village of the same name, is the valley lying to the east of the Lorettoberg.

give concerts. After the meal we set out for Güntherstal. The glorious path enticed us to walk further and further, until we arrived at the village and the inn.[1] Talkative, amiable host, who told us much about the beautiful area up the valley towards Todtnau. He recommended us to walk along the forest path, which we also took on the return journey. It was delightful. Scarcely had we arrived back home and rested a little, than we went to the theatre[2] to attend the advertised concert. *It should have been given by Alex Graefle, and was to have included amongst other things an Auverture by Rhigini, and a duet from Billini's 'Norma'.*[3] Once there, however, we were informed that it would not take place for lack of an audience. Felix did some more writing (music). Supper.

Sunday, 16 April

A shock on waking up—as a heaped measure of misfortune the tooth cement had fallen out. Short, slow walk to the exercise ground *(Fig. 1)*.[4] First lunch in our room. The little waiter with his 'O definitely!' Walk to Welz's shop to order this book.[5] Felix played to me downstairs in the

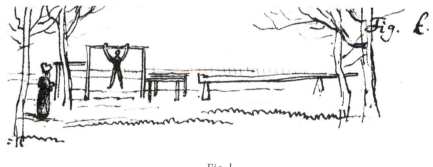

Fig. 1

---

[1] The inn was presumably the 'Kibburg' (or 'Kibfelsen'), a popular destination for Freiburgers.
[2] The theatre at this time was in the church of the former Augustinerkloster, and was opened in 1823.
[3] The odd spelling perhaps reflects that of the advertisement; nothing is known of Graefle.
[4] Its location is unknown, perhaps near the river. To judge from the drawing it also has the appearance of being a 'Rast' or halting-place, where carriers with heavy loads on their backs could rest using the cross bars.
[5] Franz von Welz is listed as a general trader in the *Freiburger Adresskalender auf das Jahr 1837*. The diary was thus not procured until nearly three weeks after the start of the honeymoon, and events up to this time were written up in Freiburg.

parlour, where I met Fräulein Rehfuss.[1] She sent camelias up to me.[2] I began to get toothache. It was, however, bearable until

Monday, 17 April

when nothing more could help; the cement had run out, and I had to spend the entire day at home. It was raining; the piano was brought upstairs. Felix looked after me, despite which I passed a dreadful night, and didn't doze off until about five o'clock. *(Here belonged the figs 'cooked in milk', the saffron and caetera animalia. (See the next day).)*[3]

Tuesday, 18 April

Things were better. As the weather was clear again, we walked to the paper mills[4] for the first time, and in the afternoon drove to Ebnet[5] in a cab. A pretty place at the foot of the hill with a view of the Höllental. Strong wind. Had scarcely arrived home than I had the most dreadful pain. Kindness of the landlady, who sent figs, saffron, and milk up to me. Felix had the dentist summoned, who turned out to be ill himself. The pain eased up and I went to sleep all of a sudden on the sofa. Felix conveyed me to bed, and I slept very well until around two o'clock when I once more began to torment Felix and myself. Firm decision to have the tooth extracted.

Wednesday, 19 April

In its final hours it behaved very well, and did not hurt for the whole morning. When, however, we were sitting at table, its executioner came swaggering in. Herr Schwerer, a large, stout man.[6] *He pulled it out (Fig. m).*

[1] Presumably the daughter of the proprietess.
[2] Although the German 'Camellien' means 'camelias', perhaps Cécile intended to write 'Camille' meaning 'camomile', which might have helped her toothache.
[3] This is one of a number of indications that even after the diary was obtained, it was not necessarily written up every day, but often a few days in arrears. Felix is here correcting Cécile's entry for 18 Apr.
[4] By the river Dreisam to the east of the old town.
[5] A village on the right bank of the Dreisam about 5 km. east of Freiburg.
[6] Probably Ignaz Schwörer (1800–60), physician and professor at Freiburg University.

Fig. m

The consequences of this heroic deed were a swollen face, and an inability to go out during a whole day of the most beautiful weather. Herr Schwerer only returned towards evening to enquire after my state of health, and suggested 'H'm, h'm, rub some sweet cream on your cheek'. I slept splendidly once more, so that on

Friday, 21 April

in the morning we embarked on a long drive to Hugstetten.[1] It was not particularly beautiful there, but from a hill in the castle garden, on which the tasteless owner, Herr von Andlaw, had

[1] A village 6 km. north-west of Freiburg. Freiherr Konrad Karl Friedrich von Andlaw-Birseck (1763–1839) was a Baden politician, who rebuilt the old Schloss at Hugstetten, and became sole landowner in the village. He was succeeded by his son, Heinrich Bernhard (1802–71), who was also in residence there from 1830. The 'tower', known as the 'Belvedere', was built in the style of a Chinese

built a preposterous tower *(Fig. n)*, there was an extensive view of the mountains. We saw the Feldberg, Belchen, and the Kandel[1] right in front of us. Strong wind at the top and on the way back. We ate at three as usual.

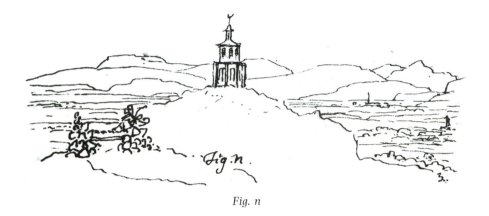

Fig. n

Afterwards we inspected the Minster more closely, which is certainly another with many very beautiful things about it. It is on the whole more consistent in style than that of Strasbourg. The windows are mostly modern, but most beautifully executed, particularly in the two small chapels. The pulpit is not bad, and the choir is in better taste than that of Strasbourg. The air was too musty and cold for us to remain there long, and Felix therefore suggested going to Gaiser,[2] the instrument maker, in order to try out his pianos. We found a dispirited quiet man, for whom things appeared not to be going well. He had three uprights and one grand for sale, and was giving them away for ridiculously low prices. Felix was disturbed by this visit, because he could not help the poor man. We spent the evening writing and drawing until supper time, after which there was nothing more to relate.

Saturday, 22 April

A delightful walk in the morning to the paper mills in warm sunshine. The path followed the stream as far as the first mill *(Fig. o)*.

garden temple in 1829, as was a single-storey tea house part-way up the hill. Only the remains of the tower's sandstone foundations can now be seen, but the tea house is still there. The Schloss, next to the old church, is now owned by the von Mentzingen family, descendants by marriage of Andlaw-Birseck.

[1] The Feldberg (the highest peak in the Black Forest) and Belchen are to the south of Freiburg, the Kandel is to the north.
[2] Valentin Gaiser (1804/5–1874); he lived in the Löwengasse (No. 392).

Fig. 0

The many mill-wheels made the Dreisam very lively; it leaped and produced a host of little waterfalls. On the other side of the path a hill rose up. At the house directly opposite, where the sun shone on the grass, a host of violets stood in the open. I saw them first and picked those I could reach through the hedge, and put them in Felix's buttonhole. He in turn climbed over the hedge and passed me over whole bouquets.[1] That was nice, but not as nice as the little song that he afterwards wrote about it.[2]

[1] A nosegay of pressed violets, originally in the diary, is still preserved in the Bodleian Library (MS MDM d. 69, fo. 1).

[2] Another manuscript of this *Lied ohne Worte*, bearing the same date is in the Staatsbibliothek zu Berlin (MS autogr. Mendelssohn 29, pp. 53–4). It would appear to be Mendelssohn's first draft, and the version in the diary displays certain modifications and refinements. See p. 200 for a modern transcription. The piece remained unpublished until 1927, when the Berlin version was printed in the Berlin periodical *Jede Woche Musik* (29 Oct. 1927, pp. 165–6), edited by Leopold Hirschberg.

We continued to the point where one can see the old Carthusian monastery,[1] with Ebnet in the distance. The mountains still had a heavy covering of snow (Fig. p).

Fig. p

[1] The 14th-cent. former Carthusian monastery is built at the foot of the Johannisberg overlooking the Dreisam 3 km. east of the centre of Freiburg. The monastery was dissolved in 1782 following an imperial decree, and sold in 1783 to Freiherr Anton von Baden. It was partially rebuilt as a private residence, and inherited in 1830 by Freiherr Christian von Türckheim (1782–1846), a major in the Austrian army. In 1894 it was taken over by the town as an old people's home, which it continues to be.

Felix spent the afternoon composing. (In connection with which, it is from now on to be understood that I also do things, which, however, are so unimportant and not worth relating, that I need not remind myself of any of them.)

Formal protest, which wishes to be included in the text.

'In so far as it is not unimportant and even less unworthy of being related, that holes be darned and a man go out no more ragged than his wife, then it must also then be gratefully acknowledged by the former that it is in this way that his outward appearance is patched and otherwise improved. This occurs daily; it does not only happen when the wants and deficiencies are too large and unmendable. Then the pants end up in shreds. It is, however, not at all unimportant, and has more lasting worth than a good many contrapuntal twists and devices. For the sake of truth I protest against the above decision, as a dissentient voice.' My wish was, as you see, complied with (cf. J. P.).[1]

Short walk on the Freiburg town ramparts.

Sunday, 23 April

We remained indoors on account of the bad weather. Felix wrote to Birmingham,[2] while I watched the farmers and townspeople coming out of mass. After lunch Felix flirted with Fräulein Rehfuss *(God forbid!)* and bought her violets from two shy little girls (to their great delight) just as we were preparing to go out. Our intention of climbing up to Loretto was not fulfilled. We were scarcely half-way up the hill, when I could not proceed any further and Felix turned back with his good-for-nothing wife. Back home it very quickly became dark, for the sky was overcast.

Monday, 24 April

Penetrated as far as the Carthusian monastery for the first time. There was a very fine view up there; the building itself is old and ruined; an old monastery garden, newly cultivated, and many cottages and sheds belong to it. Herr von Dürkheim[3] appeared to have a housekeeper there. I would rather live there, than in his country house further down. Right behind the monastery a very beautiful forest begins, which completely covers the mountain; below is the green valley and the Dreisam, and opposite are the now snow-covered hills. On the return journey, in order

---

[1] The reference must be to the writer Jean Paul (1763–1825), but does not appear to be a direct quotation. Felix's sisters gave him a copy of Jean Paul's best-known work, *Flegeljahre*, to take with him on his first journey to England in 1829.

[2] He had been invited to conduct *St Paul* at the Birmingham Musical Festival in Sept. (see Introduction, p. xxv).

[3] See p. 20 n. 1.

to add to yet more newly gathered violets, Felix bought me a beautiful bunch of hyancinths, roses, and other spring flowers, which continued to smell sweetly in our room all day and often at night too (Fig. q).

Fig. q

In the afternoon went for a long drive to the Suggental.[1] On the way we met a very pretty peasant girl. Felix immediately took notice of her and cast a backward glance at her a couple of times. After that it only needed a few casual facial expressions and words to make me quite stubbornly melancholic and jealous by the time we arrived at the inn at the entrance of the valley. We climbed up the hill behind the inn, where Felix complained about pains. I, however, behaved very badly. After some time I began to blink, without Felix being able to discover why; he pressed me about it, but my thoughts became more and more gloomy, and he more and more exasperated. Meanwhile it had started to rain, and we sat by the inn doors as mute as two fish. We walked

[1] The Suggental is a small valley off the Elztal about 8 km. north of Freiburg towards Waldkirch. The inn at the entrance to the valley was owned by Fidel Reich at this time, and known as Bad Suggen. It was burnt down in 1913, and in its rebuilt state is now the Gasthof Suggenbad.

up the hill, but nothing helped—Felix's asking and his irritation made me ever more silent and obtuse. I did nothing but weep, tormenting him and myself. The carriage was harnessed in the meantime, and we drove home, at first accompanied by a fine sunset, then by pelting rain, and only when back home did we completely become our old selves again. I told Felix my absurd thoughts, and he was once more kind and affectionate towards me. A firm resolution never to be sulky again without being able to give a man the reason.

Felix spent the whole evening playing all my favourite pieces to me so beautifully. Thus was the matrimonial quarrel settled.

Don't be angry with me, dear Cécile.

Tuesday, 25 April

Felix worked in the morning on his 'Lieder ohne Worte' in order to send them off, along with letters to London.[1] It became too late to go for a walk, and so we left going to the Loretto until after lunch. It had rained during the morning, and the benches and paths were wet. We entered the little inn parlour, formerly a hermitage, and ordered coffee, after spending a long time admiring the strange and very fine effect of the setting sun *(Fig. r)*.

Fig. r

[1] The 6 *Lieder ohne Worte*, Op. 38, published in 1837 by Simrock in Bonn, and by Novello in London. Felix was now sending them to Simrock (see letter of 25 Apr. 1837 to Simrock in *Briefe an deutsche Verleger*, ed. Rudolf Elvers (Berlin, 1968), 210).

Following this portent Felix predicted a rainstorm, while I claimed that we would be lucky and reach home still dry, wherein I was proved so right that I was able to do some shopping without needing the umbrella that had been forced upon me. It rained in the night.

Wednesday, 26 April

In the morning a walk and sketching at the paper factory. Then the lovely path and the splendid weather led us a good way through woodland in the direction of Ottilien. On a bench Felix drew my likeness, a gnarled root.[1] We were so enchanted with the beautiful forest path that we

Fig. s

---

[1] 'Knörzerchen' (little gnarled one) was the pet name given to Cécile by her brother Carl (see Petitpierre, *Romance of the Mendelssohns*, 137). Felix's sketch is preserved in the Bodleian Library, MS MDM c. 21, fo. 185, and reproduced as Pl. 8.

went back home only for a quick meal, had a carriage harnessed and once again drove along the road to Ottilien. Where the road became too steep we got out, and still had about an hour's walk in the wonderful forest.

At the top was a very prettily situated inn, and an old church dedicated to St Ottilien.[1] The saint herself is hewn in stone in an adjoining chapel, kneeling before the Cross *(Fig. s)*. The only view was of the glorious nearby forest, and the summits of the Black Forest mountains. After we had rested and refreshed ourselves in the garden of the inn, we turned back, for it was already becoming dark and cool. Our carriage was still waiting below, and the driving pleased us so much that we had ourselves taken right round the town of Freiburg again. In the evening we both wrote to Mother in Frankfurt, from whom I had received a gloomy letter in the morning.[2]

Thursday, 27 April

Felix wrote to Herr Doerrien[3] in the morning, whilst I sewed. After lunch we walked for a good hour along the Basle highway as far as the first village. The cherry trees are beginning to turn white, and the little clusters of buds are ready to burst open, but the sun does not encourage it.

Friday, 28 April

In the morning we walked once again to the paper mills, our most usual stroll, since it stays on level ground. The weather was fairly clear, but windy. After lunch, served by the new timid waiter, we went to the Schützenhaus[4] on the Neustadt road for the first time. Felix was gloomy and unwell. We consumed the inexpensive coffee in the pavilion. On the return journey we saw our first tree in full blossom. Letter to Mother in Berlin.[5] Felix went to bed early in order to sleep off his indisposition.

[1] The pilgrimage church of St Ottilien in the hills about 7 km. north-east of Freiburg. The subterranean chapel at the west end of the church is fairly accurately depicted here, except that there is only a single window in the wall above (now containing modern stained glass). It was dedicated in 1508. The water issuing from the cleft was supposed to be beneficial to the eyes.

[2] Elisabeth Jeanrenaud's letter is not extant, but its contents are clear from Felix and Cécile's replies (see pp. 142–6).

[3] Heinrich Doerrien (1786–1858), Doctor of Law, senior civil servant at Leipzig, and member of the Directorium of the Gewandhaus.[3]

[4] Now the Gasthaus Schützen in the Schützenallee to the east of the old town.   [5] See p. 146.

We spent the morning at home. Felix worked on the Psalm 'As the hart pants for fresh water'.[1] It rained the whole morning. After lunch we ventured again to the Schützenhaus, but had to sit indoors and read newspapers. On the way back the rain caught us out, and we arrived home wet. Felix wrote to Herr Rosen[2] in the evening.

Sunday, 30 April

Once again the bad weather kept us at home for the entire morning. In the afternoon we walked to the Minster, and took a little stroll on the Freiburg promenades. Conversation about Faust. We arrived at the Dreisam just as the sun was setting most beautifully; it illuminated the meadows and hills wonderfully in several places. The confectioner. Felix wrote to Herr Klingemann.[3]

Monday, 1 May

The weather was glorious. On waking we took a decision to make use of the fine day for a drive into the Höllental.[4] The carriage was ready at half past nine; various things were packed into the travelling bag in case we were able to travel across from Höllsteig to Todtnau, and we ourselves installed in the carriage. The sun beat down fiercely. We drove by way of Ebnet through a delightful valley abounding in water to the Himmelreich.[5] Final view back towards Freiburg and the plain. The Kandel. The Himmelreich is a very large and splendid inn, completely Swiss in style, with galleries and an overhanging roof; below is the Dreisam, and above yet more cultivated hillsides with fruit trees and firs. These latter become ever more numerous and darker. Soon the rocks begin to close in on one another, so that a way through is scarcely to be found. Here the real hell begins. It is magnificent, and the vertically rising rock walls are rather frightening. Little streams create waterfalls and plunge into the Dreisam that is making its way below. Everything is a very beautiful dark colour.

---

[1] Psalm 42, Op. 42, published in 1838.

[2] Friedrich Rosen (1805–37). Appointed Professor of Oriental Languages at King's College, London in 1828 at the age of 23, he was one of Felix's close friends. The letter is found in Bodleian Library, MS MDM c. 42, fos. 35–6.

[3] Karl Klingemann (1798–1862), German diplomat and amateur poet. Secretary at the Hanoverian Chancery (and subsequently Legation) in London. One of Felix's closest friends throughout his life, he had been the composer's companion on his visit to Scotland in 1829. The letter is printed in Klingemann, *Briefwechsel*, 213–15.

[4] The dramatic 8-km.-long defile of the Höllental (Hell Valley) lies about 15 km. east of Freiburg on the road to Neustadt.

[5] The Himmelreich inn, built in the style of a large Swiss chalet, is still in existence.

The Höllental comes to an end at the Höllsteig, where we had lunch. There is an excellent inn there.[1] Before the meal we were guided to the waterfall via a hair-raising path, and were not greatly rewarded for our trouble. During lunch we chatted with the landlord, who declared the Todtnau road impassable, and advised us to drive to Lenzkirch, which Felix then decided to do. Sketching. The landlord conversed with me in French, while Felix prepared the carriage. We drove up a steep mountain in zigzag fashion, and then remained high up almost all the way to Lenzkirch. The region is very attractive, especially in springtime, when one does not yet long for the shade, and it is similar to the wild parts of the Jura. The only trees to be found here too are fir trees, and possibly maples. We passed by the Titisee, which pleased me greatly. It is almost black in colour. An Englishman has been living there, winter and summer, for three years. We did a little drawing and went up the hill on foot. The pretty grey houses. The man who brought me water and had been in Hamburg. Towards evening we arrived in Lenzkirch. The Gasthaus zum Rössle[2] was very pretty, the landlord very droll. After Felix had sketched the attractive newly built village, he showed us his straw hat workshop, and became quite heated about it. His hats were very fine and rivalled the Italian ones. At supper he had his large musical box *(Fig. t)* play

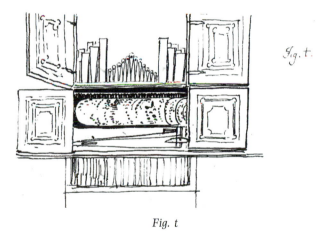

Fig. t

[1] The inn, now called the Hofgut Sternen at Höllsteig, and rebuilt, is still in business. Goethe and Marie Antoinette were among earlier notable guests. The waterfall is in the Ravenna gorge, to which a path behind the inn leads. The drawing which Felix made of the inn (in a now lost sketchbook) was subsequently redone as a watercolour, and inserted into the album he had given Cécile the previous Christmas (Bodleian Library, MS MDM c. 21, fo. 127)—see Pl. 2. He also produced a watercolour version in association with his artist friend, Johann Wilhelm Schirmer, perhaps about the year 1839, where Felix painted the buildings and Schirmer the landscape. This picture is now in the Staatsbibliothek zu Berlin.

[2] The Gasthaus 'Zum weissen Rössle' is first recorded in 1643, and in 1837 was run by Johann George Tritscheller (d. 1855), who also owned the well-known 'Stroh-Handels-Gesellschaft Faller-Tritscheller & Cie'. Although the inn closed in 1858, the building retained the Rössle name, and in a heavily rebuilt form is still in the centre of the village.

waltzes and overtures, and then the man who made it entered.[1] A real Black Forest bumpkin, who looked as if he could not count up to three, and who stood quite dumb and awkward in front of us, and let the landlord rant and rail on his behalf.

In the night I had the following hideous dream. Fig. u!![2]

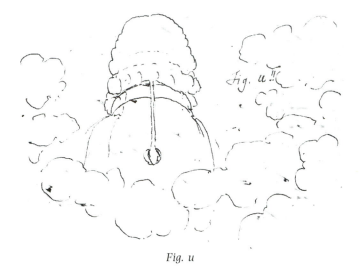

Fig. u

Tuesday, 2 May

Left Lenzkirch in the morning. The weather was glorious just like yesterday. We drove uphill for a long time. The snow was still lying around in several places along the way. Having arrived at the cross right at the top, we saw the Swiss Alps quite clearly, and in front of us the <u>wilds</u> of the Black Forest. Felix gradually established that they were the mountains near Constance and Schaffhausen that lay before us. They made a wonderful impression. We then headed downhill as far as the Schluchsee, where an isolated inn was to be found, which reminded one of those found in murder stories. From there the road proceeded in an exceedingly beautiful way up a high mountainside; beneath was a racing forest torrent which drives many sawmills, opposite were rocks covered with great fir trees, and in front of us the mountains of Lake Constance in the blue haze. The mountain up which we had to go must have been still higher at one time, and has probably been subjected to a landslide in the distant past, for tremendous boulders lay strewn

[1] Probably made by Peter Ganter, a renowned local maker, who turned the most unlikely objects into musical boxes.

[2] The figure is presumably intended to be J. S. Bach. In the original diary the drawing appears below that of Fig. t, so that he seems to be listening to the musical box.

over the whole countryside; they are, however, already covered with moss and trees. Conversation about Goldau[1]—the Universal Land Peace.[2]

In the valley St Blasien *(Fig. v)* astonished us with the round cupola of its church.[3] Formerly there was a well-populated abbey there, under whose jurisdiction the whole neighbourhood lay. We had lunch there and went for a walk. A girl offered to show us the cotton mills of Herr von Eichtal,[4] but led us instead into a room where there were only men sitting and writing, from whom we withdrew again immediately. We extracted ourselves with difficulty from the labyrinth of passages and vestibules and visited the church, which was quite attractive. The old chief official told us much about the beautiful Wiesental.

The afternoon. Continuation of the journey through the splendid Bernauertal over the watershed. The streams from there on (downhill) had a quite different and much lighter colour. The

Fig. v

---

[1] A Swiss village in Canton Schwyz near the Rigi, which was destroyed in an enormous rockfall from the Spitzenbüel in 1806. Felix had passed the site during the family's Swiss trip in 1822 (see Christian Lambour, 'Ein Schweizer Reisebrief aus dem Jahr 1822 von Lea und Fanny Mendelssohn Bartholdy an Henriette (Hinni) Mendelssohn, geb. Meyer', *Mendelssohn Studien*, 7 (1990), 171–8).

[2] The legal measures in force up to the end of the old German Empire in 1806 which were intended to prevent feuds and to preserve public order.

[3] The wealthy Benedictine abbey, founded in the 10th cent., was secularized in 1807. Its church, modelled on the Pantheon, was begun in 1772 and consecrated in 1783. Following the dissolution of the monastery, the interior of the church was despoiled and would have been in a somewhat ruinous state by 1837. It was restored after being severely damaged by fire in 1874, and has undergone further substantial alterations in recent decades.

[4] Situated in the former monastic buildings, they were founded in 1809 and survived until 1931. Freiherr David von Eichthal (1776–1851), one of the leading Baden industrialists of the first half of the 19th cent., became a partner in the mill in 1810, and eventually sole owner.

timber carts, which held us up for half an hour *(Fig. w)*.[1] Then the cart with the coarse fellow. By that time evening was upon us, and we arrived late at the River Wiese and drove on up to Todtnau and to the Gasthaus zum Ochsen.[2] Cheaply panelled small room and after a few minutes, what was only to be expected, the infestation of the Black Cavalry.[3]

Fig. w

[1] A view of the 'Wacht' or watershed of the Bernauertal and Wiesental between the villages of Bernau and Präg.

[2] Like most of Todtnau, the Ochsen was burnt down in a disastrous fire of 19 July 1876. Although subsequently rebuilt, it was demolished in the 1970s.

[3] The bedbugs! Felix, in his letter to Eduard Devrient begun in Lörrach on 3 May, says that 'it was so uncomfortable at the Ochsen that I could not settle to write' (Devrient, *My Recollections*, 200).

Felix took an early walk to the waterfall of the Wiese, and witnessed a religious procession.[1] I did a little drawing from the window, which Felix later corrected and finished off.[2] We departed besieged by a swarm of Todtnau boys.[3] It was raining gently, and so we were not able to see just how beautifully the village is situated. The valley was narrow and wild as far as Schönau; there it became more appealing. I liked Schönau a great deal. We then drove through Mambach and Zelle, past Hausen where Hebel was born,[4] and on to Schopfheim. With few interruptions it had rained the whole time, but once there it became quite dreadful. On top of that we ended up in a distasteful inn, with food which one could not eat, so that Schopfheim did not especially please us.

In the afternoon the sky cleared, and between Steinen and Brombach it became quite bright. We saw the Rötteln castle[5] *(Fig. x)* and at five o'clock arrived in Lörrach at the end of the Wiesental.

Fig. x

[1] The waterfall is 2 km. out of the village on the Geisköpfle behind the church. It flows into the Schönenbach and thence into the Wiese. The procession would have been for the Rogation Day preceding Ascension Day, which that year fell on 4 May.

[2] The drawing is preserved in Bodleian Library, MS MDM c. 6, fo. 27, and was the basis of the small pen and ink sketch that Felix included in his letter to Devrient—see Pl. 9. The illustration is only reproduced in the German edition of the Devrient letters.

[3] The German 'Wir reisen unter einem Schwarm von Todtnauer Chnabe ab' contains a reference to Hebel's poem, 'Die Wiese', which opens his *Allemannische Gedichte*:

Wo der Dengle-Geist im mitternächtige Stunde
uffeme silberne Gschirr si goldeni Sägese denglet
(Todtnau's Chnabe wüsse's wohl) am waldige Feldberg.

This was quoted by Felix, in a version of his own, at the head of his letter to Devrient.

[4] Although the family home was in Hausen, Hebel was actually born in Basle, where his parents usually spent the summer months.

[5] On a hill about 3 km. east of Lörrach, the large Schloss Rötteln, once the residence of the Margraves of Hochberg and later the Margraves of Baden, was blown up by the French in 1678. It was thus still in ruins in 1837, but was restored in 1867. Felix included a pen and ink sketch of it in the same letter to Devrient.

Lörrach is an attractive place with a splendid hotel.[1] We drank coffee, and the fine sunshine enticed us to travel further. Hardly had we arrived at the top of the road than a frightful thunderstorm started—the sky was greyish-yellow and horrible to behold—the thunder and lightning scared me. Felix told me about the cloudburst in Switzerland. The rain persisted until we arrived at Schliengen, our stopping place for the night.[2] No one in the hotel there paid any attention to us until Felix had bawled out a large company of women. We were led up a spiral staircase to a damp room. We demanded to be given another one. Felix went to the chemist's *(Fig. y)* and then wrote to Herr Devrient. I read legends of the Rhine.[3]

Fig. y

Thursday, 4 May

After a bug-ridden night*,[4] we departed at ten up the splendid Basle highway. Had lunch in Krotzingen. Beautiful flower garden, and cherry trees in blossom by the roadside. Arrived in Freiburg at two o'clock in the rain. Felix immediately went to the post office and returned with seven letters. We did some writing ourselves in the evening and went to bed early.

[1] This would have been the 'Hirschen', which was also a posthouse station.
[2] At Schliengen, on the Basle–Freiburg road, the Mendelssohns must have stayed at the Gasthof Baselstab, which is now the Weingut Blankenhorn. The stone spiral staircase (an unusual feature in the area), is still extant, and dated 1656. The letter to Devrient was evidently begun at Lörrach and continued at Schliengen; it was not finished, however, until 15 May in Frankfurt (see Devrient, *My Recollections*, 198–203).
[3] Probably Karl Joseph Simrock's collection *Rheinsagen, aus der Munde des Volkes und deutscher Dichter*, first published in 1836.
[4] In the original diary the word 'bug-ridden' is represented by a tiny depiction of the creature.

This is much too nicely put—the washing bowls looked like this:

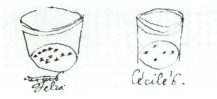

Felix   Cécile'6.

Friday, 5 May

Spent the time writing and packing.[1] The weather threatened to be bad for the journey.

Saturday, 6 May

Left Freiburg at eight in the morning, having found another seven letters together with parcels from Leipzig at the post office. Owing to our reading of the letters, which took a good hour, we neglected to observe the lovely surroundings. Emmendingen was the first stopping place, where the Freiburg horses returned. On the way to Offenburg we came to Ettenheim with the customs house where the Duc de Enghien was seized in the night.[2] Monument to Stulz, the tailor, quite delicately worked in bronze.[3] Had our midday meal in Offenburg. Set off again at three o'clock, and arrived in Rastatt about seven, where we decided to spend the night. On the way saw the Strasbourg Minster once more, and the valley of Baden-Baden. The whole day was very cold and windy, and we froze in the rooms of the Goldenes Kreuz.[4] Felix recognized the landlord as the famous waiter of the Schwan about whom Eckermann wrote.[5]

[1] Letters of this date from Cécile to her mother, and from Felix to Julie Jeanrenaud are extant (see pp. 149–53).
[2] Louis Antoine Henri de Bourbon, Duc de Enghien (1772–1804), lived in Ettenheim as an exile from 1801 until he was seized on Napoleon's orders at the Customs House on the Landstrasse on the night of 15 Mar. 1804, and shot at Vincennes six days later. The customs house in question was destroyed in 1840.
[3] At Kippenheim. Johann Georg Stulz (1771–1832), born in this small market-town, made his fortune as a fashionable tailor in London, but bestowed considerable benefactions in his native land, where he was ennobled. The monument, which is still in existence, was erected in 1834.
[4] The Goldenes Kreuz was in the Hauptstrasse (now Kaiserstrasse), and survived into the 20th cent. The Mendelssohns strangely make no mention of the large Baroque Schloss.
[5] The Schwan inn was the Weisser Schwan in Frankfurt. Johann Peter Eckermann (1792–1854) was Goethe's companion and secretary at the end of his life. He passed through Frankfurt in 1830, and gave an enthusiastic account of the waiter's remarkable abilities in his *Gespräche mit Goethe* (entry for 25 Apr. 1830). Felix had known the inn since 1822, when he stayed there with his parents on the way to and from Switzerland (see F. Hiller, *Mendelssohn, Letters and Recollections*, 3). Murray's *Hand-Book* (1836) describes it as having 'good attendance, and one of the best tables-d'hôte in Germany; very good quarters for a single man'. Felix read Eckermann's work just after publication in the summer of 1836 whilst in Frankfurt (cf. his letter to Lea, 14 July 1836, printed in *Letters . . . from 1833 to 1847*, ed. P. and C. Mendelssohn Bartholdy (London, 1863), 114–20).

Left the dull town of Rastatt at nine the next morning. The weather was better than yesterday, but we still had to keep the coach windows shut. We had breakfast in Karlsruhe and had a look at the picture dealers' shops. Felix gave a false name at the town gate in order to avoid any subsequent reproaches by the musicians of the place. The journey was very tedious through Bruchsal and Wiesloch etc. to Heidelberg, where we didn't arrive until after four o'clock! The Prinz Carl hotel[1] pleases us greatly; our room has an alcove and a most splendid, red velvet sofa. Felix immediately went in search of Fritz Schlemmer, but failed to find him at home. His princely mannered servant Franz said that he was at the castle and took us there.[2] Superb view of the setting sun from the terrace. The air was most pleasant and the sky clearer, which promised us fairer weather. After Fritz and ourselves had pursued one another in vain the whole evening, we returned home and settled very comfortably into our room.

Monday, 8 May

Fritz came to see us quite early at ten *(Fig. 2)*. Our intentions to put a stop to his talk and teasing. We walked together over the Neckar to Aunt Becher's,[3] who was very surprised to see us. Here in Heidelberg we present ourselves for the first time to society as a married couple. Our expectation of fine weather is thwarted.

After lunch it rained again. In addition, before lunch Fritz had played the organ for us in the church *(Fig. 1)*[4] and then joined us for our meal. We then walked together up to the castle, and

[1] The Prince Carl hotel was in the Kornmarkt below the castle, just round the corner from the Heiliggeistkirche. It closed in 1915, and was used as municipal offices from 1917. The old building was demolished in 1978, and new municipal offices built, although with a façade modelled on that of the old hotel.

[2] The medieval-Renaissance castle on a spur of the Königstuhl overlooking the old town, was largely destroyed by the French in 1689 and 1693. Partially restored by the Electors Palatine in the 18th cent., it succumbed to a lightning strike in 1764, and once more became ruinous, which is how the Mendelssohns saw it. The 'broken-off tower', mentioned in the entry of 9 May, is not the spectacular south-east tower (the 'Pulver Turm' or 'Gesprengter Turm'), which the French blew up in 1693, resulting in half of it falling in one piece into the moat, but the now ivyless north-west 'Dicker Turm', blown up in 1689. The two 'knights', which reside in niches, are in fact figures of the Electors Ludwig V (1508–49) and Friedrich V (1610–32).

[3] Caroline Becher, née Schunck (1779–1870), great-aunt of Cécile. Married Georg Ludwig Becher (d. 1815), a Frankfurt lawyer, and had a daughter, Ida (1804–88). From 1828 to 1844 she lived in part of the house 'Zum Waldhorn', Neuenheimer Landstrasse 18, with a garden behind extending up the hill, where the summer house shown in Fig. 2 would have been situated. 'Zum Waldhorn' was a wine tavern owned by Johannes Frisch. After many alterations the old building finally disappeard in 1965.

[4] Fritz Schlemmer is playing, with Felix conducting. Cécile is in the middle of the group of onlookers, the other two being unknown, though probably relatives. The drawing of the organ is problematical in various ways. It is generally assumed that they were playing in the principal church of Heidelberg, the Heiliggeistkirche in the Marktplatz just around the corner from the Mendelssohns' hotel. From 1705 to 1936 this church was divided between the Reformed Church and the Catholics by a wall separating the nave and choir, the nave being the Reformed part. Each congregation had an organ built on either side of the dividing wall. The Reformed one was

Fig. z

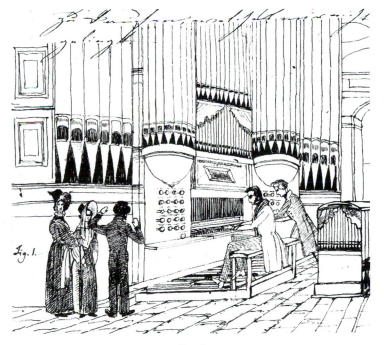

Fig. 1

later on to Aunt Pickford's.[1] I stayed there the whole evening. Felix and Fritz attended the lectures of Herr Schlosser[2] and then picked me up again. It was raining in torrents, and a coach had to be summoned from the town. This delay gave the two men topics to argue about fiercely in the coach. Agreeable look of our room on our return.

Tuesday, 9 May

Fritz on his daily visit to us at ten o'clock brought very nice flowers and music manuscript paper with him. We strolled together to see Mme Benecke,[3] who was not at home, and then up to the castle. Felix wanted to sketch the broken-off tower, where the young and old knights protrude from beneath the ivy, but it was so wet and windy that it proved impossible. Visit of the aunts and cousins—a most excellent lunch. Afterwards a walk on the Philosophenweg[4] from where there is a wonderful view of the castle, the Engelswiese[5] and Stift Neuburg.[6] Returned by

originally a two-manual instrument of 1744 by Liborius Müller, which in 1815 was extended to become a three-manual organ of 41 stops. This is certainly the size of organ suggested by the pipework in the drawing, with its large façade pipes, many stop knobs, and separate Rückpostiv division behind the player. The background of the drawing, however, shows what appears to be a Baroque church with round arches, whereas the Heiliggeistkirche is a 15th-cent. Gothic building with pointed arches. But neither of the two Baroque churches, the Lutheran Providenzkirche and the Catholic Jesuitenkirche, had organs at all like this. It would seem most likely that the drawing is simply incorrect in its architectural details, as it most certainly is in some of the details of the organ. For though it is clearly a large instrument, it has been drawn with only one manual, instead of the three it must have had. The general perspective too shows many deficiencies, especially with regard to the music desk and the alignment of the pedalboard. Would Felix himself have made such elementary mistakes in depicting an instrument like this, or did Cécile perhaps at least partially contribute to it? Since it would have been drawn some time later, back in the hotel, it may well be that the details were imperfectly recollected. Since Schlemmer himself came of a Reformed family, the Heiliggeistkirche is also the most likely church on grounds of religious adherence.

[1] Friederike Pickford, née Schunck (1783–1851), great-aunt of Cécile. She married John Middleton Pickford (c.1779–1830), by whom she had 10 children. Their large house was on the Schlierbach road east of the Karlstor. As a widow she took in English families as paying guests.

[2] Friedrich Christoph Schlosser (1776–1861), Professor of History at Heidelberg from 1817.

[3] Louisa Benecke, née Falck (1782/3–1876). Second wife of Wilhelm Benecke (1776–1837), businessman and author, who was born in Hamburg, but who later lived in England, where he founded a chemical factory in Deptford (with his brother Friedrich). In 1828 he made over the business to his son, Friedrich Wilhelm Benecke, and retired to Heidelberg, where he died on 8 Mar. 1837 shortly before the Mendelssohns' visit. They lived in the Märzgasse.

[4] A favourite promenade on the north bank of the Neckar along the slope of the Heiligenberg, providing superb views of the town and its surroundings. Its name perhaps suggests that it provided a source of inspiration for Heidelberg's academic community.

[5] 'Angel Meadow'. Strictly speaking the Engelswiese was a small meadow on the north bank of the river to the east of the old bridge. It is not named on present maps, but was the western part of the area described as 'Untere Judenhütte'. However, a path labelled 'Engelswiesen Fussweg' to the east of the Engelswiese proper, suggests that perhaps the whole of that area of the hillside was unofficially known as the Engelswiese.

[6] A former convent at Ziegelhausen, 3 km. to the west of the old town on the north bank of the river. It was secularized in 1799, and in 1825 was acquired by the Frankfurt lawyer and politician Johann Friedrich Heinrich Schlosser, a nephew of Goethe, who made it a meeting point for the Heidelberg Romantic movement. It was reconsecrated in 1926.

way of Aunt Becher's hill and drank coffee there.[1] Rehearsal for 'Die Jahreszeiten' which was to be performed in the castle.[2] Mme Kiné[3] etc.

Wednesday, 10 May

More dreadful rain. Fortunately this time Fritz brought us newspapers and books with which we could pass the time. At noon the two men went off to the organ once again. I paid a visit to Ida Ruth,[4] and made an unsuccessful attempt to buy a straw hat.

Felix came back late for dinner at three. Afterwards the visit of Aunt Becher, who stayed with me while Felix went to see Herr Hetsch and Herr Thibaut,[5] and remained with the latter for a very long time. We drank tea together, and conversed very pleasantly about the usefulness or uselessness of women. Felix accompanied our aunt across the bridge. By the time he returned it was already half past nine.

Thursday, 11 May

Fritz arrived with the eau-de-Cologne and the news that 'Oberon'[6] was to be performed in Mannheim. As Felix had never been there, we decided to drive over at twelve, after the prelude, which all three of us had been writing out, was completed.[7] Fritz brought a very spirited coach, and in no time at all we were in Mannheim, where we discovered that 'Oberon' was not to be

[1] The next sentence originally read: 'Felix spent the evening writing out preludes and fugues with Fritz'. This was crossed out, presumably because it properly belonged to 11 May.

[2] The 4th Heidelberg Musical Festival was celebrated by a performance of Haydn's oratorio on 17 May in the castle courtyard, with about 400 performers drawn from many local choirs.

[3] Possibly Mme C. Kiené, mother of the pianist Marie Bigot, who had given Felix lessons in Paris in 1816. Kiené corresponded with Felix, but all the surviving correspondence is from Paris. There is no trace of a Kiné or Kiené in Heidelberg itself.

[4] Ida Ruth, née Pickford (1809–45). Daughter of John Middleton Pickford and Friederike Schunck. In 1833 she married Emil Ruth (1809–69), who eventually became a Professor of Modern Languages at Heidelberg. She was an able harpist.

[5] Ludwig Hetsch (1806–72), composer, 'Akademischer Musikdirektor' in Heidelberg, 1836–46, and director of the Musik- und Singverein. He gave annual large-scale oratorio performances in the castle ruins. Anton Friedrich Justus Thibaut (1772–1840), German academic lawyer and amateur musician. Professor of Law at Heidelberg from 1805, he was an enthusiastic collector and advocate of older sacred music, particularly that of Palestrina and Handel, and directed a private singing group. Mendelssohn had first met him in Heidelberg in 1827.

[6] Weber's opera, first performed in London in 1826. Weber's music, and especially *Der Freischütz* (1821), was one of the greatest influences on the young Mendelssohn. According to the playbill for that day, the performance was cancelled owing to the indisposition of one of the singers, and Zschokke's tragedy *Die eiserne Larve* substituted.

[7] Felix was presumably providing Schlemmer with a copy of his recently completed organ preludes and fugues, Op. 37.

performed after all. Pre-lunch visit to the picture shop of Herr Artaria.[1] Lithographs of the 'Thief's Confession' and of 'Judith' by Horace Vernet,[2] and several Düsseldorf School pictures.[3] At lunch Fritz and Felix gave me cause to fear that they were trying to become intoxicated on champagne, and they then lurched and swayed so much afterwards in the street, when we were heading for the picture gallery,[4] that it was quite unseemly. As luck would have it the streets of Mannheim were as empty of people as the picture gallery was of art. Apart from some drawings by Albrecht Dürer and Adrian von Ostade there was nothing there worth looking at.[5] And the exhibition of modern pictures was even worse!

Stroll in the Schloss garden down by the Rhine,[6] where the Hardt Mountains[7] can be seen very clearly. At half past *five (I had to refloat the diary, it having been driven on to a sandbank, because it was so sandy in Mannheim) we drove back again.*[8] *Being tired out, Felix made ridiculous faces and yawned a thousand and one times. We laughed at him for so long that we fell asleep ourselves, and when we drove into Heidelberg, Fritz, who was woken up by the rattling, stretched himself and asked: 'Is this the learned village?' I, however, slept on until we stopped in front of the hotel, and the attendants came out with light. Then I found myself wide awake once more, and we ate further in the evening.*

Friday, 12 May

Argument in the morning over the visit to Frau Niess.[9] *Felix behaved in an unmannerly fashion—Fritz wanted to correct him but aggravated the situation, and almost made me angry. All three of us finally went out in the strong wind, but met Frau Niess and her little Amalie, and returned with*

[1] Artaria & Fontaine, art-dealers. Originally founded in Mainz by the same Artaria family as the famous Viennese print and music publishing firm, it moved to Mannheim in 1792, and rose to become one of the leading art establishments in Europe.

[2] Horace Vernet (1789–1863), military painter and lithographer. He was Director of the Académie de France in Rome, 1829–35, where Mendelssohn met him, and then returned to Paris.

[3] The Düsseldorf School of painters based on the Kunstakademie there, which came to prominence in the 1820s under the direction of Peter von Cornelius and his successor Wilhelm von Schadow.

[4] Founded in 1803 by Grand Duke Carl Friedrich in the Schloss.

[5] It is uncertain whether these were really drawings by Dürer and Adriaen van Ostade rather than engravings, since there is no evidence that the collection possessed drawings by these artists. There was a large collection of engravings, acquired in 1810 from Anton von Klein, and this included works of both artists. The Schloss collections were dispersed in 1937. The engravings, which remain uncatalogued, are now in the Städtische Kunsthalle in Mannheim. The paintings (which included 4 by or attributed to Ostade), are now partly in the Staatliche Kunsthalle in Karlsruhe, and partly in the Reiss-Museum in Mannheim.

[6] The vast 18th-cent. Schloss with gardens extending down to the Rhine was the residence of the Elector Palatine until 1778.

[7] The Hardt range lies on the west bank of Rhine in the neighbourhood of Bad Dürkheim and Neustadt an der Weinstrasse.

[8] Although the diary 'voice' continues to be that of Cécile, Felix actually wrote the text from here until part-way through the account of 13 May.

[9] Cornelie Charlotte Nies, née Du Fay (1783–1841), a widowed aunt of Cécile's friend Marie Bernus (see p. 42 n. 4). She lived in Villa Charlottenberg on the Ziegelhausen road.

them. Afterwards to Aunt Becher's, who wasn't at home, but who then joined us in the summer house (Fig. 2) in which we sat ourselves down.

Fig. 2

Fritz had to go to his beloved,[1] with whom he had arranged a rendezvous and a tête-à-tête with 16 feet; we walked along the Philosophenweg to the point where one turns the corner and sees Handschuhsheim[2] and Mannheim; then back again through the delightful neighbourhood. Lunch with Fritz at three o'clock. Afterwards to Mme Benecke for tea, where Fritz drank seven cups of tea, and courted the young ladies. Felix tried out the English grand piano, and I recalled the previous year, when I had often stood at the same place by the window and admired the view.[3] Stroll up to the castle. Pickfordian twinge of conscience—decision to pay a final visit. It was very succinct. Then Felix swore like a trooper; and then the day came to an end.

Saturday, 13 May

Left Heidelberg at nine, since Mother in her letters (both of which, through a postal mistake, we received yesterday, instead of on the 9th and yesterday) had very much wanted us to get to Frankfurt.

---

[1] i.e. the organ.
[2] A village on the east side of the Heiligenberg, 2 km. north of Heidelberg.
[3] The view from the Benecke house (Märzgasse A 232, now No. 16), would have been principally of the large 'kurfürstliche Herrengarten' (now built over) and towards the castle.

Fritz on the coach-box with us as far as Aunt Becher's. Counted nineteen bakeries in Bensheim and bought four rolls; added a sausage in Auerbach (Fig. 3).

Fig. 3

Thus far the countryside and weather were everything one could have wished for; in Weinheim we had the coach opened up, as a result of which we swallowed a fair amount of dust, which was expelled again by fresh oranges. With the intention of having lunch in Darmstadt we drove to the Darmstädter Hof,[1] but found the room there so disgusting and full of men and offensive smells that it made me quite wretched, and I went out into the street, while Felix cancelled the meal. We awaited the horses in front of the repulsive hotel and drove along the roads from Darmstadt to Frankfurt. Unpleasant country—Langen—the Frankfurter Wald.[2] It was raining as we passed by the watch-tower. On the way downhill we met Julie, who came to meet us alone in the coach. At five we arrived together at the Fahrtor.[3] We found the house empty. Grandfather and August are in England,[4] Grandmother is in Koblenz for the baptism.[5] Mother

---

[1] In the Rheinstrasse. Dating from 1791–3, it was torn down in 1903 when a new 'Darmstädter Hof' opened in a neighbouring building; this in turn was destroyed in 1944.

[2] The extensive forest to the south of the town. A popular hostelry within it was the old Forester's House (Oberforsthaus), which the Mendelssohns visited more than once, and which survived in rebuilt form until 1963 (a remnant still exists). This was the 'Jägerhaus' of Goethe's *Faust*.

[3] See Introduction, p. xiv.

[4] Cécile's grandfather, Cornelius Carl Souchay, was in England throughout the summer, and Felix met him in Birmingham (see diary entries for 19 Sept. onwards). August was evidently his servant (see letter of Cécile to Elisabeth Jeanrenaud, 5 May 1837, p. 150).

[5] Cécile's aunt, Emilie Souchay, daughter of Cornelius Carl and Helene Elisabeth Souchay, had married Friedrich Fallenstein, and lived in Koblenz (see p. 47 n. 5). Their first child, Ida, was born on 29 Apr. 1837.

was very glad to have us back again. We drank tea, allayed the day's hunger to some extent, cleaned ourselves up, and looked over our room with the Armide and Venus. I brought out the presents from Strasbourg, which gave much pleasure. With this and much conversation evening soon arrived. Supper. To bed.

Sunday, 14 May

First day of the Whitsun holiday. In the morning we were alone. Mother and Julie went to church[1] for Communion. At eleven we went to visit Aunt Schlegel[2] and Aunt Elise Schunck.[3] The lovely family portrait[4] at the former's house. The rain caught us just as we were about to go to Mme Hiller's.[5] We therefore visited her in the afternoon. Mlle Toye. Herr Hiller[6] was at the music festival in Heidelberg.[7] It rained the whole day right up to the end.

Monday, 15 May

Decision to drive to Bonames[8] to visit Aunt Helene,[9] which we carried out in the afternoon. The weather was very pleasant. Felix was happy in the garden, having a long conversation with Uncle Eduard about the Düsseldorf painters and Herr Veit.[10] Windy return journey rather late in the evening.

---

[1] The French Reformed church in which Felix and Cécile were married.

[2] Dorothea von Schlegel; see Introduction (p. xiii).

[3] Elise Schunck, née Harnier (b. 1781), great-aunt of Cécile by marriage. Wife of Heinrich Schunck (see p. 110 n. 2).

[4] Presumably the drawing of Dorothea von Schlegel with the Veit family by Franz Brentano (see p. 163 n. 3 and Carola Stern, 'Ich möchte mir Flügel wünschen': Das Leben der Dorothea Schlegel (Reinbek bei Hamburg, 1990), 296–7). According to Norbert Suhr's Philipp Veit (Weinheim, 1991), it is now in private ownership.

[5] Ferdinand Hiller's mother, Regine Hiller, née Sichel (1786–1839) had an apartment on the Pfarreisen (Hiller, Mendelssohn, Letters and Recollections, 54).

[6] Ferdinand Hiller (1811–85), German conductor, composer, writer, and teacher. He first met Mendelssohn in his native Frankfurt in 1822, and the two soon became close friends. He acted as conductor of the Cäcilienverein for the 1836/7 season, deputizing for the sick J. N. Schelble, as Mendelssohn himself had done in the summer of 1836. He was to spend most of the next six years in Italy.

[7] See p. 37 n. 2.

[8] Village 10 km. north of Frankfurt.

[9] Helene Souchay, née Schmidt (1804–85). Wife of Eduard Franz Souchay (1800–72), maternal uncle of Cécile, and a Frankfurt senator.

[10] Philipp Veit (1793–1877), German Romantic painter of the Nazarene school. Son of Dorothea von Schlegel by her first marriage to Simon Veit, and hence a cousin of Felix. Director of the Städelsches Kunstinstitut in Frankfurt, 1830–43.

Julie's songs[1] arrived from Leipzig. Her delight and pride at seeing her name in print. In the afternoon a drive into the Frankfurter Wald, where on that particular day the whole town gathers.[2] Felix was amused by all the carriage driving and riding beneath the beautiful trees, which, however, are only just beginning to come into leaf. We returned home again by way of Niederrad.[3] Felix sat in his room and wrote a good many little noteheads for the rest of the day.

Wednesday, 17 May

In the morning we received visits until some time before lunch, when we intended to take a little walk and were caught out by the rain. After lunch we paid a visit to Marie Bernus,[4] whom I maintain should have married Felix. We then collected Julie and went for a drive in the direction of Bornheim,[5] where there was today the same chaos as there was yesterday in the forest (just downright vulgar folk). I then continued on with Julie to see Victoire, while Felix returned home just in time to greet the disagreeable, strange maid of Frau Mylius.[6] Nice, calm evening.

Thursday, 18 May

Lunch at Aunt Elise's.[7] Felix and I were separated at table for the first time, and consequently felt the bad effects of it and great joy when it was over. We had a good stretch out in the carriage and in this state made a visit to the Gogels,[8] who fortunately were not at home. Julie went to the theatre,[9] while the rest of us stayed quietly at home, and continued to chew over lunch

[1] Felix's *Sechs Gesänge*, Op. 34 (Leipzig, Breitkopf & Härtel, 1837), which are dedicated to Julie Jeanrenaud.

[2] Tuesday after Whitsun is 'Wäldchestag', when it was (and still is) the custom for Frankfurters to go out into the Frankfurter Wald for a picnic and other entertainment.

[3] In the forest just across the Main from Frankfurt.

[4] Marie Bernus, née Du Fay (1819–87), wife of Franz Bernus (see p. 44 n. 1).

[5] Then a village 3 km. north-east of Frankfurt.

[6] Wife of Carl Mylius (see p. 50 n. 5). [7] Elise Schunck.

[8] Johann Noë Gogel (1788–1865), married Marie Sophie Elisabeth v. Loevenich (1791–1862) in 1816. Their daughter Sophie (1817–96), a childhood friend of Cécile, married the banker Georg Adolf Heinrich Hauck (1812–84) on 20 May 1837.

[9] The theatre was in the Komödienplatz (now the Rathenauplatz). It was demolished in 1902. Bellini's *Die Puritaner* in Friederike Ellmenreich's German translation was performed that day.

and its boredom. At supper Bury[1] aroused our curiosity through the concealment of a piece of news which she believed only she had been told about, and which we should only learn of the next day.

Friday, 19 May

Herr Hiller, who had returned from Heidelberg, came to see Felix. Scarcely was he here, and I had gone to my old drawing master[2] again, then all of a sudden and to our great surprise Mme Veit[3] appeared with Felix's two small cousins, Marie and Margarethe Mendelssohn.[4] They had arrived from Berlin with their father, and were passing through on their way to Bonn. Since last autumn they had altered, much to their advantage, and are very lovable and pretty and nicely dressed. After the first astonishment, greetings, rejoicing, and many questions from Felix, Frau Veit produced the idea of spending the afternoon together at the Mainlust,[5] which duly happened. We drank coffee there with Aunt Schlegel and went for a walk in the garden. At half past six we called for our very dear cousin at the Hotel de Russie,[6] and then drove together almost as far as Höchst.[7] This was a very great but all too brief pleasure. End of the day—beginning of the night.

Saturday, 20 May

At half past ten Mother, Julie, and I went to church to see, or rather to hear, Sophie Gogel[8] get married. Then we picked up Felix for breakfast from the company of Herr Hiller, where he had been greatly enjoying himself. It was raining in torrents and the weather was the sole topic of conversation. In the afternoon Felix and Herr Hiller played on the piano, sang psalms, and made fun of a good many people. Herr Hiller stayed for supper and late on into the evening.

[1] Sara Bury, formerly governess to Elisabeth Jeanrenaud's children.
[2] Anton Radl (1774–1852), Frankfurt landscape painter and copperplate-engraver.
[3] Philipp Veit's wife, Caroline née Pulini.
[4] Marie (1822–91) and Margarethe (1823–90), daughters of Joseph Mendelssohn's son Alexander (1798–1871) and Marianne, née Seeligmann.
[5] A well-known inn on the bank of the Main outside the town walls to the west of the Unter Main Tor, now the site of the Westhafen.
[6] At this time it was probably Frankfurt's most luxurious hotel, situated in the Zeil.
[7] Then a village on the Main about 8 km. west of Frankfurt.   [8] See p. 42 n. 8.

I missed church by oversleeping. At eleven Herr Bernus[1] arrived to take Felix off to see his pictures. I received a visit from my friends. After lunch Mother, Julie, and I took a drive and went visiting, while the two friends once more created a great din on the piano. We drank tea together, and then listened to the recital. Disturbed by a great row from the kitchen. The man-servant had been teased over his sweetheart and had become enraged because of it. Evening.

Monday, 22 May

In the morning I had a English lesson. News from Koblenz that Grandmother had fallen ill there, and will come back later. Felix did a lot of composing. Frau Hiller's and Mlle Toye's visit in the afternoon. In the evening Felix read aloud to us the 'Fräulein von Scuderi' from Hoffmann's writings, and we were terrified by it.[2]

Tuesday, 23 May

In the morning visits to Herr Appia,[3] whose wife displayed immense enthusiasm about 'St Paul', and to old Herr Harnier.[4] Herr Perret,[5] returned from Koblenz, had lunch with us and fell asleep over it. The rest of the day must have been of no interest since it has slipped from my memory.

Wednesday, 24 May

I drove in the morning with Mother to the cemetery;[6] the weather was very rough. Everything there is green and very pleasant; we did some tidying up of my little sister's grave, and then

[1] Franz Bernus (Bernus Du Fay) (1808–84). Frankfurt senator and head of a large trading house. He spent much of his youth abroad in England, Italy, and Russia, and developed a strong interest in art.

[2] 'Das Fräulein von Scuderi', a Novelle by E. T. A. Hoffmann (1776–1822), first published in 1819. It involves a Parisian goldsmith of Louis XIV's time, who murdered his clients, and was then killed himself.

[3] Paul Joseph Appia (1782–1849), Pastor at the French Reformed Church in Frankfurt from 1819 in succession to Cécile's father, Auguste Jeanrenaud. He married Caroline Develay (1787–1867), and officiated at the Mendelssohns' marriage.

[4] Louis Harnier (1768–1855), Frankfurt banker, father of Eduard von Harnier (see p. 48 n. 1).

[5] Presumably François Perret, partner in the Frankfurt import business of Souchay & Perret until 1811, and then the firm's representative in London.

[6] The Hauptfriedhof, on the Eckenheimer Landstrasse, opened in 1828, and designed by Sebastian Rinz. Cécile's younger sister, Augustine, born in 1819, had died in 1832. Her grave is apparently no longer extant, but Cécile, her mother, and her brother Carl and his family are all buried there.

returned home again. Felix in the meantime had been with Franz Bernus to see Herr Brentano's miniatures[1] and to Herr Leerse's[2] to see an old family portrait by Van Dyck. Lunch. In the afternoon, or rather towards evening, a small gathering that dearly wanted to hear Felix play. He was all too obliging and played wonderfully. Everybody, especially my friend Marie,[3] was quite enchanted. So the day ended.

Thursday, 25 May

Franz Bernus came once again to take Felix off to view pictures. Together they saw the Two Marys by Herr Veit,[4] and the studios of the Düsseldorf artists, and in the afternoon the decoration round a goblet which was due to be presented to Rückert.[5] Short drive round the town. Felix worked a great deal and in the course of these days completed his Psalm 'As the hart pants for fresh water'.[6]

Friday, 26 May

I had another English lesson. I am reading Pelham[7] and have already reached the first page. In the afternoon we went for a drive to the Oberräder Wald;[8] lovely forget-me-nots, which tempted us to get out. We picked a whole sunshadeful of the pretty little blue flowers, which continued to give us great amusement in the carriage (Fig. 4). The wood was a wonderful light

[1] Franz Brentano (1765–1844), Frankfurt merchant and senator. In 1798 he married Antonie Birkenstock (1780–1869), who inherited in 1809 a fine art collection from her Viennese father, Johann Melchior Birkenstock, much of which, however, was sold in the years immediately following. Half-brother of the poet Clemens Brentano (1778–1842). During a stay in Vienna, 1809–12, the Brentanos became good friends of Beethoven, and Antonie is generally accepted as the most likely addressee of Beethoven's 1812 letter to the 'Immortal Beloved'. They lived at 22 Neue Mainzergasse.

[2] Jakob Philipp Leerse, called Sarasin (1762–1840). He was a banker, and partner in Chiron, Sarasin et Cie.

[3] Marie Bernus.

[4] The 1837 version of *The Two Marys at Christ's Tomb* is the earliest of three that Veit painted; it is now in a private collection.

[5] For Friedrich Rückert's birthday on 16 May, a group of his Frankfurt admirers, including Philipp Veit and Xaver Schnyder von Wartensee, sent him a letter of congratulation, and had commissioned an inscribed silver goblet to go with it. Rückert, however, did not actually receive the goblet until the autumn.

[6] Psalm 42, Op. 42.

[7] *Pelham, or the Adventures of a Gentleman*, by Edward Bulwer Lytton (1803–73), published anonymously (London, 1828).

[8] The eastern part of the Frankfurter Wald to the south of Oberrad (between Sachsenhausen and Offenbach).

Fig. 4

green, all sorts of little birds were singing delightfully, the sunlight peeped so brightly through the slender small trees—in short it was a glorious afternoon. We arrived back home late—Felix did some writing—Herr Appia's visit.

Saturday, 27 May

In the morning writing—sewing—reading. Uncle Eduard,[1] who is on his way to Munich, ate with us. In the afternoon another drive into the forest to the Forsthaus,[2] where we once more enjoyed ourselves enormously and found a host of flowers.

[1] Eduard Souchay (see p. 41 n. 9).   [2] See p. 40 n. 2.

To church in the morning. Lunch at the Bernuses with Veit, Hessemer,[1] and Grieck.[2] Drive afterwards to the Sachsenhäuserberg[3] and along the roads we used yesterday. Franz Bernus's allusions. Marie and I promised to share with each other our observations on this matter, which I have not yet mentioned in this volume, but which is nevertheless the main subject of our conversations and thoughts.[4]

Returned to the garden, where we drank tea and then took leave of the Bernuses, who are going to Kreuznach tomorrow. Mother called for us. Grandmother arrived late in the evening from Koblenz with Herr Fallenstein.[5] Strange impression that was made on Felix by this much talked of man.

Monday, 29 May

Spent the day with the new arrivals until four o'clock in the afternoon, when Herr Fallenstein departed. Felix was very industrious; I spent my time mostly with Mother and Julie.

Tuesday, 30 May

In the morning a bulky letter was written to Berlin, I writing to Mother, Felix to his sisters.[6] Stroll in the evening.

Wednesday, 31 May

In the morning we paid visits to the St Georges,[7] on account of their daughter's wedding, to old Frau Koch,[8] who behaved very strangely and immediately sat Felix at the piano in

---

[1] Friedrich Maximilian Hessemer (1800–60), architect and writer on architecture at the Städelsches Institut from 1830. He also published poetry.

[2] Perhaps Georg Ludwig Kriegk (1805–78), Professor at the Gymnasium in Frankfurt, later town archivist.

[3] Sachsenhausen was then a small suburb of Frankfurt on the opposite bank of the Main. A group of hills to the south formed the Sachsenhäuser Berg, on top of which was the Sachsenhäuser Warte ('watch-tower').

[4] Both women were then pregnant.

[5] Friedrich Fallenstein (1790–1853), civil servant in Koblenz 1832–42. He married Emilie Souchay (1805–81), an aunt of Cécile.

[6] Cécile's letter is actually dated 28 May (see p. 157). Felix wrote letters not only to his sisters, but to his mother as well; all are dated 29 May (see pp. 158–63).

[7] Johann Georg Konrad Saint-George (1782–1863), banker. He married Margarete Luise Bethmann-Hollweg (1793–1831) in 1810. Their daughter Susanne Elisabeth Ida (1815–96) married another banker, Johann Georg von Heyder (1812–88) on 19 Sept. 1837.

[8] Probably Susanne Elisabeth Koch, née Perret (1775–1843), who married Heinrich Koch (1772–1828) in 1800.

order to give him some good tuition, and to Bürgermeister Harnier.[1] Felix conducted himself exceedingly well, whilst I was quite furious. Herr Hiller ate with us and invited us to go to the Cäcilienverein in the evening, where the choruses from 'St Paul' were to be sung.[2] I enjoyed myself greatly, and Felix was very satisfied, particularly delighted by the contralto part. Fräulein Arnold's trial aria. We returned home rather late, and went to bed tired out.

Thursday, 1 June

Felix started off this month with great courtesy; he sent me to the milliner's in order to buy a hat for Grandmother, with whom yesterday he had become somewhat exasperated, so that grass, or rather flowers, could grow over his anger. Then as always he was very industrious; my activities were so unimportant that I cannot recall them.

Friday, 2 June

At ten I had a drawing lesson, and sketched out the pretty picture which Schirmer had painted for us as a wedding present.[3] Lunch. Afterwards Felix engaged in composition. In the evening, just as we were about to go out together, an unexpected visit by Herr President Verkenius[4] from Cologne, a very genial old music lover and admirer of Felix, who was travelling to Karlsbad on account of his health. He gave us all great pleasure and stayed until fairly late in the evening. On top of that Herr Schnyder von Wartensee[5] came along and had supper with us, during which he did not forbear to provide us with long explanations about the various kinds of clouds, canons, counterpoints, <u>that is to say</u> things which people like me cannot understand, especially when they come from the mouth of Herr Schnyder. He also set the most unintelligible arithmetical

[1] Eduard von Harnier (1800–68). Doctor of law, and a Frankfurt senator; he was junior Bürgermeister in 1837.

[2] Hiller, *Mendelssohn, Letters and Recollections*, 94, recalls the occasion.

[3] Johann Wilhelm Schirmer (1807–63). He was a pupil at the Düsseldorf Akademie from 1827, and a friend of Felix from the latter's Düsseldorf days. He specialized in landscapes, engravings, and lithographs. The whereabouts of Schirmer's painting is now unknown, but it is described in Felix's letter to Rebecka of 29 May (p. 163).

[4] Erich Heinrich Wilhelm Verkenius (1776–1841), Appeal Court judge in Cologne. He possessed a fine music collection, and organized the Lower Rhine Music Festivals.

[5] Xaver Schnyder von Wartensee (1786–1868), Swiss composer and teacher, who settled in Frankfurt in 1817.

problems. The only comprehensible thing (very much so the next day) was his prediction of bad weather.[1]

Saturday, 3 June

At ten in the morning we departed for Homburg,[2] and sure enough it rained several times on the way, but once there the sun shone again. Herr Hiller is living very congenially with his mother in a pretty little house with grounds outside the town. We were very warmly received. Mlle Toye is very courteous. Dr Weil,[3] an absent-minded schoolmaster, took Julie firmly by the arm, and led her off to eat in Homburg. Walk in the castle garden. Felix inspected dwellings which did not appeal to him. On the whole Homburg did not impress us favourably, although the Hiller family maintained that it did not lack charm, and spoke very highly of their stay. We drove back at half past seven, a little perturbed by the bad weather.

[1] This puzzle is a magic square. Using all the numbers from 1 to 64, the figures in each vertical and horizontal column and the main diagonals add up to 260.
[2] Homburg, now Bad Homburg, in the Taunus mountains 16 km. north of Frankfurt. The Baroque Schloss at the west end of the town was the seat of the Landgrave of Hessen-Homburg, and its gardens, with an orangery, were open to the public. The Hillers had taken summer lodgings in Homburg with a Herr Mauch, probably the gardener Johann Christian Ludwig Mauch (1794–1862), at the Brunnenhaus, which was in the present Kurpark.
[3] Dr Jakob Weil (1792–1864), who ran a boys' school in Frankfurt.

Visits in the morning, when Felix met the Crown Prince of Sweden[1] in the Städel Institute.[2] To the theatre in the evening to see the play 'Kean'.[3] Felix saw Lindner[4] act for the first time. She and the entire French play amused him greatly. When we arrived back home we had to sing to the Myliuses,[5] and Felix had to play to them. They stayed to supper with us.

On Monday, 5 June we set off at eight o'clock in the morning past the Forsthaus and through the forest to Gross-Gerau.[6] Strange conversation that Felix had on the way with a farmer, who took him for his brother. We lost sight of Mother, who had climbed out of the carriage. We went back again and found her quite tired, and on the point of becoming angry with us.

Conversation between Felix and me about the journey to England on a bench beneath lime-trees in Mörfelden, where the horses were watered.

(Fig. 5.)—[no drawing present]

We arrived in Gross-Gerau at two o'clock. From there it was still a little under two hours to Hohenau[7] where Herr Touchon[8] lives, whom we intended to visit. We arrived there completely famished and shaken up by the poor roads. The Touchon couple had come to meet us. They were very happy, especially as their doubts over our arrival had gone so far that they had consumed lunch on their own. Enough, however, was still found to assuage our hunger. Herr Touchon met with Felix's approval. After the meal we went down to the Rhine and walked in the garden, accompanied by old Mme Schrimpf[9] and the whole houseful of children. It was decided that we should spend the night there. The house is most peculiar, old and dilapidated,

[1] Oscar I (1799–1859), King of Sweden and Norway 1844–59.

[2] Founded by the bequest of the banker Johann Friedrich Städel (1728–1816), and housing one of the most important art collections in Germany. At this time it was in the Neue Mainzer Strasse. In 1878 it moved to its present building across the river in Sachsenhausen. Mendelssohn's cousin, Philipp Veit (1793–1877), was its director, 1830–43.

[3] The comedy by Alexandre Dumas père (1802–70), *Kean, ou Désordre et génie*, written in 1836; given in the German adaptation of Ernst Grossmann.

[4] Karoline Lindner (1797–1863). She first appeared on stage in Frankfurt in 1816, and remained based there most of her life, despite many guest appearances elsewhere.

[5] Carl Mylius (1790–1870), partner in the Frankfurt firm of Gebrüder Mylius, wholesale cloth merchants. In 1833 he married his second wife, Emilie Fanny, née Aubin (1810–46).

[6] Town 30 km. south-west of Frankfurt.

[7] A tiny hamlet by the Rhine about 12 km. from Gross-Gerau.

[8] Auguste Touchon (1784–1850), Pastor at Hanau, 1819–32, then resigned and moved to Hohenau. Married Henriette, née Schrimpf (1794–1875), in 1817, being her second husband. A long-standing friend of the Jeanrenauds, having entered the ministry on 18 May 1808 at the same time as Auguste Jeanrenaud.

[9] Katharina Elisabeth Schrimpf, née Koch (1772–1847). Mother-in-law of Auguste Touchon.

and without any trace of elegance.[1] One large room, with many bare windows, two sofas, a few old-fashioned chairs, an old stove, and a piano, constitutes the living room, study, and dining room of the whole family, the remaining rooms are small sleeping compartments. Felix and I watched the sun set over the Rhine; afterwards Felix played on the little piano to the delight of the whole company. Supper. To bed. Felix was not able to get to sleep in his.

Tuesday, 6 June

We set out from there after breakfast. The whole family accompanied us as far as a mound,[2] from where they could still watch us for a long time. Beautiful road from Hohenau to Gustavsburg, where the Main is crossed by a flying bridge.[3] Felix bought a superb breakfast in Ginsheim, which we consumed in the carriage. We passed by Mainz on the other side of the Rhine, and drove to Wiesbaden, where we arrived at the Rose[4] at three o'clock in a heavy downpour. Lunch at four, which Felix and Mother found excellent. Donkey ride afterwards in the direction of Sonnenberg.[5] Julie and Felix went galloping off. We only went as far as the Dietenmühle and then returned through the parks to the assembly-room.[6] It rained again. Meeting with the Crown Prince of Sweden on the way home. Felix conversed with him. Evening—night-time.

Wednesday, 7 June

Felix went in the morning to the springs,[7] and round about ten o'clock we departed for Königstein by way of Höchst. The heat on the way up the hill was considerable. Mother and Felix climbed out and surveyed the view over the plains. Arrival in Königstein.[8] Lunch. Stroll in

[1] Apparently dating back to the 15th cent., it survived until the 1950s.
[2] In fact a low dyke a few hundred metres from the Rhine.
[3] The road actually passed through Gustavsburg and Ginsheim before arriving at the flying bridge—a ferry guided by chains on the river bed—which crossed the Main shortly before its juncture with the Rhine.
[4] The Hotel Rose at the corner of the Kranz Platz and Taunusstrasse. The present building dates from 1896–1902.
[5] A hill to the north-east of the town, the Dietenmühle being about 2 km. out of the centre: with its medicinal water establishment and attendant entertainments, it was a favourite summer excursion point.
[6] The Cursaal standing in 1837 was completed in 1810 to designs by Christian Zais (1770–1820). A new Cursaal (Kurhaus) was built at the beginning of this century, designed by Friedrich von Thiersch.
[7] Presumably the Kochbrunnen—hot springs—just by the Rose.
[8] Village in the Taunus mountains 20 km. north of Frankfurt, with a ruined castle.

the village garden. Departure for Krontal.[1] Lovely shady road down the hill. When it became too steep we got out, and tried to find the path to our trees *(Fig. 6)*. Lost our way among the many small valleys.

| Fig. 6.)

Fig. 6

At last we arrived at the inn. We saw the room where we had eaten lunch, the bench were we sat afterwards, found the chestnut trees where I had waited so long for Felix, and finally the spot where we became engaged the previous autumn. Since that time new, young life has come to the trees and meadows, and also to her who today stood beneath them! Return journey in the

[1] Now part of the picturesque small town of Kronberg 4 km. east of Königstein, it was then a separate little spa at the foot of the hill. It was here that Felix and Cécile became engaged on 9 Sept. 1836. Fig. 6 is a view of Kronberg from the Königstein–Oberursel road.

evening sun and air. Wretched roads. Arrival in Frankfurt, where we were no longer expected. Wonderful night![1]

Thursday, 8 June

Herr Hiller came to see Felix in the morning. The house is like a wreck, and one can scarcely get up the staircase; we inhale more dust here than on the whole journey. For three days nothing remarkable happens. We sleep, eat, drink, work, go for walks. I have a good many clothes made for me. On Sunday I did not go to church, but began to suffer a great deal from the growing heat. On Monday I felt distinctly unwell, and spent much time lying in bed or on the sofa.

Tuesday, 13 June

It continued. I read the tedious 'Fidanzata Ligure'[2] and fell asleep over it. Felix took care of me and pampered me greatly as did Mother, in spite of which I was still not yet on my feet on Wednesday, 14 June. Herr Lejeune[3] prescribed medicine for me, which, like a child, I take with hideous grimaces. Herr Hiller visited me. In the evening Felix read Goethe to me and Julie, a piece we did not hitherto know, 'Künstlers Erdewallen'.[4] It pleased us immensely! On Thursday, 15 June visits to Felix came one after the other. Amongst others Herr Bennett,[5] the little Englishman, arriving from Leipzig. Felix ate with Monsieur Ferdinand at the Mainlust. Herr Bennett spent the afternoon with us and we drove with him into the Oberräder Wald. In the evening a gathering at Hofstadt's,[6] where Felix performed.

Friday, 16 June

Drawing lesson at ten o'clock with old Rad'l, whom Felix totally bewildered by doing him the honour of joining in the painting. Felix did some writing in the afternoon, and in the evening

[1] Presumably intended ironically in view of the state of the house.

[2] *La Fidanzata Ligure, ossia usi, costumanze e caratteri dei popoli della Riviera ai nostri tempi*, by Carlo Varese, published anonymously (Milan, 1828).

[3] Adam Franz Lejeune (1765–1854), Frankfurt doctor and Privy Councillor to the Landgrave of Hessen.

[4] 'Des Künstlers Erdewallen', a verse dialogue published in 1774.

[5] William Sterndale Bennett (1816–75), English composer. He first met Mendelssohn in 1833, who gave him much encouragement. Having left the Royal Academy of Music in 1836, he spent the winter of 1836/7 in Mendelssohn and Schumann's musical circle in Leipzig, before returning to England in July 1837.

[6] Probably Friedrich Hoffstadt (1802–46), painter, lawyer, and writer on art. He was a civil servant to the King of Bavaria at the Bundeszentralkommission in Frankfurt, 1833–42.

the Appias, Gogels, and Klings came to hear Felix play. The poor fellow was quite dreadfully tired and only recovered again in bed.

Saturday, 17 June

English lesson in the morning. At two we drove to eat at a great and merry gathering in Rödelheim,[1] where afterwards Herr P.[2] entertained us enormously with his great jollity. From there Felix had to go straight to the anniversary festival of the Liedertafel,[3] from which he did not return to me until midnight!, and then in a quite furious mood. I was still awake and succeeded after some time in calming him down, and lulling him to sleep.

Sunday, 18 June

Felix went to church in the morning. I received many visits during which Felix would in other circumstances have fallen asleep. After lunch we went to see Aunt von Schlegel who was unwell, but whom we encountered in the garden in the midst of her usual entourage, the silent painters.[4] We inspected drawings by Herr Steinle[5] from Rome. I wrote to Marie Bernus. Drive round the town in the evening.

Monday, 19 June

In the morning Felix did a great deal of writing and gave me a reading lesson. In the afternoon we paid visits together to Bernay[6] and Aunt Elise (the air suits them very well), and to Mme Eberhard.[7] We also went to see Aunt Schlegel, who was feeling better. From our windows in the evening we admired the beautiful moonlight, with its pale reflection in the water.

[1] Then a village about 7 km. west of Frankfurt.   [2] May be Perret or Passavant.

[3] Formed in 1826 by Schelble from members of the Cäcilienverein in order to cultivate the male-voice part-song repertoire. It lasted only a year in its original form, but was then revived more successfully in 1835.

[4] One of the 'silent painters' was Franz Brentano (1801–41), a portrait and religious painter, who was a pupil of Philipp Veit at the Städelsches Kunstinstitut, 1832–6 (see Felix's letter to Rebecka Dirichlet, 29 May 1837, p. 163).

[5] Eduard Jacob von Steinle (1810–86), artist. Born in Vienna, he studied in Rome 1828–33, then returned to Vienna. He travelled to Frankfurt and the Rhine in 1837.

[6] Either Johann Anton Bernay (see p. 149 n. 3) or his son Georg Ludwig Bernay (1810–56), also a spice merchant, who had married Wilhelmine Klothide Wippermann on 10 May 1837.

[7] Johanna Charlotte Eberhard, née Winter (b. 1803), the wife of Christian Franz Eberhard (b. 1791).

I had to go and assist at the dressmaker's. In the afternoon I had a piano lesson and could do nothing right. In the evening a lovely excursion on the water as far as the Grindbrunnen *(Fig. 7)*.[1] Wonderful effect of the sky, hills, and water. We picked many pretty cornflowers in the fields and returned home quite late. Aunt Helene,[2] who is very fond of Felix, had supper with us.

Fig. 7

Wednesday, 21 June

Herr Hiller came again from Homburg and had a session with Felix and his compositions and the piano, while I sewed. Aunt Schlemmer[3] was here from Hanau. In the afternoon Herr Hiller and Felix did a lot of playing. At seven, a lovely trip on the water with Mother and Felix.

---

[1] A spring with reputed therapeutic qualities, surrounded by ancient lime trees, and situated in a meadow just beyond the Mainlust inn to the west of the town. The trees were chopped down when the Westhafen was created in the 1880s.

[2] Eduard Souchay's wife (see p. 41 n. 9). The German can equally mean 'of whom Felix is very fond'.

[3] Wilhelmine Friederike Henriette Schlemmer, née Schunck (1773–1846), a great-aunt of Cécile on her mother's side. She married Georg Wilhelm Maximilian Schlemmer, pastor in Steinau, and after his death in 1825 moved to Hanau, 17 km. east of Frankfurt. Fritz Schlemmer was one of her sons.

Felix took a morning dip in the Main, returned home late at eleven, wrote and worked a good deal until about four, when we drove up the Rötherberg to eat with Lindheimer.[1] Strolls in the garden—pretty view. In the evening Herr Hiller came and played us his own compositions. He ventured down the dangerous staircase with us, and we had supper together.

Drawing lesson in the morning. The heat, the smell of the pigments, and holding the palette made me so tired that I had to stop every other minute, while Felix painted away eagerly on his view of Cadenabbia.[2] In the afternoon I dropped off to sleep, and on waking filled Felix's ears with lamentations about my idleness, his journeying to England on his own, etc. etc. Drove to Gogel's estate, accompanied by Felix as a favour. The evening was fine, with the hills superbly illuminated.

When we came for breakfast we saw in the newspaper 'Le roi d'Angleterre est mort'.[3] That may produce changes to our plans. Felix immediately wrote to Mr Moore[4] in Birmingham, and to Herr Klingemann, then in the afternoon sent a letter to Berlin and began a new quartet.[5] Julie and I paid visits across on the other side of the Main, and then awaited Felix by the water under the lime trees, and went for a long walk with him in the cornfields and picked many flowers. Felix was unwell with a cold, sore throat, and headache.

---

[1] The Rötherberg lies to the east of the old town of Frankfurt, and was then outside the town boundary. Andreas Daniel Ludwig Lindheimer (1769–1818) was a Frankfurt trader, who married Susanna Barbara Schindler (1782–1865) in 1800. A daughter, Cleopha, married Fritz Schlemmer in 1841.

[2] Felix had done a pencil drawing of Cadenabbia (on Lake Como) on 22 July 1831 during his stay in Italy, and was presumably now producing a watercolour version of it—a common practice of his. The whereabouts of the watercolour is not known, but the original pencil drawing is in the Bodleian Library (MS MDM d. 3, fo. 23).

[3] William IV died on 20 June to be succeeded by the 18-year-old Victoria.

[4] Joseph Moore (1766–1851), Birmingham benefactor of independent means, having previously been in the button trade. He had been one of the principal organizers of the Birmingham Musical Festival since the beginning of the century. At this time he lived at No. 10 Cambridge Street, Cambridge Terrace, Birmingham. The letter appears not to be extant.

[5] The String Quartet in E flat major, Op. 44 No. 3. See p. 140 n. 1.

Sunday, 25 June

Felix was still unwell today, in spite of which he painted like a Raphael, morning and afternoon. I wrote to Mother in Berlin. Drove round the town in the evening. On Monday and Tuesday Herr Hiller spent almost the entire time with Felix; they played together a good deal. Herr Ries[1] also came, the desiccated clover leaf in contrast to the other two. In the afternoon we drove to the Sandhof[2] to make enquiries as to whether we could stay there for a time, but nothing came of it. Felix had supper with Herr Hiller at the Mainlust.

Wednesday, 28 June

In the morning Mme Eberhard came to make arrangements about a surprise for Herr Hiller in his final concert today.[3] Long conversation between her and Felix until he went to see Herr Ries, who played and sang him his oratorio 'The Ghost of Samuel'.[4] 'Upon my so-o-ul, fah-ah-ar be it.' Lunch at the Harniers.[5] Felix went to the Mainlust on his own. Concert at the Cäcilienverein in the evening. Felix was saddened. Long talk about the Cäcilienverein.

Thursday, 29 June

We made preparations for a stay in Homburg. At eleven we set off, arriving after lunch was over. Felix immediately became very angry over the uncivil innkeeper, and we were altogether dissatisfied by Homburg. Long deliberations with Mme Hiller. Walk in the castle garden. We decided to drive back again, and to stay in Frankfurt despite the wrecked state of the kitchen and the dusty house.

---

[1] Ferdinand Ries (1784–1838), German pianist and composer. After an early itinerant career, he lived in London from 1813 to 1824, before returning to Germany to spend most of his later years in Frankfurt.

[2] The Sandhof was an old estate owned by the order of Teutonic Knights (*Deutschherrenorden*), to which an inn had been attached in 1817. It lay on the other side of the Main, west of Sachsenhausen, near the village of Niederrad, now the area of the University's medical departments.

[3] Hiller had come to the end of his temporary conductorship of the Cäcilienverein, and was about to leave for Italy.

[4] Really *Die Könige in Israël*, Op. 186, first performed at the Lower Rhine Music Festival in Aachen, 1837, and published the same year. The oratorio concerns the story of Saul and David, and hence includes the scene with the Ghost of Samuel. The phrase 'Meiner Seele sey es fern' (Upon my soul, far be it) occurs in David's solo within the chorus 'In düstrer Nacht'. The Mendelssohns are evidently poking fun at Ries and his music.

[5] See p. 48 n. 1.

Herr Rad'l came at ten. My landscape refused to make any progress. Felix hosted a great lunch at the Mainlust. Recital by Herr Tausig[1] from Vienna. In the evening Felix read Molière's 'Les femmes savantes'[2] to us.

Felix gave me a reading lesson in the morning, and did a lot of composing. Lunch at Aunt Elise's.[3] Shopping. Felix played me his piano concerto[4] and other lovely things. In the evening he went with a companion on flag-bedecked little boats down the Main to the Forsthaus. He didn't return until late at night, and I heard nothing of him when he came.

The next morning

he told me ridiculous things about the mayor and others. I went to church and then paid visits with Julie. As soon as we returned home we encountered the sudden arrival of the Beneckes[5] from Berlin. Emmeline told me a lot about Berlin and about Fanny's great gathering. Big dinner at Philipp Passavant's,[6] together with Herr and Frau Veit. The old gentleman did the honours very well, and his house and garden are most delightful. After the meal I felt unwell as usual, and filled Felix's ears with my complaining. To cheer me up he played for me a great many delightful and merry pieces by Moscheles.[7] The Beneckes left again very early the next morning.

---

[1] Aloys Tausig (1820–85), Prague-born pianist, pupil of Thalberg, and father of the famous Carl Tausig. In 1837 he undertook his first concert tour, which included a visit to Germany.

[2] Comedy first produced and published in 1672.   [3] Elise Schunck (see p. 41 n. 3).

[4] Piano Concerto No. 2 in D minor, Op. 40. At this time the work would appear to have been still basically in Mendelssohn's head. The first piano draft is dated 26 July, and the completed score, 5 Aug., although he continued to revise it after this date. It was first performed at the Birmingham Musical Festival on 21 Sept. (see entry for that date).

[5] Victor Benecke (1809–53), son of Wilhelm Benecke (1776–1837) and his first wife, Dora, née Paxmann. A Berlin merchant, he married Emmeline Schunck (1813–77) a first cousin once removed of Cécile (daughter of Cécile's great uncle, Phillip Schunck).

[6] Philipp Jakob Passavant (1782–1856), Frankfurt merchant specializing in French imports, and a partner in Wichelhausen und Passavant (founded 1804). He was unmarried, and had great interest in music, art, and science. He was a co-founder of the Cäcilienverein.

[7] Ignaz Moscheles (1794–1870), German pianist, composer, and conductor. Resident in London, 1825–46, where amongst other activities he was one of the conductors of the Philharmonic Society. Having known Mendelssohn since 1824, Moscheles and his wife, Charlotte, were amongst his closest lifelong friends.

Monday, 3 July

Start of the packing for the journey to the Rhine. Lunch with Bürgermeister Harnier, followed by visits. Ladies' gathering at the Mainlust.

Tuesday, 4 July

Visit to Aunt Schlegel. Earnest preparations for the departure, which ensued at one o'clock. Fine though windy weather as far as Mainz. We rested and had lunch at the Rheinischer Hof, where we had spent the first nights of our honeymoon. Fond reminiscences on the sofa, while Mother and Julie went and did some shopping.

The weather grew uncertain as we continued our journey. Glorious road along the heights behind Mainz. Ingelheim, the Johannisberg, Rüdesheim.[1] In wind and rain we reached Bingen, which has grown a great deal since I saw it last. We put up at the Weisses Ross,[2] run by the most insufferable person, Herr Soherr. The building, the rooms, the view, the little garden, are all very nice. As it was late in the evening we drank tea and then went to bed.

Wednesday, 5 July

We got up fairly late.

This is the view from our windows. From one side we can see the Rossel, the Niederwald, and Ehrenfels castle,[3] from the other, that is to say through the very curious little window pictured here, the Johannisberg and Rüdesheim.

---

[1] They would have passed through the village of Ingelheim on the left bank of the Rhine, and observed the Johannisberg and Rüdesheim, which lie on the other side of the river.

[2] The Weisses Ross (White Horse) hotel in the Obere Vorstadt dated back to the 17th cent. At the time of the Mendelssohns' visit it was a handsome free-standing building under the proprietorship of Joseph Soherr (1781–1850). On the other side of the road, running down to the Rhine promenade, it had its own enclosed garden with two corner pavilions. At the beginning of this century other houses and hotels replaced the garden, and the Weisses Ross lost its view of the river, and also had properties joined onto it. In 1910 an attempt was made to revive the hotel's fortune by renaming it the Goethehaus, including a small museum, capitalizing on Goethe's visit in 1814. The enterprise failed, and the building eventually assumed its present use as private apartments, bearing both the Weisses Ross and Goethehaus names on its façade.

[3] The Niederwald is the wooded hill on the other side of the Rhine from Bingen, the Rossel being an artificial ruin built on its highest point in 1774 (centre of Fig. 8). Ehrenfels is the ruined castle to the left. Dating from the 13th cent. and situated at a strategic point of the Rhine, it was destroyed by the French in 1689.

Fig. 8

Fig. 9

Unfortunately I felt distinctly unwell this first day. After lunch I took my medicine again with dreadful grimaces. It is a strange business with such a small person! In the morning we had already visited the Klopp,[1] a garden with a ruin perched up high in the middle of Bingen. Towards evening we went by water (needless to say) to the Mäuseturm *(Fig. 10)*.[2] The glorious Rhine,

Fig. 10

[1] Burg Klopp, perched on a hilltop above the town, stands on the site of a Roman fortress. The medieval castle was destroyed in 1711, and heavily restored in the second half of the 19th cent.

[2] The 'Mouse Tower', a 13th-cent. watch-tower on an island in the Rhine just downstream of Bingen. Its name derives from the legend of Bishop Hatto, the 10th-cent. bishop of Mainz. According to one version he was hated by all, both man and beast, for having incarcerated the poor in one of his barns during a famine, and set fire to it. Pursued by an army of mice, he took refuge on this island, thinking himself safe, but the mice swam across and ate him up. The tower was in a ruined condition in 1837, assuming its present appearance through a restoration of 1855. Although the only mention of the tower is in this entry for 5 July, and the drawing in the original diary is located in the middle of the entry for 6 July, Felix in his letter home of 13 July (p. 174) says that he had drawn Bishop Hatto being eaten by the mice on the previous day. This suggests that the events of around 5 July were only written up about a week later.

the old greyish tower, the many boulders on which it is built, all covered with beautiful flowers, and the pleasant sunset breeze wafting over us banished all taste of medicine.

Thursday, 6 July

In the morning came the effects of the medicine and complete idleness, walking up and down in the garden. In the afternoon we sailed on the water as far as the foot of the hill on which the Rochuskapelle[1] lies. A very steep and arduous footpath led upwards, which I would never have climbed if Felix had not constantly pushed and supported me from behind. Having finally reached our goal, we learned that the chapel is always shut except when a service is being held, which we greatly regretted because Felix would have liked to have seen once again the little organ upon which as a child he had played for the first time in his life. It was, however, so lovely outside that we soon forgot church, picture, and organ. The weather in the evening was glorious, and objects in the furthest distance lay free of haze before us. We rested beneath the young trees which surround the church, lay for a long time on the dried grass, counted the many islands in the Rhine, observed the Feldberg and the Main valley, the Donnersberg,[2] and all the fertile country around us here, and enjoyed ourselves greatly. The path down was even more tiring than on the way up. Arrival in Rüdesheim. Inspection of the raft which lay at anchor there, and which is very large and splendid. Vast quantities of bread lay piled up in the small hut. The three boatmen were very talkative. Return journey and a weary evening in Bingen.

Friday, 7 July

Nothing special happened. We didn't go on any big expedition, nor play great tricks, nor make jokes at the table d'hôte, but allowed ourselves to experience the view and the comfort at Mother's bedside, who was feeling a little unwell. In the evening Felix, Julie, and I walked to

---

[1] A pilgrimage chapel on the Rochusberg just to the west of Bingen. The one seen by the Mendelssohns had been built in 1814, superseding the original chapel destroyed in 1795. This too was destroyed by lightning in 1889, and replaced by the present elaborate neo-Gothic edifice in 1893–5. The picture would have been that of St Roch on his travels by Louise Seidler, which was presented by Goethe following his visit to the annual festival of St Roch in August 1814. Felix had visited it as a child with his family in 1820.

[2] The Feldberg is the highest peak of the Taunus hills (880 m.); the Donnersberg is the highest peak of the Pfälzer Bergland to the south of Bingen (687 m.).

the Nahe, and had a look at the old bridge, which the Romans are supposed to have built.[1] In the middle is an inscription on the pedestal of a fallen-down statue of St Nepomuk. It reads:

> Behold this and consider then,
> that it is no more than a stand-in;
> he is an intercessor with God
> for whoever calls upon him in every time of need.

On Saturday, 8 July Mother felt better. At midday we met the Schadows[2] on the staircase. Felix recognized him from behind, little Rudolph jumped round his neck and took him to his old grand-father, who has come from Berlin with his 16-year-old daughter and a young son. Mme Schadow, a very genteel woman of the world, visited us in the pavilion in the afternoon. In the even-ing we went together as a party up to the Rochuskapelle. The ancient 70-year-old was particu-larly cheerful and merry; he cackled away to Julie, and drove back again alone with her along the stony path. Letter from Marie Bernus, and an invitation to go to Kreuznach tomorrow, Sunday.

Sunday, 9 July

Departure at 11.30 in the mail coach. Arrival in Kreuznach just before lunch. The little wolf. Stroll in the afternoon and chat with Marie Bernus. Mme Heitweiler and her little daughter, Amalie, who was greatly enjoying herself.[3] Herr and Frau Bernus and ourselves went to the Casino[4] and in broad daylight attended the depicted ball *(Fig. 11)*. Glorious return journey at nine through the many lively villages of the Nahe valley.

---

[1] The old bridge (the so-called 'Drususbrücke') over the Nahe, which joins the Rhine at Bingen, was basically a medieval structure of the 10th or 11th cent., built on the foundations of a Roman one. Largely destroyed in 1945, it was reconstructed in 1951–2. St John Nepomucen, *c*.1340–93, a native of Nepomuk in Bohemia, was martyred by being thrown from a bridge; he was canonized in 1729, and was invoked as a protection against floods and slander.

[2] Gottfried Schadow (1764–1850) with his daughter Lida (1821–95) and youngest son Richard by his second marriage to Henriette Rosenstiel (d. 1832), as well as his painter and sculptor son Wilhelm (1788–1862) by his first marriage. Wilhelm was teacher at the Akademie in his native Berlin, 1819–26, and then moved to Düsseldorf as Cornelius's successor at the Akademie there. He married Charlotte Groschke (1795–1882), and became Schadow von Godenhaus in 1845. Their son was Rudolph (1826–96).

[3] The 'Unterhaltungen' of Bad Kreuznach, No. 26, 30 June 1837, records the arrival of 'Frau Landrath Heydweiler, mit Frl. Tochter u. Bedienung, a. Mannheim'. Evidently Ernestine Heydweiler, née von Göll (b. 1788), who was married to Friedrich Heydweiler, a Prussian Royal district counsellor in Mannheim.

[4] The foundation stone of the Casino building was laid in 1834, and it still exists in the 'Neustadt' area of Bad Kreuznach, where it is now used by the town administration. According to Felix's letter to Lea of 22 July (p. 176), Cécile was responsible for the draw-ing, although the 'Fig. 11' at least is in Felix's hand.

Fig. 11

Monday, 10 July

Felix took his first bathe in the Rhine, which greatly disagreed with him.[1] We saw him come up through the garden looking quite pale, but after a sleep he was fine again. In the course of the day[2] we took a ride to Schloss Rheinstein,[3] which gave me much pleasure.

Tuesday, 11 July

The Bernuses came to visit us. We went off together for a very pleasant boat journey as far as the island off Rüdesheim. Marie was feeling very well and cheerful; nevertheless she, like me, often has dreadful thoughts, which our husbands sweep away from us. Return journey and tea. Departure of Herr and Frau Bernus. Night-time.

Wednesday, 12 July

Spent much time in the garden in beautiful clear weather. In the afternoon I searched through Goethe's poems for something suitable for Marie's birthday on the morrow.[4] Felix set it to music and I quickly made a little garland for it. The whole thing went off early the next morning(!)

---

[1] George Grove in his original *Dictionary of Music and Musicians* article mentions for 1837 that 'at Bingen, while swimming across to Assmannshausen, he had an attack of cramp which nearly cost him his life, and from which he was only saved by the boatman'. Grove cites no source for this incident, and it appears to be unrecorded in printed letters and memoirs, but his article in part derives from material gathered personally from Mendelssohn's acquaintances. If the incident occurred on this particular day, then it would appear that Felix did not reveal the full extent of his danger to Cécile. On the other hand, in his letter to Rebecka of 24 July (see p. 182) Felix specifically reassures his mother that this summer he has not been taking any risks when swimming, as if to suggest that there had been a life-threatening situation a year or so previously.

[2] After 'day' the original text finished with the words 'no long walk', but this was altered/crossed out and the present ending substituted—see p. 67 n. 1 (13 July).

[3] Perched on a rock above the Rhine, 5 km. downstream from Bingen, the castle probably dates back to the 14th cent. After many years as a ruin it was bought in 1823 by Prince Friedrich Ludwig of Prussia (1794–1863) and restored to designs of Claudius von Lassaulx, who was also the architect of Joseph Mendelssohn's tea house at Horchheim (see p. 75 n. 2).

[4] 'Die Freundinn'. Although published posthumously as by Goethe in vol. 47 of the *Ausgabe letzter Hand* in 1833, the poem is in fact one of those by Marianne von Willemer. The copy sent to Marie Bernus is now in the Goethe-Museum, Düsseldorf, and was published in facsimile as *Lied einer Freundin*, ed. Max F. Schneider (Düsseldorf, 1960). It has a number of differences from the version in the diary. See p. 203 for a modern transcription of this version.

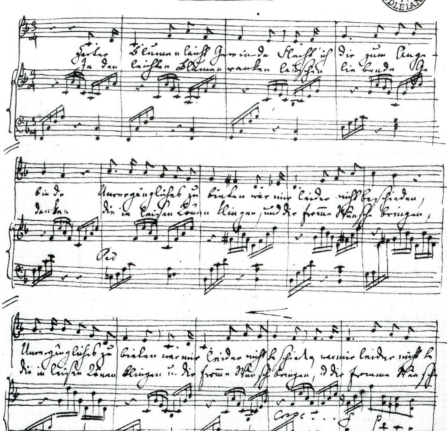

at six to Kreuznach. Answer at midday.[1] Evening stroll up the Rhine. My indisposition, which kept both Felix and me awake until midnight. The next day I slept on for a long time.

I felt well again round about midday. In the evening the Bernuses came to stay here for a couple of days, and struck it unlucky with the weather. It was windy and overcast for the entire three days, so that nothing came of our grand plans for trips by land and water. On Saturday, 15 July the two men went for a muddy walk up the Elisenhöhe,[2] and we spent the evening in the pavilion, laughing about Franz Bernus. On Sunday, 16 July the weather was quite awful, so that we didn't even have a chance to cross over to Rüdesheim for a meal. Big dinner in the salon. Walk up to the Klopp in the afternoon. In the evening poems by both men, and a great performance by Franz Bernus of 'The English lord and the German professor'.

Early morning departure of the merry couple. I had a read of the 'Makamen' by Hariri[3] which Bernus left behind for Felix. In the afternoon I felt unwell again and cured myself by sleeping. The next day

I didn't get up until eleven. In the afternoon we received a visit from Locher, the postmaster, and his daughter. They stayed till late in the evening. Even then Felix read to us from the 'Barber of Seville'.[4]

---

[1] Originally after this sentence came another, reading 'Trip to Rheinstein', which was crossed out and transferred to 10 July.

[2] The hill above Bingerbrück on the left bank of the Nahe.

[3] Friedrich Rückert's free translation of al-Ḥarīrī's collection of tales, the *Maqāmāt*, first published in 1826. A second edition appeared in 1837. Abū Muḥammad al-Qāsim ibn ʿAlī al-Ḥarīrī (1054–1122) was an Arabian language and literature scholar and government official, best known for these tales.

[4] The play by Caron de Beaumarchais, first performed and published in 1775.

Wednesday, 19 July

I had another English lesson, and began to read Bulwer's 'Rienzi'[1] (the sound of the holy bell). Felix wrote a good deal of music and many letters. It rained. We travelled to Rüdesheim for the first time, which pleased us very much.

Thursday, 20 July

Felix went on his own to the Niederwald, and was so delighted again by it that he would like to take me there as well, but how? I cannot ride on an ass, and to drive would be dangerous. Mother, Julie, and I in the meantime went for a stroll on the Ingelheim road. The strange old Englishman who travels around with endless boxes and cases, an ugly wife (who had burnt her eyes with <u>vitriol solution</u> in Schwalbach), a lark, and a thousand sordid stories. In the evening he was a little drunk and assailed Felix with his great nonsense. 'J'ai eu l'honneur d'entendre votre superbe opéra de Paulus, ah, monsieur, c'est la musique de l'âme, moi, j'ai senti ça en dedans là' [I have had the honour of hearing your superb opera 'St Paul'. It is, sir, the music of the soul; as for myself, I have felt it right there inside] he said in his ridiculous Polish jacket. He called me nothing less than 'Ce petit Mademoiselle, qui est le génie' [This little genius of a lady], and asserted that St Peter's in Rome had cost three hundred thousand million Louis d'or.

Friday, 21 July

Letters from Berlin.[2] Felix answered them immediately. I drew the view from our window for Becky. Bad weather.

---

[1] *Rienzi, Last of the Tribunes*, novel by Edward Bulwer Lytton (1835). The opening description of Rome contains the passage 'from concealed but numerous convents, rolled, not unmusically, along the quiet landscape and the rippling waves, the sound of the holy bell'. By coincidence in this very same month Richard Wagner was reading it for the first time, and in the following year began to use it as the basis of his opera.

[2] Lea's letter of 17 July (GB VI 57) and Fanny and Rebecka's of 10 July (GB VI 56). Felix's reply to Lea is in fact dated 22 July, though he refers to the visit to the Niederwald as taking place 'yesterday'. Separate letters to Fanny and Rebecka written jointly by Felix and Cécile are both dated 24 July (pp. 178–83).

Travelled with Felix's favourite boatman, Anton, to Assmannshausen[1] in glorious weather. The village is shabby but most beautifully situated. We climbed some way up the road to the Niederwald, and met a poor old woman, who sold us the most wonderful strawberries and raspberries. We lay down at the first pleasant spot. Felix and I sketched Assmannshausen. Mother and Julie knitted zealously for Felix's little feet. Lines of asses passed by and the breeze was as gentle and peaceful as our hearts. Delightful return journey.

Sunday, 23 July

Visited the convent of Eibingen,[2] deserted buildings above Rüdesheim. The old nuns are dead. The spirit indeed of one of them has still not found peace. Below there lives a schoolmaster with his family, and the Catholic priest who looks after the church; up above there is also a Protestant church. The garden has run wild and the courtyard is overgrown with grass. Felix drew the convent. Encounter with the drunken men[3] (see Felix's sketchbook). Tea in Rüdesheim on the way back in the Engel[4] with the painter Grabau[5] who lives there. Late night trip on the Rhine.

Monday, 24 July

The weather was again unpropitious. We went for a walk in the evening up the hill in the direction of Ingelheim, and were caught out by the rain. Felix whiled away the evening for us by reading from Schiller's 'Turandot'.[6]

---

[1] A village about 3 km. downstream from Bingen on the right bank of the Rhine.

[2] A village lying on the slopes just above Rüdesheim. The old convent, founded by St Hildegard of Bingen as a daughter house to her main convent at Rupertsberg, was on the site of the present parish church. The convent (subsequently dedicated to Hildegard) was secularized in 1802, but the nuns were allowed to remain until 1814, and one was still there in 1837 caring for the old graves. A Protestant chapel was temporarily housed in the old east wing, which still survives, now serving as the Catholic priest's house. The old convent church became the parish church, but was burnt down in 1931 and replaced by a new building, in which Hildegard's remains are still to be found. A large new convent was built on the hillside above the village at the beginning of the 20th cent.

[3] See letter of Felix and Cécile to Rebecka Dirichlet of 24 July (p. 182).

[4] Built in 1743 on the Rheinstrasse (now No. 11) at the corner of the Drosselgasse, and by 1837 the leading inn of Rüdesheim. Converted to other uses after 1867, the building was reconstructed after a fire in 1883. The present Weinhaus 'Zum Engel' in the Drosselgasse itself, founded in 1955, has connections with the original business.

[5] Christian Grabau (1810–74), painter, especially of landscapes and animals. He was a pupil at the Düsseldorf Akademie in the early 1830s.

[6] Schiller's verse adaptation of Carlo Gozzi's play *Turandot*, first published in 1802.

We planned to drive to the Morgenbach, which, however, was once again thwarted by the rain. Since we were under way anyhow, we sailed in the covered boat to Rüdesheim. Felix sketched us on the way. In Rüdesheim we went to see Herr Grabau and were shown his pictures. He was at work on a large picture with horses and the view towards Bingen and the neighbouring hills for the Leipzig exhibition.[1] Stroll in the direction of Eibingen with the sky brightening up.

Wednesday, 26 July

Felix went to bathe today just like every other day. In the entrance hall he met Herr Appia and Victor Benecke with his wife, both having come up on the steamer. I felt unwell before lunch, and so saw them for the first time in the afternoon as Mother and Julie, Herr Appia and his English lady[2] were just on the point of going to the Niederwald. Felix then took me for a walk. We found one of the vineyards open,[3] in which stood such a lovely boulder, that we went in and sat down on the withered grass and flowers of the large rock. Felix picked harebells, carnations, and ivy for me, and we recalled pleasant things from the past year. By these means I recovered completely again. In the evening a mouldy supper with the Beneckes.

Thursday, 27 July

Felix went on a morning trip with his Anton to the Morgenbach.[4] Trip to the village of Johannisberg[5] in the afternoon. We climbed up the hill and were shown over the fine Schloss of Prince Metternich by a melancholic man from Oestreich. Wonderful view from the balcony. Lovely effects of the light during our return journey on the Rhine. Felix bought some wine there, which we sampled in the evening at supper in the pavilion. Herr Appia did not need much persuading.

---

[1] The Leipziger Kunstverein came into being early in 1837, and held its first exhibition at the Deutsche Buchhändlerbörse in September and October of that year with works of German, Dutch, and French artists.

[2] The English lady is probably the 'Mme Burne' mentioned in the entry for 30 July. Frau Appia and 'Mme Burne' occur in the same sentence of a letter of Cécile to her mother written in April 1838 (Bodleian Library, MS MDM d. 18, fos. 85–6).

[3] The vineyards are usually closed for the 6–8 weeks before harvest.

[4] A wild narrow valley off the left bank of the Rhine, about 6 km. downstream from Bingen.

[5] The village lies on a hillside above the Rhine east of Rüdesheim. The Schloss, the centre of the famous vineyard, was built in 1757–9, and presented by the Austrian emperor to Prince Lothar von Metternich (1773–1859) in 1816. Metternich had been born in Koblenz, and spent his youth in the Rhine/Moselle region.

The morning was spent in the garden. Mme Greis,[1] an acquaintance of Felix from Cologne, arrived from Kreuznach at midday, with her sister and two youngsters. We travelled with her and the Appias on the steamer to Oestreich to see the picture gallery of Prince——;[2] it was, however, closed, and even Felix's finest eloquence could not open the doors. Attractive inn in which there was a piano, on which Felix played to the delight of the entire company. Wonderful stormy journey on the water. Rüdesheim. Visited the Brömserburg.[3] Confusion at teatime. Departure of Frau Greis—Mother's headache—the damp room.

Saturday, 29 July

Felix bathed in the Nahe and found the water much pleasanter and warmer than that of the Rhine. Then he worked on his concerto. In the afternoon the Appias wanted to go to the Morgenbach, but they likewise returned soaked. Felix had discussions with Mr Novello,[4] who had arrived on the steamer and who brought plenty of interesting news with him. In the evening they drank tea with us, and argued with the French. Felix was in quite a cheerful mood.

Sunday, 30 July

Herr Appia read out homilies to us in the morning. We spent the afternoon in the pavilion. I read 'Fiesco's Conspiracy';[5] Mme Burne drew Julie and told us her strange story. Then we went for a walk, crossed the Nahe and strolled along on the road to Koblenz. From there we had a very fine view of Bingen. Gruesome night.

---

[1] Probably Johanna Greiss, née Weyhe (1805–80), wife of Jakob Greiss (1800–53), Gartendirektor in Cologne and teacher of botany, whom she married in 1827.

[2] This would have been the well-known picture collection of Erwein Franz Damian, Graf Schönborn (1776–1840), at Schloss Reichardshausen just to the east of Oestrich-Winkel. Schönborn, an art connoisseur and collector had a strong interest in scholarship. His picture collection was mainly divided between his properties at Pommersfelden and Reichardshausen, the latter being his favourite abode at the end of his life.

[3] The massive rectangular fortress dating from the 10th or 11th cent., now the Rheingau museum. The old visitors' books, preserved in the archives, do not include the Mendelssohns' signatures on this visit, although Felix had signed when he had visited it with his family in August 1820.

[4] Joseph Alfred Novello (1810–96), English music publisher, eldest son of Vincent Novello.

[5] *Die Verschwörung des Fiesco zu Genua* (Fiesco, or the Genoese Conspiracy), historical tragedy by Schiller, published in 1783.

Monday, 31 July

Herr Appia departed in the morning with our boatman. Felix played at Herr Ernst's and did plenty of composing. Letter from Carl[1] in Vienna; drawing by the Nahe. Felix read to us in the evening.

Tuesday, 1 August

Felix wrote to Paul[2] and to Mme Novello.[3] Packing and preparations for the journey. Rain and thunderstorms.

Wednesday, 2 August

Departure from our beloved Bingen at ten in the morning, the sky being murky, and remaining overcast for the whole day. The Morgenbach. Glorious road along the Rhine. Bacharach—the Wernerkirche.[4] Drawing. Lunch. Afterwards drove slowly on past the Pfalz and Kaub,[5] visited the church in Oberwesel.[6] The place is very beautiful, with many Roman antiquities, towers, and walls still standing. The echo of the Lorelei rock.[7] Arrived in St Goar at five. After a short rest Felix climbed up to Burg Rheinfels[8] and did some drawing there. I continued resting on the sofa, and observing the beautiful view of St Goarshausen, the hills, and the river. We decided to spend the night in the pleasant Rheinischer Hof[9] inn run by the son-in-law of the busy Herr Soherr.[10] Attractive walk to a small valley leading to Werlau.[11] In the evening the Lorelei horn was played again in front of our windows; the echo here is almost finer still. Night-time.

[1] Carl Jeanrenaud (1814–91), Cécile's brother, who was a lawyer.
[2] Paul Mendelssohn Bartholdy (1812–74), Felix's younger brother, who dealt with his banking business. The letter appears not to be extant.
[3] Mary Novello, née Hehl (c.1789–1854), wife of the organist and music editor Vincent Novello, whom Mendelssohn had known since his first visit to England in 1829. Felix's letter is preserved in the Library of Congress.
[4] A graceful ruined Gothic church, part-way up the hill to the castle. Built in the 13th–15th cent., it was partly destroyed in 1689 during the attack on Burg Stahleck above.
[5] The 'Pfalz' is the well-known 14th-cent. island fortress in the middle of the river, characterized by Victor Hugo as 'a ship of stone', near the ancient town of Kaub.
[6] Of the two main churches it was probably the lofty and slender 14th-cent. Liebfraukirche at the south end of the town which attracted their attention, rather than the Martinskirche. The town has the most complete old town walls in the area.
[7] Opposite the Lorelei rock a man demonstrated the famous echo with the aid of a horn and a gun.
[8] Burg Rheinfels lies just above the town. Although Felix's drawing is not extant, a subsequent watercolour version, dated 1 Aug. 1838, is in private possession, and is reproduced as Pl. 11. Felix himself presented it to his daughter Marie.
[9] The Gasthof zum Rheinischen Hof lay at the northern end of the town, and was also the post station. The building was destroyed in the 1970s.
[10] See p. 59 n. 2.   [11] A small village north of St Goar.

On the morning of the King of Prussia's birthday[1] we took a trip in a small boat adorned with flags to St Goarshausen, and walked from there into the Schweizertal.[2] A glorious path, passing many mills, which were driven by the most flower-bedecked stream that I have yet seen. We could scarcely tear ourselves away from the lovely valley, but the rain allowed us no respite. Returned to St Goar, packed up, and set off in a heavy downpour. On the way the sky sometimes cleared, but poor Felix had to hold the umbrella aloft a good deal. We saw the Cat and Mouse,[3] the Brothers,[4] and all the castles lying on the right bank of the Rhine. We arrived in Boppard at midday, where we visited the church[5] and had a lunch befitting the birthday with the doctor, the pastor, and the chemist in a very nice inn, and then drove on further, through all the Spays,[6] past Braubach and the Marksburg[7] to the fortress at Koblenz[8] and across the bridge into the Ehrenbreitstein valley.[9] After a wash and brush-up we took our seats in a carriage for the drive to Horchheim.[10] On the way, after an argument with the ill-mannered coachman, we climbed out and walked. Met Benny[11] on his white horse. Horchheim—Auntie[12]—Rosa on the balcony *(Fig. 12)*—Uncle—Evening—Return home.

[1] Friedrich Wilhelm III (1770–1840).

[2] A rocky gorge-like valley leading off from St Goarshausen near Burg Katz. A hasty pencil sketch by Felix survives in Cécile's drawing book (Bodleian Library, MS MDM c. 6, fo. 29), and a subsequent watercolour made from it is in one of Cécile's albums (MS MDM c. 21, fo. 130)—see Pl. 12.

[3] The castle at St Goarshausen is popularly known as Burg Katz, its real name being Neu-Katzenelnbogen. Its builder, Count Wilhelm von Katzenelnbogen, supposedly gave the nickname of the 'Mouse' to the rival castle of Thurnburg above Wellnich, 4 km. downstream.

[4] The twin castles of Sterrenberg and Liebenstein, which face each other above the town of Bornhausen opposite Boppard. The nickname derives from the legend of the two rival brothers, Conrad and Heinrich, sons of Ritter Bayer von Boppard.

[5] The main churches are the Romanesque church of St Severus and the Gothic Carmelite church.

[6] Osterspay, Oberspay, and Niederspay.

[7] Braubach, ancient town on the right bank, dominated by the large castle of the Marksburg above it.

[8] The fortress referred to would not have been the massive one still seen across the river at Ehrenbreitstein, but the Kaiser Alexander fortress on the Karthause hill, then by the main Mainz–Koblenz road. Built in 1817–22, today only traces of the walls and the main entrance, the so-called 'Löwentor' remain. With its neighbouring Grossfürst Konstantin fortress, it guarded the approaches to the Hunsrück.

[9] In 1819 a bridge of boats was thrown across the Rhine on 36 barges. The Mendelssohns stayed at the Weisses Ross, Ehrenbreitstein, as is confirmed by the 'Fremdenliste' in the *Rhein- und Mosel-Zeitung* for 6 Aug.

[10] Now a suburb of Koblenz, Horchheim was then a village 4 km. south of Ehrenbreitstein. Felix's uncle, the banker Joseph Mendelssohn (1770–1848), acquired an estate with a vineyard at Horchheim in 1818, including a large imposing house (shown in Fig. 12). The house eventually passed into institutional use, and survived until 1970, when, having been unoccupied for some years, it was pulled down following a fire caused by youthful vandals. The site is now a park in the Emserstrasse with a small monument recording five visits of Felix to Horchheim.

[11] Benjamin Mendelssohn (1794–1874), eldest son of Joseph Mendelssohn. He married Rosamunde ('Rosa') Richter (1804–83).

[12] Henriette Mendelssohn, née Meyer (1776–1862), Joseph's wife.

Fig. 12

Friday, 4 August

Visit to the Fallensteins.[1] Lunch in Horchheim. Rain. The garden house.[2] Pleasant afternoon. Drive to Lahnstein and the Johanniskirche[3]—the community bull.[4] On the return journey darkness fell before we expected it. Night-time.

Saturday, 5 August

At nine in the morning Felix took me out with him; we almost got wet. Breakfast in the garden room. Felix composed, while I sat with Auntie and Rosa until lunchtime. Lunch. Afterwards it rained continuously once again. We ladies chatted about various things, while the men played billiards and did some writing. Then came the evening and we drove back home in Uncle's carriage.

Sunday, 6 August

Auntie's visit to the inn, then lunch at the Fallensteins. Afterwards Felix and I returned home and indulged in a variety of mad pranks. In the evening a big gathering at the Fallensteins where Felix played and several Berlin ladies pursed their lips.

The next morning, Monday, 7 August, great argument over an invitation to Horchheim. Finally Fräulein Hehl came and unravelled the knot. We set off at three. Everyone was immensely affable towards me. Felix played and became so excited by it that it gave him a headache. Little Gritti Thormann also played very nicely. We drove to the Fallensteins, whom Felix had promised to visit, but stayed there only a very short time. Felix went to bed and slept everything off.

---

[1] See p. 47 n. 5.

[2] Joseph Mendelssohn had a tea house (or garden house) built by Claudius von Lassaulx in the grounds overlooking the Rhine. It is still in existence, but now forms part of a Protestant church. Felix's own family home in the Leipzigerstrasse in Berlin also had a famous garden house, in which Sunday concerts were regularly given.

[3] Lahnstein lies 3 km. to the south of Horchheim, and the Romanesque Johanniskirche lies at the mouth of the Lahn river outside Niederlahnstein. At this time it was partly derelict, its ruined towers forming a prominent feature of the landscape.

[4] The Lahnstein community bull, which serviced all the local farmers' cows, was known as 'Heinz'. It lived in a meadow ('Heinzewiese') between the church and the Rhine, and from it the inhabitants of Oberlahnstein obtained the nickname 'Hainze'.

By Tuesday, 8 August

he was quite well again. We awaited the Mendelssohns and then rode in three carriages to Sayn[1] in glorious weather. We first went up to Friedrichsberg where there was a lovely view towards Koblenz and into the little valleys. The hill is laid out like a pleasure garden and very well maintained. We had breakfast in an arbour and then walked along the pretty shaded paths down into the valley. Drive to Isenburg.[2] Delightful road alongside a stream and by the side of high crags. Climbed up to Schloss Isenburg where, apart from the old walls and a small tidily kept garden established on the ruins, there was nothing much to see. Return journey to Sayn. Lunch. Visit to the iron foundry of the Rhine Schloss. Late return to Koblenz.

Wednesday, 9 August

Early morning visit of Herr Lenz,[3] who brought Felix his compositions. Lunch at home. The great heat made going out impossible; our rooms with their splendid view were unbearably warm. In the evening an excursion to Belzig[4] on the estate of a Dutchman. Beautiful view of the Rhine valley with the setting sun and an approaching thunderstorm. Felix was feeling unsociable. Lovely return journey.

Thursday, 10 August

Bathing in the Rhine. Felix was very industrious and in the course of these days completely finished work on his piano concerto. The heat continued yet again and made me feel quite wretched. Evening at Horchheim. The plan to visit the Ahrtal was abandoned.[5]

[1] At that time a village 10 km. north of Ehrenbreitstein, it was famous for its ironworks, close by the Schloss. In the 19th cent. it was one of the three most important in Germany, and supplied armaments and other material for the Koblenz/Ehrenbreitstein fortresses. Started in 1769–70, a new foundry hall was erected in 1828–30, being the first cast-iron hall-type construction in Europe, to designs by Carl Ludwig Althans. The buildings are still preserved, and it is now a museum. Friedrichsberg is the hill overlooking the village on the north-west.

[2] In the Saynbachtal 7 km. north of Sayn. The castle ruins are still there.

[3] Joseph Lenz (1813–65), composer and director of the Koblenz Musik-Institut, 1847–65. Born in Koblenz, he studied in Paris under Habeneck and Anton Reicha, and returned to Koblenz, where by 1837 he was conducting the Cäcilienverein and Liedertafel. Mendelssohn clearly encouraged him, for in the autumn of 1837 he went and spent a year in Leipzig studying and taking in the musical life; he then went to study law in Breslau and Berlin before returning to Koblenz in 1842.

[4] Evidently a mishearing of Besselich, an estate north of Ehrenbreitstein, between Urbar and Vallendar. A former monastery, it was acquired in 1834 by the Dutchman Carl Stedman (1804–82), who quickly turned it into a favourite meeting place for a wide mix of Koblenz society. The estate is still owned by Stedman's descendants.

[5] The Ahrtal is a valley off the left bank of the Rhine north of Koblenz. Rebecka had suggested a visit in her letter of c.10 July 1837 (GB VI 56), adding that Felix never took notice of her recommendations. In the letter to Lea of 22 July (p. 177), Felix, by way of an

Friday, 11 August

An invitation to Horchheim arrived. We ate there in the company of General Hehl's wife. After lunch a billiards party interrupted by the visit of Mme Schliengen. Evening drive via the Kartause to Van Gelder's.[1] Tea at the farm—the balcony—the green book—moonlight. Return in the dark.

Saturday, 12 August

We wanted to see the Telegraph.[2] Benny picked us up, but we arrived too late, and it was already shut. The law courts.[3] The trial. Mother and I paid a number of visits. Felix went for a bathe. Lunch at home. A walk to the little Mühlental[4] in the evening.

Sunday, 13 August

Spent almost the whole day in Horchheim. After lunch great discussions about Uncle's birthday, as to how it should be celebrated. Felix played—comical canons. The storm kept us out until about midnight.

Monday, 14 August

Mother and Julie passed the time at the Fallensteins. Benny came to us with his poem which he had written overnight. Felix argues against the dignity of the Rhine. Spent the afternoon alone with Felix. In the evening a big rehearsal held in Horchheim. The wife of Professor Hasse.[5]

---

aside to Rebecka, teases her by saying that as a penance he will take in the Ahrtal on the way to Cologne, and is determined to declare it detestable, even if it is in fact beautiful. Although the planned visit was apparently abandoned on 10 Aug., the letter to Berlin on 13 Aug. (p. 183) again mentions the idea of travelling to Bonn by way of the Ahrtal, but in the end they took the steamer direct from Koblenz.

[1] Friedrich Anton van Gelder (1794–1854), Koblenz landowner, wine merchant, and innkeeper.

[2] The 'Optische Telegraphen-Linie Berlin-Koblenz', set up in 1833 for military use. As it was an optical system it only worked in fine weather, but it survived until the arrival of the electric telegraph. The end station was on the Koblenz Schloss and the next on the Ehrenbreitstein fortress, There is a picture of it in the Mittelrheinisches Museum, Koblenz. Felix had a lasting curiosity concerning the inventions of the burgeoning industrial era.

[3] Situated in the Schloss.   [4] There is a small 'Mühlental' in Ehrenbreitstein.

[5] Possibly the widow of Johann Christian Hasse (1779–1830), Professor of Law in Berlin 1818–21, and then at Bonn 1821–30.

Great confusion at supper caused by Herr Ackermann.[1] I travelled back with the professor's wife, her daughters, and Clementine Lassa.[2] Felix and Julie soon followed.

Tuesday, 15 August

The Feast of the Assumption. Uncle's birthday. Wedding of the gardener's daughter. We set off at eleven; the children's celebration was already over. We all went into the church, and witnessed the Catholic wedding, then were driven to Braubach. Uncle was very talkative, while Felix was still learning his lines. Lunch in a large hall. Afterwards came our dressing-up and presentation of the tale, which we will all continue to remember. Felix looked wonderful as the river-god with his flaxen wig. Stroll along the Rhine. Glorious journey on the water with a sunset sky and moonlight. Ball at Horchheim. Return home.

Wednesday, 16 August

In the morning packing and visits until about half past eleven when we went over to the steamer. Uncle and Benny accompanied us as far as the quay. On deck we immediately found Ritter Neukomm,[3] who talked to us so incessantly, that we saw little of the surroundings. The many passengers returning from the Mainz Gutenberg Festival[4] combined with the great heat made this form of travelling disagreeable. Arrival in Bonn at three o'clock and parting from the Ritter. Put up at the Stern hotel.[5] Felix went to visit Herr Simrock,[6] who showed him every courtesy, and came in person to beg us to refrain from travelling further and to spend the evening with him. After I had satisfied my longing for an ice, we actually went there and encountered his very pleasant

---

[1] Possibly J. A. Ackermann, a civil servant in Koblenz.

[2] Clementine Maria Christine von Lassaulx (1812–77), younger daughter of Claudius von Lassaulx, who built the Mendelssohns' tea house at Horchheim. She became a nun and ended up as matron of the Hospital Sisters of St Elisabeth in Luxembourg.

[3] Sigismund, Ritter von Neukomm (1778–1858), Austrian composer who settled in Paris from 1809. He made frequent visits to England from 1829 onwards, fulfilling commissions and conducting his works at all the major festivals.

[4] On 13–16 Aug. 1837 Mainz celebrated the 400th anniversary of Johannes Gutenberg's invention of printing. Elsewhere it was celebrated in 1840, including Leipzig, for whose festivities Felix wrote the *Lobgesang* and *Festgesang*. On 14 Aug., after a service in the Cathedral, the present statue of Gutenberg by Albert Thorwaldsen was unveiled in the Gutenbergplatz, and Cécile had an opportunity to see it during her return journey on 28 Aug. Neukomm himself was returning from the Gutenberg Festival, where he had conducted his Military Te Deum for massed forces, and, like Felix, was heading for England and the Birmingham Festival.

[5] The 'Gasthof zum goldenen Stern', as it was then properly known, is still in existence as the 'Sternhotel' in the Marktplatz. Queen Victoria stayed there in the 1840s. It was heavily damaged in 1944, but reopened in 1945.

[6] Peter Joseph Simrock (1792–1868), music publisher. In 1832 he took over the Bonn firm that his father, Nicolaus Simrock, had founded. The firm published all of Mendelssohn's books of *Lieder ohne Worte* as well as *St Paul* and *Elijah*.

wife[1] and a well-ordered household. Felix and Herr Simrock played his 'Lieder ohne Worte' arranged by Czerny.[2] A fat man, Herr Pröbstin,[3] was there. Supper—weariness. Home and to bed.

Thursday, 17 August

Felix felt unwell early in the morning, brought about by the heat and all the drinking of the previous day, and also by the news of Herr Schelble's death.[4] Nevertheless we departed from Bonn at nine o'clock. Improvement produced by the fresher air. The landscape between Bonn and Cologne could no longer be considered beautiful. Arrival at the table d'hôte in the Kaiserlicher Hof.[5] Afterwards a visit to the wonderful cathedral,[6] of which the completed choir is the most glorious thing one can see anywhere. The old painting of the 11,000 virgins.[7] The fine stained-glass windows. The monument of the Three Kings.[8] The grave of Queen Maria de' Medici.[9] The picture gallery with the 'Mourning Jews' by Bendemann, and the 'Winter Landscape' by Lessing.[10] Saw the church of St Gereon[11] outside the city, a very fine sumptuous church with a crypt, and

[1] Elisabeth Wilhelmine, née Peipers.

[2] The 4-hand arrangements by Carl Czerny (1791–1857) of the first two books of Mendelssohn's *Lieder ohne Worte*, Opp. 19 and 30, published (separately) by Simrock at the end of 1837.

[3] A business associate in the Simrock firm. Mendelssohn spells him 'Pröbsting' in a letter of 10 July 1838 (*Briefe an deutsche Verleger*, 220).

[4] Schelble (see Introduction, p. xii) had died on 6 Aug.

[5] The 'Gasthof zum römischen Kaiser' was one of Cologne's best hotels, situated at Hahnenstrasse 31. It survived until about 1855.

[6] The immense Gothic cathedral was still unfinished at this time. Building had ceased in the 16th cent., with the nave, transepts, and towers only partly erected, and the crane on the tower was to remain there as a prominent city landmark for over 400 years (until 1868). Having become rather ruinous by the beginning of the 19th cent., restoration was begun in 1821, so that it was in rather better condition when the Mendelssohns saw it. It was not, however, until 1842 that a start was made on completing the building to the original plan, which was finally achieved in 1880.

[7] The *Dombild* of the patron saints of the city, a triptych by Stephan Lochner (1400–51). Formerly in the Ratskapelle near the old Town Hall, it was moved to the cathedral in 1809, and displayed at that time in the Agneskapelle. The left-hand panel shows St Ursula with a crowd of women. According to legend, this British princess was murdered in Cologne with her 11,000 virgin attendants during a return journey from a pilgrimage to Rome.

[8] Shrine of the Three Kings. A superbly wrought 12th-cent. reliquary, now behind the high altar. In 1837 it stood in the central chapel (Axis Chapel) of the choir ambulatory.

[9] Marie de' Medici, widow of Henri IV of France, died in exile in Cologne in 1642. Her 'heart' (really her entrails) was buried under the floor in front of the Axis Chapel. It appears that by 1837 there was little there to record the fact, and excavations in 1947 found no trace of a casket or urn.

[10] The Wallraf Museum, Trankgasse No. 7, on the north side of the cathedral. As the Wallraf-Richartz-Museum it now occupies a modern building to the south of the cathedral. It still houses the two paintings mentioned, Eduard Bendemann's early masterpiece *Die trauernden Juden im Exil*, and Carl Friedrich Lessing's *Klosterhof im Schnee*, which were acquired in 1832 and 1835 respectively.

[11] The church of St Gereon, in the northern quarter of the old town, was built to an unusual plan. A long Romanesque choir is joined onto a Gothic decagonal nave with a square vestibule at the west end. The 11th-cent. crypt under the choir contains a mosaic pavement.

viewed yet others from outside. Visited J. M. Farina[1] and then drove to the water-meadow by the Rhine. Meeting with Felix's acquaintances. Tea in the very popular garden. Lovely return journey and encounter with the Gutenbergers.

Friday, 18 August

Felix went early to the Rhine baths at Deuz,[2] and at nine we followed on and had breakfast in the Bellevue hotel. Felix had heard a young man play who gave him great pleasure. The weather was all too fine for such a terribly unshaded road. Mühlheim, Langenfeld stage-coach stop. Dreadful heat all the way to Düsseldorf. Arrived at one o'clock and went straight to the table d'hôte. Herr Rietz's[3] visit after the meal, bringing Felix the édition de luxe of 'St Paul'.[4] Visit to the Schadows.[5] Evening spent in the Hofgarten at the Eisberg.[6]

Saturday, 19 August

In the morning we briefly visited the picture exhibition,[7] and then the studios of Schrötter,[8] Lessing,[9] Steinbrück,[10] and Hildebrand.[11] Saw all the painters; Steinbrück was particularly

---

[1] Johann Maria Farina, the firm which had originated the commercial production of eau-de-Cologne in the early 18th cent. Its premises were opposite the Jülichs-Platz (Obermarspforten 23).

[2] Deuz was then a village facing Cologne on the other side of the Rhine, with a river bathing area. The Bellevue was a hotel next to the bridge of boats, and a favourite evening resort of Cologne's inhabitants.

[3] Julius Rietz (1812–77), German cellist, conductor, and editor. Born in Berlin, he had known Mendelssohn since childhood. In 1834 he went to Düsseldorf as Mendelssohn's assistant at the opera, and then succeeded him as the city's music director in 1835.

[4] A special copy of the published full score, printed on fine paper, with illustrations contributed by various artist friends of the composer. See Felix and Cécile's letter to Lea, 24 Aug. (p. 186) for a description of it. It is at present in private hands. Mendelssohn had conducted the première of the work at the 1836 Lower Rhine Music Festival in Düsseldorf.

[5] From 1835 the Schadows (see p. 63 n. 2) lived in an imposing new house in the Flinger Steinweg, designed by Rudolf Wiegmann after the model of an Italian Renaissance palazzo. Their salons were renowned for the mixture of artistic and social circles.

[6] A park originally laid out in 1769, and extended in 1802. The Eisberg, or Eiskellerberg (ice cellar mound), by the harbour was a restaurant much favoured by Düsseldorfers in the evenings.

[7] An annual exhibition was held in the gallery of the Akademie.

[8] Adolf Schrödter (1805–75), painter and illustrator. Became a pupil of Ludwig Buchhorn at the Berlin Akademie, where he soon entered the circle of Schadow's pupils, and in 1829 followed Schadow to Düsseldorf to continue his training especially in oil painting.

[9] Carl Friedrich Lessing (1808–80), painter. Trained first at the Berlin Bauschule; he became acquainted with Schadow and followed him to Düsseldorf in 1826. Specialized in landscapes and historical (especially religious) paintings.

[10] Eduard Steinbrück (1802–82), painter. He studied from 1822 in Berlin before going to Düsseldorf in 1829. His stays in Rome (1829/30) and Berlin (1830–3), before returning to Düsseldorf, corresponded closely to Mendelssohn's own places of activity in these years.

[11] Theodor Hildebrandt (1804–74), painter. A pupil of Schadow, he moved with him to Düsseldorf in 1826; from 1836 he was a professor at the Akademie.

obliging. Also went to see Herr Schadow's pictures; he is engaged in painting 'The Wise and Foolish Virgins'.[1] Herr Rietz dined with us as did Herr Killmann,[2] who had arrived that morning. Felix went to Herr Rietz in the afternoon and played there. In the evening a gathering at the Schadows, with only the princely and aristocratic present. Ate in the dew-laden little garden beneath a moonlit and starry sky. Then Felix delighted the company with his playing, which was followed by supper.

Sunday, 20 August

Herr von Woringen[3] came to breakfast, having just returned from his short journey. He expressed great joy in seeing Felix and at the same time delighted us all very much. Visits to Hildebrand and Frau von Dobeneck, sister of the fat Herr Fränkel,[4] our daily table companion.

Lunch with Herr Killmann, von Woringen, and Rietz. Coffee at Herr von Woringen's. He sang the aria 'Sei getreu bis in den Tod'[5] quite splendidly. Saw Frau Steinbrück for the first time, and went to the exhibition with her husband. Portrait of Mme Schadow by Hildebrand,[6] landscape by Lessing, Miriam by Köhler,[7] portraits of Steinbrück etc. in the studios, Job by Hübner,[8] Madonna by Deger,[9] etc. etc. Walk in the Hofgarten. Had an ice—thunderstorm—went to the Schadows

---

[1] Schadow's *Die Parabel von der klugen und die thörichten Jungfrauen* was commissioned by the Städelsches Kunstinstitut, Frankfurt, in 1835, but not completed and delivered until 1842. The Mendelssohns presumably saw one of its preliminary stages, such as the cartoon known to have been exhibited in 1838, or the small colour study now in the Kunstmuseum, Düsseldorf.

[2] Probably Karl Gottlieb Kyllmann (1803–78), a manufacturer in Solingen-Wald. The family's musical interests had led to friendship with Mendelssohn during his Düsseldorf period.

[3] Ferdinand von Woringen, son of Otto von Woringen (1760–1838), who was an appeal court judge and judicial counsellor in Düsseldorf and involved in the 'Musik-Akademie und Konzert-Gesellschaft' as well as being secretary of the Lower Rhine Music Festival. Ferdinand took over this task from his father, and became a good friend of Mendelssohn. In 1837 he left Düsseldorf to become a senior government official in Liegnitz (now Legnica in Poland).

[4] Joseph Maximilian Fränkel (Fränckel) (1788–1847), partner in the Mendelssohn family bank, 1821–7, when it was known as Mendelssohn & Fränckel.

[5] 'Be thou faithful unto death', tenor aria from part 2 of *St Paul*.

[6] Painted in 1837, now in the Kunstmuseum, Düsseldorf.

[7] *Mirjams Lobgesang* by Christian Köhler, painted in 1836, now in the Kunstmuseum, Düsseldorf. Köhler (1809–61) studied at the Berlin Akademie with Schadow, and then followed him to Düsseldorf in 1826.

[8] *Hiob mit seinen Freunden*, painted 1836–8 for the Städelsches Kunstinstitut, Frankfurt am Main, where it is still to be found. Carl Wilhelm Hübner (1814–79) went to Düsseldorf in 1837 to become a pupil of Karl Sohn, and later of Schadow.

[9] Ernst Deger (1809–85), historical painter of religious themes. He trained first at the Berlin Kunstakademie in 1828, and then under Schadow from 1829. There are various paintings of the Madonna by him, including a *Madonna with the Christ Child* and an *Annunciation*, both painted in 1835, and both now in the Düsseldorf Kunstmuseum.

and examined their albums. Herr Schadow was very loquacious. In their company we watched the magnificent sheet-lightning. Night-time.

Monday, 21 August

The immense heat made going out impossible. In the evening a big gathering at the Steinbrücks. Frau von Linzer, Herr and Frau Backhausen,[1] a cheerful small woman. The silent hostess. Felix and Herr Rietz played together quite superbly. The spider.[2] Supper.

Tuesday, 22 August

I went with Felix in the morning and afternoon to the Steinbrücks to keep him company during his sitting. Towards evening the picture was ready and a very good likeness.[3] Herr Steinbrück presented it to me. Visit to Backhausen. In the evening a party at Ferdinand von Woringen's, with more or less the same people as yesterday. Felix and Herr Rietz played again; Herr von Woringen sang a little and was very fine. The supper—the pineapple punch—the leave-taking.

Wednesday, 23 August

The Killmanns arrived early amidst the most awful rain, he, his wife, and child. Then the Backhausens and the Schadows paid visits. Hildebrandt came to dine. I wrote to Mother and packed. In the evening we went together to the Singverein, where nearly the whole of 'St Paul' was sung.[4] Ferdinand von Woringen sang both tenor and bass solos and in all the choruses. We ate again at his house afterwards.

[1] Herr Backhausen has not been indentified, but his wife was Malwine, née Schleiden (1810–80), who is found described as the owner of the Nettehammer estate.

[2] Elise Polko, whose reminiscences rely entirely on reports from others for events outside Leipzig, has an account of this evening in which the spider has been transformed into a mouse: 'After supper there was music. While Mendelssohn was playing Beethoven's "Kreutzer Sonata" with Rietz, and all were reverentially listening, a little mouse glided out of a corner and sat in the midst of the circle motionless, as if spellbound by the magic tones. No doubt it would have remained in the same position till the playing ceased, had not one of the ladies made an abrupt gesture in horror of the formidable monster, which caused a slight commotion, and drove away the four-footed enthusiastic amateur' (*Reminiscences of Felix Mendelssohn-Bartholdy*, 67–8).

[3] The whereabouts of Steinbrück's 1837 portrait of Felix (probably in pencil) remains unknown. An 1836 watercolour portrait is now in the Pierpont Morgan Library, New York.

[4] Wednesday evening was the Singverein's usual meeting time.

Felix let me sleep on late, and had his coats folded together by the boots. The drawn curtains. At ten, accompanied by the Herr and Frau Killmann and Ferdinand von Woringen, we went to the steamer. There we still had to wait around a good while. Many acquaintances continued to arrive, Schadow, Rietz, etc. Alas the smoke finally appeared, and we were soon already far apart. The handkerchief. The large, kind von Woringen took us back to the hotel, presented us with a basket of apricots, and helped us pack and carry our things. The Killmanns took their leave and invited us yet again most generously. At eleven we departed back along the tedious road. We met the Killmanns once more. Fortunately it was windy and overcast, and thus not too hot. We had a cold breakfast at Deuz and completely avoided travelling through Cologne. Round about five o'clock we were in Bonn. My unreasonableness at the sight of our former room. Stroll to the old toll-house,[1] where we met the Simrocks. Lovely view. Mother and Julie went to pay another visit, while I wrote to Felix. Supper. Sleepless night.

[24 August]

The smoke appeared, and I had to board the steamer. Immediately the whistle sounded. I could still hear Cécile speaking, then the whistle sounded again and the ship left the river bank. I saw her still standing there, then waving with the handkerchief, then only the white handkerchief, then nothing more. I thought that would have been the worst moment, but on the following evenings there was worse to come. Consistorial Counsellor Brüggemann[2] was on board the steamer—conversations with him particularly about Catholicism in the Rhineland, which he portrayed as very bigoted and intensified by the priests. I was surprised at these opinions coming from a Catholic and a Consistorial Counsellor into the bargain, and wondered what the Royal Prussian Government would have had to say about it. He disembarked at Emmerich, to be greeted most reverently by two schoolteachers. There was to be a school inspection at a new grammar school. I watched him turn into the street chattering with the black-clad men and disappear, and then it was time to continue on our way. Brightly coloured flags and cannon-shots now came from all directions. It was the King of Holland's birthday,[3] the same day on which a

---

[1] An old bastion in a park by the Koblenzer Tor, commanding a fine view over the river.

[2] Johann Heinrich Theodor Brüggemann (1796–1866). Having been headmaster of the Gymnasium in Düsseldorf from 1823, in 1832 he became a government counsellor in Koblenz, before being called to the Ministry of Culture in Berlin in 1839.

[3] William I (1772–1843), King of the United Netherlands from 1815 until his abdication in 1840.

year ago I was in the same place but travelling up the Rhine, heading for Cécile and our engagement. In Nijmegen a dreadful throng, and barbaric music from a violin, and a cello which only ever played on the open strings. Tiny room. Letter to Cécile. Short night.

Friday, 25 August

Departed from Bonn at nine. A cold morning. Much mist on the Siebengebirge.[1] Saw Godesberg[2] for the first time. On the whole the overland journey is far more agreeable than the steamer. Many Gothic monuments, wells, and crosses along the highway. Alighted at the inn in Rolandseck, and were led into the garden. From beneath a pear tree we had a glorious view of all the seven mountains and the island of Nonnenwerth. Continuation of the journey in a constant cold wind through Remagen to Andernach.[3] An attractive place with many Roman gateways and a fine church. Stopped there for lunch at a nice inn. The organ-grinding girl. Arrival at the Fallensteins in Koblenz in the afternoon. Wrote to Felix in the evening.

[25 August]

Left Nijmegen at eight. Argument between a man from Cologne and a Dutchman as to whether Schiller or Hugo Grotius[4] was the greater, and which nation, the German or the Dutch the more important. The Dutchman won, to be quite honest. In Rotterdam at half past four (Fig. 13). Letters to Cécile and to Rietz in reply to his handed to me on my departure from Düsseldorf. Beautiful clearer evening. Walk along the Boompjes;[5] saw a three-master, hawsers and the Lions' Harbour.[6] Small hovel in the garden house,[7] damp and unpleasant. Low spirits and reflections on the past filled my mind.

---

[1] The 'Seven Mountains', a range of hills along the east bank of the Rhine around Königswinter.

[2] Now Bad Godesberg and part of Bonn, then a village 5 km. south of the town.

[3] Small town about 16 km. north of Koblenz. Although once a Roman fort (Antunnacum), the 'Roman gates' are in fact medieval. The Liebfrauenkirche, with its four towers, is a fine late Romanesque building. The principal inns were the 'Lilie' and the 'Kaiser von Russland'.

[4] Hugo Grotius (Huigh De Groot) (1583–1645), Dutch jurist, statesman, and historian.

[5] The Boompjes was the main quay, extending for 2 km. along the river. It was lined with elms (Boompjes = little trees), and was a popular promenade. The trees perished in the German air raids of 1940.

[6] The Leuvehaven, the old dock near the Boompjes.

[7] Presumably the garden annexe of one of the inns, of which there were several on the Boompjes itself.

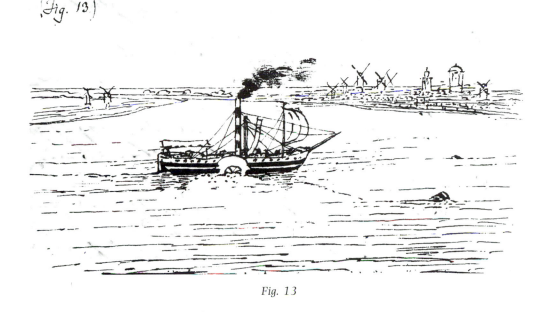

Fig. 13

At ten o'clock the carriage arrived to take us to Horchheim. A dreadful box of a cart. We alighted in Ehrenbreitstein and I showed Mother the lovely footpath by the water going as far as the chapel.[1] Gritti Thormann greeted us at the gateway. There were visitors in the garden, a gentleman from Paris and an officer from Cologne. Breakfast in the garden room. Uncle's polonaise. Auntie was upset about Rosa and Benny's departure. Felix's portrait was declared a very good likeness. Return journey in all the heat. Lunch. Coffee party at Aunt Emilie's, whose husband was angry about his books. The old couple's delight with the sunshade. Packing. Supper.

Sunday, 27 August

Left Koblenz early along the lovely road through Boppard to St Goar and Bacharach. Here we met the Steinbrücks, who were both very agreeable. We did not, however, delay long, because

---

[1] The chapel, now a wayside shrine, is still there at the corner of Hermannstrasse and Ellingshohl in Pfaffendorf, at the highest point of the old road between Ehrenbreitstein and Horchheim. It features in a view over Koblenz which Felix had sketched at this spot in 1827 (Bodleian Library, MS MDM d. 9, fo. 15).

horses are in great demand everywhere. We arrived in Bingen at four o'clock, ate at the chatterbox's inn,[1] had the carriage repaired, and drove to Ingelheim with a French postilion, who told us his whole life-story, how he had had a duel with his superior and therefore had had to flee, and now had only another couple of years to wait before he could return to his beloved France again. Arrival in Mainz, and given rooms high up in the Rheinischer Hof.[2] I wrote to Felix until late in the night.

[26/27 August]

Boarded the Attwood[3] at seven o'clock in the morning. The same ship on which I had made my first sea voyage from Hamburg to London eight years ago. It has now been demoted, and is in service here in Holland, unloved by all on account of its decrepitude. The same steward with whom I then made my first attempts at the English language, who first bawled at me in English, whose English I first failed to understand, here he was still, just as uncivil and coarse as before. Race between our Attwood and a French steamer at Brielle.[4] The English were victorious and I was seasick. Before that I asked the captain whether I could collect my things at the Customs House on a Sunday, and how I should go about it. Answer: "You are not yet there." And indeed I went to bed at ten, and did not hear the longed-for name of Margate[5] announced until three o'clock in the morning, and sensing that fresh water was at hand then went to sleep. Woke early on Sunday, got out of bed at seven o'clock, had breakfast, looked about me, and was at the Customs House[6] at half past twelve. There I caught sight of Klingemann coming towards me in a small boat. Klingemann came on board, took me off into his boat, and there I was once more on the island (Fig. 14).

I am staying with Klingemann, 4 Hobart Place, Eaton Square, Pimlico. The curious cabriolets,[7] the noise in the streets, everything astonished me anew, but above all I was glad once again to see Klingemann unchanged. We drove to his house; soon Rosen[8] came too. We had lunch with him and Wilhelm

---

[1] i.e. the Weisses Ross, owned by Joseph Soherr.

[2] The same hotel that Felix and Cécile had stayed in on their wedding night.

[3] The *Attwood* was operated by the General Steam Navigation Company, which ran a twice-weekly service between London and Rotterdam. The same company also operated the London to Hamburg and other routes to the Continent.

[4] Brielle was a small fortified town on the left bank near the mouth of the river Maas.

[5] The first place to be passed on the English coast when heading for the Thames.

[6] The company's boats sailed from off the Customs House, near the Tower of London.

[7] The cabriolet was then a fairly novel form of carriage, introduced in 1823.   [8] See p. 26 n. 2.

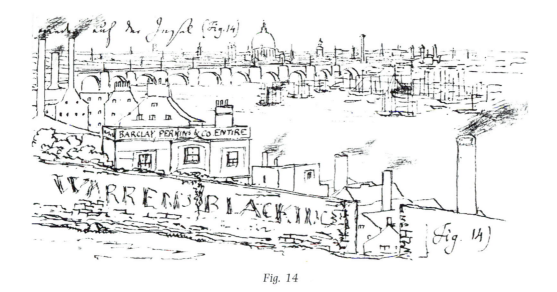

Fig. 14

and Victor Benecke.[1] *Beforehand I had a meeting with the Exeter Hall people,*[2] *and a walk to see Novello.*

Monday, 28 August

After a nasty bug-ridden night we went into the cathedral[3] and to the Gutenberg monument,[4] and then departed for Frankfurt in beautiful weather. Arrival at one o'clock and ate dinner straight away. After the meal came unpacking and laundry matters. Received various letters. The house was all ready, and has turned out very nicely. Evening time.

[1] Friedrich Wilhelm Benecke (1802–65), eldest son of Wilhelm Benecke (see p. 36 n. 3), and also known as Wilhelm. He married Henrietta Souchay (1807–93), an aunt of Cécile. After running the family chemical business for 4 years from 1828, he sold it in 1832 on being made a partner in the London branch of his father-in-law's trading firm of Schunck, Souchay & Co. The Beneckes lived at 6 Lewisham Road, Deptford, from 1830. A son, Carl Victor Benecke, married the Mendelssohns' daughter, Marie. For Victor Benecke see p. 58 n. 5.

[2] Exeter Hall in the Strand, with a main hall apparently accommodating an audience of 3,000 was built in 1829–31 and demolished in 1907, the site now being occupied by the Strand Palace Hotel. The 'Exeter Hall people' or 'Exeter Hall society' as Mendelssohn always refers to them here, were properly called the Sacred Harmonic Society. This amateur chorus, with strong working-class links, was founded in 1832 and moved its concerts to Exeter Hall in 1836. Unusually it also had its own orchestra, with professionals to lead each section. Joseph Surman was the conductor from 1832 to 1848. The Society had already given the first London performance of *St Paul* on 7 Mar. 1837.

[3] A Romanesque cathedral, with six towers and choir at both east and west ends.   [4] See p. 78 n. 4.

Sent a letter in the morning to Birmingham.[1] *The problem was that I had found a letter from there on my arrival, which expressed to me in rather unseemly terms the jealousy of the Birmingham people toward the Exeter Hall organization. The latter had also invited me to conduct 'St Paul', and (if I am not mistaken, for it is now two years later that I write this) were offering £25 for it. The Birmingham letter contained a resolution "that Mr. Mendelssohn be prohibited etc." On this point I now replied to them that there could be no question of prohibition, and if they stood firm by the prohibition I would stand firm by conducting. If on the other hand they feared financial loss because of the performance in London coming first, and had asked me about it, then, since they had engaged me first, and paid my travelling expenses, I would have declined the London performance, although it would have been to my disadvantage. The Novellos,*[2] *to whom I went for advice over the letter, as publishers and connoisseurs of the English public, suggested in the strongest terms that I should at least demand monetary compensation from the Birmingham people. That, however, did not please me. I considered it was something they could do by themselves, but I did not want to demand it. In fact it annoyed me afterwards that I had not done it, for they gave me not a single word of thanks. The Exeter Hall people (an amateur society drawn from the working classes, whose principal director, Mr Bowley,*[3] *is a shoemaker) had immediately sought me out yesterday. I had told them about the Birmingham resolution and said that I would have to await an answer to my letter of today before I decided.*

I then wrote my first letter to Cécile from London, visited Rosen in Conduit Street, and at noon we drove out to the Horsleys,[4] *whom I found again to be good, dear, unchanged friends, and enjoyed their company.*

Tuesday, 29 August

Atrocious weather. I spent the morning writing and sent off my letter to Felix. Visits in the afternoon. Did some work with Grandmother and gave an account of the journey. Evening and night in my maiden bed.

---

[1] Neither the letters to nor from Birmingham appear to have been preserved.

[2] Presumably Vincent and his son Alfred.

[3] Robert Bowley (1813–70), bootmaker. A very active member of the committee of the Sacred Harmonic Society, his official position was Librarian, 1837–54, and Treasurer, 1854–70.

[4] William Horsley (1774–1858), organist and composer especially of glees. He married Elizabeth Callcott (1793–1875) and had five children. The family had been good friends of Mendelssohn from his first English visit in 1829. They lived at 1 High Row, Kensington Gravel Pits. The house still exists as 128 Kensington Church Street, Kensington.

Atrocious weather—a swirl of fog and cloud, as in the witch's kitchen, and a downpour over St James's Park. I had to pay visits, first to Brunel,[1] *but found only his wife, frightfully elegantly dressed, then to my former host, the ironmonger Heincke,*[2] *103 Gt. Portland St., to Smart*[3] *(who had gone off on a journey), to Novello and Ayrton.*[4] *Wrote to Mother,*[5] *ate at Klingemann's, and in the evening went with Rosen to the 'St Paul' rehearsal in Exeter Hall. It took place in the small hall. We were taken through the committee room into the large hall in order for it to be shown to us. It looks like a huge warehouse. Rosen, on account of his short-sightedness, lingered behind half absent-mindedly in the committee room. He found his way back to us again with difficulty and embarrassment. His perplexed and stoical manner both struck and grieved me. We returned to the rehearsal and listened in. The choruses very good, the orchestra not. I wanted to correct a wrong note in the double-bass parts, and as I got to the first bass desk tremendous yelling, rejoicing, calls for three cheers and hat waving broke out, lasting several minutes, so that at first I was quite alarmed and subsequently delighted at such a reception. Such a thing is unknown in Germany, where nevertheless Englishmen are termed 'the cold English'.*

Went out in the morning in cold weather, then made garlands for the engagement dinner. Great feast in honour of Fräulein Fez.[6] Saw Sophie Hauck[7] for the first time since her marriage. In the evening went to the theatre to see the French company. They performed 'Un duel sous le cardinal Richelieu' and 'Le mari et l'amant',[8] the latter splendidly. Franz Bernus came into the

---

[1] Isambard Kingdom Brunel (1806–59), civil engineer, designer of the Clifton Suspension Bridge, the Great Eastern steamship, and the Great Western Railway. Married Mary Horsley (1813–81), the eldest daughter of William Horsley in 1836. They lived at 18 Duke Street, Westminster, overlooking St James's Park. Not to be confused with Duke Street, St James's, this street lay on the east side of St James's Park, parallel to the present Horse Guards Road, and thus just round the corner from the Houses of Parliament. It disappeared later in the 19th cent. when the government offices were extended.

[2] Felix had lodged with the German ironmonger Friedrich Heinke on his first four visits to London (1829–33).

[3] Sir George Smart (1776–1867), English conductor and composer, and one of the founders of the Philharmonic Society in 1813. He conducted the first English performance of *St Paul* at the Liverpool Festival in 1836.

[4] William Ayrton (1777–1858), English impresario, writer, and composer. By 1837 he was amongst the most senior of English musical journalists, having been editor of the *Harmonicon*, a contributor to the *Morning Chronicle*, and from 1837 to the *Examiner*.

[5] See p. 187.

[6] Charlotte Sophie Feetz (b. 1812), a music teacher in Frankfurt. She married Jacob Friedrich Hamburger, a master lace-maker, on 9 June 1838.

[7] See p. 42 n. 8.

[8] A visiting French troupe under MM. Doligny and Alix performed the 3-act drama *Un duel sous le Cardinal de Richelieu* by Lockroy and Edmond Badon, and the 1-act comedy *Le Mari et l'amant* by Jean Baptiste Charles Vial.

box and invited me to visit his wife the next day. We signed to each other with our handkerchiefs and behaved in a slightly unseemly way. Afterwards I wrote to Felix again.

[30 August]

Morning visits to the Misses Alexander,[1] Hanover Terrace, Regents Park [Fig. 15].

Fig. 15

Then to Taylor.[2] Also in the morning began to draft the 'Elijah' oratorio text[3] with Klingemann. In the evening out to Horsley's and music-making there. Meeting with the Exeter Hall people. In the morning there had appeared in all the newspapers a fierce article against the Birmingham people, saying that they did not want to allow me to conduct, and printing the whole resolution "that Mr. Mendelssohn be prohibited etc."[4]

[1] Daughters of Claud Alexander (1752–1809), who served in the East India Company. The three unmarried Alexander sisters, Margaret (1791–?), (Anna-)Joanna (1793–?), and Mary (1806–67), had known Mendelssohn since 1833, and Mary fell in love with him. Hanover Terrace, designed by John Nash, was finished in 1823, and the Alexanders came to live at No. 12 in 1827.

[2] See p. 95 n. 5.

[3] Mendelssohn first suggested Elijah to Klingemann as a possible subject for a new oratorio in a letter of 12 Aug. 1836 and again on 28 Mar. 1837. Klingemann's draft, with Mendelssohn's annotations, is preserved in the Bodleian Library, MS MDM c. 27, fos. 33–44. In the end the collaboration with Klingemann came to nothing, and Mendelssohn eventually turned to Julius Schubring for assistance, as he had done previously with *St Paul*. It was, however, to be 1845 before he seriously started work on the composition and completed it for the 1846 Birmingham Musical Festival.

[4] 'In all the newspapers' is an exaggeration. A search through the main London papers (*Courier, Examiner, Morning Advertiser, Morning Chronicle, Morning Herald, Morning Post, Public Ledger, The Times, True Sun*) has turned up nothing on 30 Aug. The only account traced (including the resolution) appeared in the *True Sun* on 31 Aug., with a follow-up article the next day, and a letter from 'A

Visits to Aunt Schlegel, who wasn't at home, and to Aunt Helene.[1] At eleven o'clock drove over to Marie Bernus, and spent the whole day alone with her. Her husband was in Hanau. Dashed hopes on returning home. There was no letter for me there. I wrote myself.

[*31 August*]

Worked the whole morning on the 'Elijah' project with Klingemann (Fig. 16). Had lunch at Benecke's in Deptford, together with Herr Remenance from Antwerp,[2] Herr Schlemmer jun.,[3] and Augustus Steinkopf. The first-named was asked a lot by me about the return journey, and promised to write to Dover to find out when the steamers departed, and whether I would be able to travel straight through from Birmingham to Calais. I was already beginning to count the days until my return. Drank Monzinger[4] during the meal, which tastes good amidst all the rich port and heavy pudding. Afterwards made music on Benecke's grand piano. Wrote to Cécile before driving back.

Fig. 16

chorus singer' of the Sacred Harmonic Society on 5 Sept. The full text of the resolution, as printed in the 1838 Annual Report of the Sacred Harmonic Society ran as follows: 'Resolved, That the Chairman be requested to write to Mr F. M. Bartholdy, that the intention of performing St. Paul, in Exeter Hall, in September next, conducted by Mr F. Mendelssohn Bartholdy, *be abandoned*, being contrary to the spirit of the engagement made with the Managers of the Birmingham Festival; and that the Chairman do make a similar communication to Mr Surman, the conductor of the Exeter Hall Festival.'

[1] Helene Souchay (see p. 41 n. 9).

[2] Almost certainly Eugene Rymenans (1779–1854), an Antwerp merchant with particular interests in insurance and freight transport.

[3] August Schlemmer (b. 1815), youngest son of Georg Wilhelm Maximilian and Wilhelmine Schlemmer, and brother of Fritz; he lived in London.

[4] A well-known wine from the Nahe Valley.

Dreadful rain once again—old Rad'l did not come. I wrote and posted the letter. Work. In the afternoon drove out to go shopping, then went to a gathering at Sophie Hauck's. Found a host of girls there. A letter from Berlin, none from England. Evening time.

[1 September]

In the morning received a letter from Mr Moore in Birmingham.[1] He writes his letters on the borders of the printed music festival programmes, which go post free, and so his letters do too. "To cheat the post", he said. "I would be very well advised to cancel the Exeter Hall performance; it would do them far too much harm if I conducted there before Birmingham." The affair is becoming doubly embarrassing, since today's paper had another article answering that of the day before yesterday, and agreeing with the Birmingham people.[2] I pondered with Klingemann as to whom I could go for advice, someone with a good knowledge of England and English customs in such situations. In Sir George Smart's absence he proposed Mr Ayrton, to whom I went and presented him with the facts. He unreservedly advised me to stick with the Birmingham people and not to accept the Exeter Hall performance. (I only discovered several weeks later that he was, through various circumstances, on bad terms with the latter and on good terms with the former, and had himself written the article in today's paper; so I had really gone to a good adviser!) I followed his advice, believing it to be impartial, and my lovely guineas were lost and gone. I wrote a note to the Exeter Hall people, which again was printed in the paper,[3] and I likewise wrote to Moore in Birmingham[4] and indicated that the matter was settled, and that the newspaper article against them had prejudiced me more in their favour than anything else, which was true after all. Then I wrote to Ferdinand Hiller in Italy, and had lunch at Coventry's,[5] where I met Bennett, who must have been preoccupied, dejected and ill-humoured, for I was surprised at seeing him so changed. He escorted me home in bad weather after the meal; the conversation was about things of little import, and I did not see him again in London.

[1] The letter, postmarked 26 Aug., is in the Bodleian Library (GB VI 62).

[2] This article has not been traced. An account in the *True Sun* on that day does not correspond with Mendelssohn's description of it justifying the Birmingham position.

[3] This letter is printed in the 1838 Annual Report of the Society, but no trace of its newspaper appearance has been found. Although Mendelssohn regretfully withdrew from the Exeter Hall performance on 12 Sept., he did offer to conduct it on Saturday 23 Sept. if the performance could be postponed. It is difficult to see how he could have managed this given his already very tight schedule for the return journey to Germany.

[4] The letter is not extant.

[5] Charles Coventry, partner in the English music publishing firm of Coventry & Hollier, and Bach enthusiast. The firm was later to publish Mendelssohn's Organ Sonatas, Op. 65, and his editions of Bach's chorale preludes.

Saturday, 2 September

Letter from Felix in London. Cheerful morning. In the afternoon Aunt Schlegel came to see the copy of 'St Paul'. She found Steinbrück's leaf the most beautiful. Her fine attire and healthy appearance. Spent the evening upstairs with Sophie.

Saturday, 2 September

Morning visits to Erard,[1] Stone, and Benedict[2]—found none of the three in town. Dinner at five o'clock with Klingemann at Mme Novello's—not particularly pleasant.

Sunday, 3 September

In the morning went to church, then paid visits, wrote, ate, and went out for a drive. In the last few days I have felt life stir within me for the first time. It is far too great a delight to be my Felix's wife!

Monday, 4 September

Wrote to my aunt in Leipzig,[3] to Mother in Berlin,[4] and to Felix. After lunch went for a walk on the other side of the Main, and consumed plenty of fruit in the gardens. The weather was autumnal yet still fine. I spent the evening alone upstairs and pined dreadfully for my husband.

[3/4 September]

Wrote out the piano part of my D minor Concerto. Received a visit from Mr Neate.[5] Drove in the cabriolet to Erard about a piano and to Novello on other business. A nice peaceful dinner at home

---

[1] French firm of piano and harp makers, who also established a branch in London in the 1790s. By the 1830s the firm was run by Pierre Erard (1796–1855) in Paris, the London branch being managed in 1837 by J. J. Bruzand.

[2] Sir Julius Benedict (1804–85), English composer and conductor. After an early career on the Continent—where Mendelssohn met him in Naples in 1831—he settled back in London in 1835, and was made conductor of the Opera Buffa at the Lyceum Theatre in 1836, before becoming musical director at Drury Lane in 1838.

[3] Julie Louisa Schunck, née Bauer (1789–1862), Cécile's great-aunt by marriage. Married the Leipzig merchant, Philipp Schunck.

[4] Cécile must mean the letter to Lea of 2 Sept. (see p. 189)—it is postmarked in Frankfurt on that day, so cannot have taken more than one day to write. Presumably the diary here was written in arrears.

[5] Charles Neate (1784–1877), pianist and composer. He studied under John Field, and was one of the original founders of the Philharmonic Society in 1813. He went to Vienna for 8 months in 1815 and became a friend of Beethoven.

with just Klingemann and Rosen: fish, steak, and pudding. Pleasant evening. Angry note to the Exeter Hall people because of the publication of my letter of the day before yesterday. They came and apologized, saying that it was quite the usual thing in England, that they had had to do it on account of the public, since my name had already been announced everywhere in large letters and so on. I'm sick of the whole business. An attractive slim lady with her husband paid me a visit and brought a letter of recommendation from Smart: her name was Mrs Alfred Shaw.[1] She was very keen to come to Germany, and I assured her that if what Smart had written about her were true, then the German public would be even more delighted with her than she would be with the country. She invited me to hear her sing at home; I gladly accepted and was intrigued. Meanwhile I had discovered that Mme Dulcken[2] had just arrived from the Rhineland, and I hastened over but did not meet her, and left a message that I very much wished to talk with her about David.[3] Unfortunately the next day, Monday 4 September, I had occasion to discover that she had been obliged to hurry over to see the Queen and God knows what other "nobility" at Windsor, and I was thus not able to see her. I was feeling unwell, probably as a result of all the walking around in the bad weather. Visits in the cabriolet to Erard, Novello, etc. Wrote to Cécile and to Birmingham. Continued with the piano part of my concerto. Pleasant dinner with Rosen and Klingemann, just like yesterday.

Tuesday, 5 September

I went shopping for various things with Mother. I returned home weary, and could not do much work in the afternoon as my back hurt. I read and re-read Felix's charming letter a hundred times, and rejoiced that he had not forgotten me.

Wednesday, 6 September

Today I still did not yet feel completely well, and on that account was grumpy. I wrote to Felix, received visitors, worked, and went to bed, and did not wake up in the night as I did in the beginning.

[1] Mary (Mrs Alfred) Shaw, née Postans (1814–76), English contralto. She married the painter Alfred Shaw in 1835. Mendelssohn invited her to Leipzig, where she sang in 12 concerts in the 1838/9 Gewandhaus season to considerable acclaim.

[2] Louise Dulcken, née David (1811–50), German pianist, sister of Ferdinand David. She lived in London for the latter part of her life, where she was a sought-after piano teacher.

[3] Ferdinand David (1810–73), German violinist. He had been a friend of Mendelssohn since the mid-1820s, and in 1836 went to Leipzig as leader of the Gewandhaus orchestra.

Out to Horsley's at half past eleven. Made music with Horsley senior and his daughters,[1] chatted, had lunch there and passed the whole day nice and quietly. Drove with Charles[2] to the rehearsal at Exeter Hall at eight o'clock in the evening. The following morning I again had to pay many visits: Cramer,[3] Altridge,[4] Erard, etc. etc. Continued working [on the concerto]. Visit to the Alexanders, where father's portrait sat between flowers on the small table. On to Benedict's, whom I again failed to meet. To Judd Street in the omnibus, and from there to dinner at Edward Taylor's.[5] He had invited none other than Herr Kiallmark[6] to meet me. His wife lay ill upstairs, and comforted herself with her husband's wisdom, whom she called a very "scientific man". After dinner he sang me a song by Spohr[7] so badly that I felt like running away, and was altogether a loathsome, underhand, servile Jesuit. Let the Devil take him! He railed like a trooper about the Birmingham people, and continued to do so after the Festival in all the newspaper articles he could. Home and supped further with Klingemann, and recovered myself in his company.

Thursday, 7 September

Went to the Städel Institute in the morning to see the fresco and the painting of the Two Marys by Veit.[8] Encounter there with Herr Stieler,[9] who took me for an unmarried girl. His wife,

---

[1] The unmarried daughters were Frances Arabella (Fanny) (1815–49) who was to marry Dr Seth Thompson in 1841, and Sophia Hutchins (1819–94). The third daughter, Mary, was already married to Isambard Kingdom Brunel.

[2] Charles Edward Horsley (1821–76). He became a composer and studied with Mendelssohn in Leipzig.

[3] Johann Baptist Cramer (1771–1858) or his brother Franz (1772–1848). Both were resident in London, the former as composer, pianist, and music publisher, the latter as a leading orchestral violinist, and, from 1835, Master of the King's Music. Franz Cramer led the orchestra for many of Mendelssohn's concerts with the Philharmonic Society, and was one of the leaders of the orchestra at the 1837 Birmingham Musical Festival.

[4] Presumably really Aldridge, but unidentifable.

[5] Edward Taylor (1784–1863), English bass, lecturer, and writer on music. He became Professor of Music at Gresham College, London, in 1837. Music critic of the *Spectator*, he also wrote for the *Morning Chronicle*. His report on the Birmingham Festival in the *Spectator* (23 Sept. 1837) included criticism of *St Paul* for over-reliance on the models of Bach and Handel.

[6] George Frederick Kiallmark (1804–87), pianist, whose playing was admired by Mendelssohn.

[7] Louis Spohr (1784–1859). German composer, violinist, and conductor. Kapellmeister at Kassel from 1822, in which year the young Mendelssohn first met him, and began a lifelong friendly association.

[8] The three-part fresco by Philipp Veit, *Die Verherrlichung des Christentums* (The Triumph of Christianity), was painted in 1834–6 and its room opened to the public in Aug. 1837. In 1877 it was transferred to canvas and moved from the old Städelsches Kunstinstitut in the Neue Mainzer Strasse to the present building. The centre panel represents the Introduction of the Arts into Germany through Christianity, whilst to left and right are allegorical figures of Italy and Germany respectively. *The Two Marys*—see p. 45 n. 4.

[9] Joseph Karl Stieler (1781–1858), painter, whose portraits included ones of Cornelius Carl Souchay and his wife, Helene. He married Luise Becker in 1818 and settled in Munich in 1820, where he was responsible for the Gallery of Beauties in the Nymphenburg Schloss. They had a daughter Ottilie, and three sons.

who looked younger than her daughter—all wanted to come to us in the evening. The large picture pleased me more than ever, except for the frame. I did a lot of writing during the day. The Stielers came in the evening. A comical misunderstanding. Frau Stieler is a most pleasing woman, who told us much about Munich and Felix, whom she saw there.[1]

Thursday, 7 September

Rosen had told me that today he would like to bring along the young Edmond Spring Rice,[2] who wanted to make my acquaintance. Klingemann had summoned them both to breakfast, and they came at nine. It was Rosen's last outing. He complained of having a fever, of a swollen arm which greatly hampered and hurt him. He wanted us to present his apologies at Brunel's in case he could not get there at midday. We advised him to stay away, since he looked pale and exhausted, and I told him that he ought to go to bed, as it might then be gone by tomorrow. He hoped so too. I played the piano to him and his young friend, who was a good-looking tall fair-haired English boy of whom Rosen seemed to be very fond. I was called away, since Miss Wesley,[3] the organist's daughter, together with another lady were in the parlour, and had brought album leaves, which they wanted me to inscribe for them. When I returned, Rosen and his young friend were gone. About one o'clock Hogarth[4] arrived, with his usual friendly manner, unaffected and very pleasant toward me. I had not visited him first because he is a journalist with the Morning Chronicle—but he makes one forget that, he is so decent and honest. Then wrote to Cécile and rejoiced that the time of having to correspond is diminishing. Visits to Collard,[5] Novello, and Erard, but encountered none of them. At seven in the evening to dinner at Brunel's in the Park with Klingemann. O what should man request? If friends are not well, that causes distress, and if they are well, then there is still no lack of distress. For example, as here, where everything was

---

[1] Mendelssohn visited Munich in 1830 and 1831 on his way to and from Italy.

[2] Stephen Edmund Spring-Rice (1814–85). Eldest son of Thomas Spring-Rice (1790–1866), he eventually became deputy chairman of the Board of Customs.

[3] Eliza Wesley (1819–95), daughter of Samuel Wesley, and posthumous editor of his letters. Her autograph album is in the British Library (Add. MS 35,026). Felix's contribution (fo. 66) was a 9-bar four-part canon (4 in 2), set out with the two written-out parts headed 'Quartett?' It is reproduced in facsimile in Gordon Phillips and Ludwig Altman (edd.), *Samuel Wesley and Dr Mendelssohn: Three Organ Fugues* (London, 1962). The contribution to the other lady's album is unknown.

[4] George Hogarth (1783–1870), Scottish writer on music. On moving to London in 1830, he wrote for the *Harmonicon*, and became joint editor and music critic of the *Morning Chronicle*. In 1838 Mendelssohn wrote testimonials on behalf of both Hogarth and John Thomson for the Edinburgh professorship of music; Thomson (see p. 113 n. 4) was the successful candidate when the appointment was eventually made in 1839.

[5] Either Frederick William Collard (1772–1860) or his brother William Frederick (1776–1866), partners in the London piano manufacturing firm of Collard & Collard.

so elegant, and aristocratic, and befitting of a Member of Parliament, that the likes of me began to feel quite sick in the stomach. What had happened to the Mary Horsley of old? And what to the former Isambard Brunel? Flown off into the world of grandeur, where there is room for everything, but pleasure for no one and concern for no one. For nothing was forthcoming from the two at dinner, except for plenty of fish, poultry, and the like. And beforehand we had to wait a while with the ladies and the baby before the man of the house arrived with his father,[1] and Mr Hawes MP[2] and goodness knows who else, still engrossed in the deepest conversation, and then we proceeded straight to the feast, and immediately after the feast we went into an elegant room, in which stood a small organ,[3] upon which I was expected to play! However, I took my hat, and walked home alone through St James's Park, and there in the dark heard the retreat sounded on trumpets and drums, and could have almost wept, so moved was I. Klingemann stayed on and sought to excuse me, and I resolved that I would not go there again, where a merry, good companion had become twisted into a grand speculator, politician, and man of quality. I know of nothing which I regret more. We had apologized for Rosen, saying that he was not very well.

Friday, 8 September

Herr Rad'l came at ten o'clock, and I worked at my Swiss landscape; then I received a letter from Felix and was very happy. Work in the afternoon. Visit of Herr Gansland[4] from Hanau in the evening.

Friday, 8 September

Young John Horsley,[5] who wanted to show me his picture and to hear me play, came to breakfast. After some music-making we went off together to Cartwright's[6] in whose rooms the picture hangs (he

[1] Marc Isambard Brunel (1806–59), civil engineer; he was knighted in 1841.

[2] Benjamin Hawes (1797–1862), Member of Parliament for Lambeth 1832–47, and then for Kinsale, 1848–62. He married Sophia, daughter of Marc Isambard Brunel, and was knighted in 1856.

[3] J. C. Bishop built a house organ for Mary Brunel in 1837 (Laurence Elvin, *Bishop and Son, Organ Builders* (London, 1984), 35–6).

[4] Röttger Ganslandt (1812–94), son of a Lübeck merchant and senator, Wilhelm Ganslandt, and Charlotte Louise Hestermann of Hanau. He was born in Hanau and became a well-known lawyer.

[5] John Callcott Horsley (1817–1903), artist and Royal Academician, eldest son of William Horsley. The picture *Rent Day at Haddon Hall in the Days of Queen Elizabeth* was exhibited at the British Institution in 1837, and helped launch him on a successful career. Its whereabouts are unknown, but Horsley returned to the same subject 30 years later, and a small sketch dated 1866 is in the York City Art Gallery; the subsequent larger version was exhibited at the Royal Academy in 1868, and was sold at Christie's, London, on 3 June 1988 (lot 151).

[6] Samuel Cartwright (1789–1864), well-known London dentist, and friend of the Horsley family.

himself was away). It portrays an old English Hall, in which figures from that period are used as back-ground, and has a nice use of light and colour. Then we went by way of Piccadilly, where we had break-fast in a cake shop, to the little church of St John, Paddington,[1] which stands alone in the field to the right of the Oxford road. There we met all the Horsleys, and Klingemann, who had been to see Rosen and said that he perhaps had rheumatic fever, and was no better yet. Then I played fugues by Bach and others on the organ for an hour. The strange parson's wife, a bluestocking, came up to the organ, requested a psalm tune, and annoyed Mrs Horsley greatly, who in turn spoke sharply to her, because she found fault with Turle[2] the organist. The strange beadle, who, as Fanny Horsley asserted, had taken a fancy to me. We then walked through Kensington Garden to an early dinner at the Horsleys. At eight o'clock in the evening I drove to the final rehearsal of my 'St Paul' at Exeter Hall.

Saturday, 9 September

Strolled round the fair[3] with Julie and made various small purchases. Then worked at home and wrote letters. Today it is a year since we became engaged, and now we are already separated! The weather was not as fine as last year, when I ran up the hill in the awful heat of the sun, heading towards my fortunate destiny. In the evening I went for a little walk with Mother and later still wrote to my husband.

Saturday, 9 September

A letter from Leipzig in the morning with the offer of an engagement for Clara Novello.[4] I went to their house and discussed the matter with her mother, who seemed to have no real enthusiasm for it, and with her brother, who had still less. Clara herself was not present. The decision will ultimately be left in her hands. I visited Rosen, who was lying in bed, apparently fairly well, then Coventry and Sir Lewis Möller.[5] Letter to Cécile. Tedious and dull evening at home with Novello. I wanted to sell him my

---

[1] The church of St John the Evangelist, now in Hyde Park Crescent. It was consecrated in 1832. The two-manual organ with an octave and a half of pedals was built by J. C. Bishop. It was moved to Ilkeston in Derbyshire in 1866.

[2] James Turle (1802–82), English organist and composer. Organist of Westminster Abbey from 1831 to his death.

[3] The autumn fair was held in the three weeks preceding Michaelmas (29 Sept.).

[4] Clara Novello (1818–1908), singer, fourth daughter of Vincent Novello. Following initial fame in England, she also triumphed on the Continent, beginning with her appearances at the Gewandhaus in the winter of 1837/8. Although Mendelssohn admired her singing, her rather superior manner did not appeal to him.

[5] Sir Lewis Möller (1770/1–1847), sometime Hanoverian Chargé d'Affaires in London.

three new things, the Psalm, Concerto, and organ pieces, for £40;[1] *he appeared churlish. I broke off the discussion and thought: I won't give you another chance.*

Sunday, 10 September

I did not go to church as I was not feeling too well. Many visitors came, and before lunch we went for a walk together to see Marie Bernus. In the afternoon a drive to Bonames[2] with Theodor Schunck,[3] who has been here for several days, and who likes it here very much. Returned late in the evening by beautiful moonlight, stood for a long time at the window, and later still wrote a letter.

Sunday, 10 September

Cooper,[4] *the deputy of old Attwood,*[5] *who had gone off on a journey, had invited me up to the organ in St Paul's*[6] *(Fig. 17) for evensong. I found a vast crowd of people gathered in the choir and elsewhere, so that I could hardly push my way through to the organ, even though the service had already ended. Every musician whom I remembered meeting in London I found again in the choir. When I had played for half an hour, and the crowd was growing rather than diminishing, I started on the great A minor Prelude and Fugue by Bach.*[7] *It was going well and everything was working out successfully, when in the closing passage of the fugue, where the pedal plays the rising figure alone, Cooper suddenly pulled on*

---

[1] Psalm 42, Op. 42, Piano Concerto No. 2, Op. 40, and the 3 Preludes and Fugues for organ, Op. 37.

[2] The home of Eduard and Helene Souchay (see p. 41 n. 9).

[3] Theodor Schunck (1818–65), first cousin once removed of Cécile. Son of Martin and Susanna Schunck, great-uncle and aunt of Cécile.

[4] George Cooper (d. 1843), London organist, Thomas Attwood's deputy at St Paul's Cathedral, and father of the better-known organist George Cooper (1820–76).

[5] Thomas Attwood (1765–1838), English composer and organist. Organist of St Paul's Cathedral from 1796. A friend of Mendelssohn from his first visit to England in 1829, he was the dedicatee of the Preludes and Fugues, Op. 37.

[6] The organ, in a case designed by Christopher Wren, was built by Bernhard Smith at the end of the 17th cent. on a screen between the dome and choir. By 1837 it was a three-manual instrument with pedals, having a Great manual compass extending all the way down to 16 foot C. The two-octaves of pedals were permanently coupled to the Great, although in 1826 J. C. Bishop had added an octave of independent 16 foot pedal pipes. Mendelssohn's very inaccurate drawing (probably done from memory) shows the instrument from the choir side. It makes the main case look much squatter than it really was, and does not hint at the rich profusion of decoration on it. The choir or 'chair' case in front also appears to be two separate cases rather than a single case with a lower central section like the main case. The screen was taken down in 1861, and Wren's case eventually divided and used to house the new Willis organ of 1871/2 on the north and south sides of the choir. Evensong was at 3.15 p.m.

[7] BWV 543. Although the St Paul's organ had only a two-octave pedalboard (CCC–C), very little adjustment of Bach's pedal part of this work would have been necessary, since it only exceeds this compass for three notes.

Fig. 17

the assistant's bell. The weights which indicated the wind supply quickly dropped down, and the wind was gone out of the organ. Cooper ran off like a madman, quite red with anger, was away a little while, and finally returned with the news that during the performance the organ-blower, on instructions from the beadle, who had not been able to get anybody to leave the church and had been obliged to stay on longer against his will, had left the bellows, locked the door to them, and departed. Cooper wanted to fetch him back, but since I had no more time I left the organ, and had an opportunity to observe something of the "public spirit" of a crowd of Englishmen. They heaved to and fro as excited as if something important had happened. Shame! shame! was called out from all sides. Three or four clerics appeared and tore the beadle completely to pieces in front of all the people, threatening him with dismissal. Cooper helped in the chiding, and while the noisy disturbance proceeded in the church, and the people formed a jostling crowd, I left the organ and reached the open air. I then took an omnibus and went to dinner at Mrs Shaw's, where I met Mr Neate but nobody else. Some of Mr Shaw's paintings were shown to me, which I praised as much as I possibly could, which wasn't that much. After dinner, however, his wife sang me the alto aria from my 'St Paul',[1] plus some Handel and some Italian pieces, all so superbly that I was able with a good conscience to furnish all the praise which before dinner I had held back. I thought to myself, O God, if only we had her in Leipzig instead of Novello, for her voice had quite a different liveliness about it—but it was now too late. All in good time, I thought. Then Neate and I played as well and walked home together. He told me on the way that he was studying Thalberg's pieces[2] very diligently, but that they were becoming very difficult for him. Nevertheless he had to do it for the sake of his pupils. The bald, ageing 50-year-old man thereby moved me more than I could admit to him.

Monday, 11 September

In the morning wrote to Berlin,[3] did some sewing, attended to the tailor and so forth. In the afternoon went to Mme Bernay[4] and shook her mirabelle-plum trees. The weather is fine and every evening the moon shines quite gloriously. I wrote to my Felix and had also today received a short letter from him.

Tuesday, 12 September

In the morning I did some sewing. At eleven an invitation arrived from Marie Bernus, and at one her carriage. At her house the painter Thöming[5] and some other gentlemen had come to dine. After the meal we looked at copper engravings of Cologne Cathedral as it is meant to turn out, and conversed as well as we could with the painter, who was from Holstein, where apparently proper German was no longer spoken. Later on we two ladies went for a walk in the garden, then Sophie[6] arrived, whom we proceeded to instruct. Marie accompanied me home—it was already dark. I did some writing.

---

[1] 'But the Lord is mindful of his own' from part 1.

[2] Sigismond Thalberg (1812–71), German or Austrian pianist and composer. One of the great virtuoso pianists of the 19th cent., his compositions consisted mainly of fantasias and variations on operatic themes.

[3] No letter of this date to Berlin has been preserved. The letter to Lea dated 8 Sept. (see p. 190) is postmarked 9 Sept., so it cannot be a continuation of it.

[4] Probably Marie Charlotte Bernay (see p. 149 n. 3) or possibly Wilhelmine Klothide Bernay (see p. 54 n. 6).

[5] Frederik Thöming (1802–73), landscape and seascape painter, actually born at Eckernförde in Schleswig, close to the border with Holstein. He studied in Rome from 1830, and then went to Munich.

[6] Sophie Hauck (see p. 42 n. 8).

I had to begin making my farewell visits; drove to Erard, Novello, Dance,[1] and Mrs Anderson.[2] Piano rehearsal at two with Bennett,[3] the tenor soloist engaged for Birmingham. He sang everything correctly and well the first time through. On the way there an acquaintance accosted me, and I began to tell him the story of yesterday's incident with the organ. He said he had read it already in the newspaper, and indeed there it was in all today's papers.[4] It passed from there to the German ones, and on my return caused me the greatest nuisance, since everyone asked me about it both verbally and by letter, wanting to know what happened. I could not see at all why people appeared so surprised about it. I could just as easily tell quite different stories of German organists and organ-blowers as this one. Dinner at Coventry's at five. The evening spent at the Alexanders in the company of Mrs Hobhouse.[5] Klingemann was with Rosen and was becoming anxious. The situation did not please him; he brought along a new doctor who made him even more concerned. It was not rheumatism but a tumour under the arm, resulting from some inner weakness—Brodie[6] or Key[7] (I believe that is how it is spelt) should be asked for their advice. In the meantime Tuesday, 12 September arrived. The danger increased. Key said it was one of the most serious of illnesses. My seat for tomorrow's journey to Birmingham at 7 o'clock was reserved. I asked whether the journey could be postponed. Answer, no. I, however, was determined not to travel in a state of uncertainty, and Klingemann was afraid that I would still be able to go. He said nothing more. I too did not ask, and we walked silently further up the road, and were doubtless both thinking for the first time of the worst, of the irretrievable loss which was imminent. I wrote a few lines to Cécile, went to see Smart and Erard, neither of whom I met, then to Rosen's at twelve. 'You see clearly', he said to me 'that there is nothing to be done with me. Indeed I already told you yesterday, you mustn't come and see me now at all. There is no joy to be gained from me'. Next to his bedroom builders and carpenters were working and making a noise with their singing and whistling. It disturbed him and he complained.

---

[1] William Dance (1755–1840), English pianist and violinist, one of the founders of the Philharmonic Society in 1813. Mendelssohn had known the Dance family since his first visit to England in 1829.

[2] Lucy Anderson (1797–1878), English pianist. In 1820 she married George Frederick Anderson, violinist and member of the Royal Household, who was responsible for the Royal Music Library.

[3] Christian name unknown. He had sung the part in the first English performance of *St Paul* in Liverpool on 7 Oct. 1836 under the direction of Sir George Smart.

[4] This incident was indeed widely reported in the press.

[5] The wife of Thomas Benjamin Hobhouse (1807–76), MP for Rochester, 1837–41, and a friend of the Alexanders.

[6] Sir Benjamin Collins Brodie (1783–1862), London surgeon. Sergeant-surgeon to William IV and then to Queen Victoria.

[7] Aston Key (1793–1849), surgeon at Guy's Hospital.

At one o'clock I had to go to Christ Church[1] to play the organ. The whole church, choir and every-where, was stuffed full of people. Some ladies I didn't know presented me with flowers. I play a good deal and it comes off well. In the sacristy refreshments of cakes and wine were served. All the churchwardens came and expressed their thanks, and mocked the churchwardens of St Paul's, where such a scandal was not wholly unexpected. There was no fear of such a thing with them. Old Wesley,[2] trembling and bent, shook hands with me and at my request sat down at the organ bench to play, a thing he had not done for many years. The frail old man improvised with great artistry and splendid facility, so that I could not but admire. His daughter[3] was so moved by the sight of it all that she fainted and could not stop crying and sobbing. She believed she would certainly never hear him play like that again; and alas, shortly after my return to Germany I learned of his death.[4] The Alexanders came up to the organ, and carried me off in their carriage so that I could return to Rosen all the sooner, and I was presently out of the crowded church, away from the organ and by his bedside. He no longer recognized me properly, and spoke in a laboured and disjointed manner. The builders were still working, but did not disturb him any more—he did not hear them. The doctor in the room next door said it was incomprehensible that he was dying so quickly. I still could not believe it and give up all hope. Walked home with Klingemann, ate there quickly; then he returned to Rosen to see what the situation was; the Alexanders called to take me to Exeter Hall for the performance of my 'St Paul'. An immense hall with galleries—completely filled—my seat was in the centre of the gallery facing the orchestra. Next to me on my right I found Smart, whom I had met four years ago in London, and Benedict whom I had met six years ago in Naples. Before we could greet each other properly and talk things over, the overture started. Smart as always looked at his watch in the opening bar and again in the last one, in order to find out how long it

---

[1] Christ Church, Newgate Street. The three-manual instrument of 1690 by Renatus Harris had undergone a number of altera-tions by Elliot & Hill between 1824 and 1834, including the addition for the first time of pedals, although their compass of only 17 notes from GG to c would have posed problems for Mendelssohn in the Bach work. Hill radically rebuilt the instrument in 1838 and Mendelssohn was to play it again on his visit in 1842. It was destroyed in 1940. According to Henry John Gauntlett's account in the *Musical World* (15 Sept. 1837), Mendelssohn played 'six extempore fantasias and the pedal fugue he was not allowed to go through with at St. Paul's'. Gauntlett admired the ease with which he overcame the limitations of the pedalboard, and noted that in the A minor Prelude 'either by accident or design, he amplified and extended the idea of the author, in a manner so in keeping and natural, that those unacquainted with its details could not by any possibility have discovered the departure from the text'.

[2] Samuel Wesley (1766–1837), English composer and organist. Acknowledged in his prime as the finest English organist of his day, he was a central figure in the promotion of J. S. Bach's music in England.

[3] Eliza Wesley (see p. 96 n. 3).

[4] Wesley died on 11 Oct. 1837. The British Library has a Fugue in B minor 'composed expressly for Dr. Mendelssohn' on 9 Sept. 1837 (MS Add. 35007, fo. 99b), whose subject is taken from the canon Mendelssohn wrote in Eliza's book on 7 Sept. (see p. 96 n. 3). Unless Mendelssohn's account here is faulty, however, it would appear that Wesley never actually played it to him. Gauntlett also only mentions Wesley as having extemporized.

lasted.[1] *The choruses went admirably and sounded powerful; the orchestra was deficient. Miss Birch*[2] *sang 'Jerusalem' and Mrs Shaw the alto aria*[3] *quite beautifully; both were encored—likewise Phillips*[4] *with the second B minor aria of Paul*[5] *and the duets of part two, and several of the choruses. The other solo parts were for the most part unremarkable. A lady who sang 'Far be it from thy path' and who persisted in entering both times a tone too low, in G minor rather than A minor, caused complete confusion and amazement.*[6] *Nevertheless the performance was altogether singularly interesting for me, since I* <u>heard</u> *my oratorio for the first time, and only one thing bothered me terribly throughout—the overlong pauses between the individual numbers, whereas they cannot follow on quickly enough for me. After the first part Smart led me to the Green Room, where the orchestra and several of the singers were assembled, who greeted me warmly, proposed my health, and drank to a return with a new "St Paul" or "St John" or anything else I fancied. When I returned to my seat in the hall the audience below began to call out my name and to applaud, and when I stood up to express my thanks and gave a bow, an unbelievable noise arose, which continued for more than five minutes, and which fairly startled me and then made me proud. The people waved handkerchiefs and hats, climbed on the seats, roared out my name and greetings, and I could not be finished with the bows and thanks. It was the greatest burst of applause that I had yet heard in my life; the whole audience to a man stood up and turned round in my direction. At that moment I wished only that Cécile were there. 'What do you say to this?' asked old Smart. Then the Claxtons*[7] *appeared, whom I thought to be in Rome, Henle,*[8] *whom I thought to be in Berlin, and Armstrong, whom I thought to be in Leipzig; and all greeted me and wished me good luck. Then the second part began. Eight numbers were encored, and at the end another round of cheering, almost as long as the first. The Alexanders took me back to Rosen in the carriage, and waited at the door for news. I arrived about midnight, but he had passed away during the performance. Klingemann*

---

[1] Although the British Library has a large collection of Smart's annotated programmes, the one for this performance is not amongst them.

[2] Charlotte Ann Birch (*c*.1815–1901), English soprano. A pupil of Sir George Smart at the Royal Academy of Music, she was first engaged by the Sacred Harmonic Society in 1836, which started her very successful career as a concert artist.

[3] 'But the Lord is mindful of his own' in part 1.

[4] Henry Phillips (1801–76), English bass. In addition to appearing regularly on the London stage and concert platforms, he was a frequent principal bass at provincial festivals. Mendelssohn wrote his Ossianic scena *On Lena's gloomy heath* for Phillips, who sang it at the Philharmonic Society in 1847.

[5] 'O God have mercy' in part 1.

[6] The part 2 chorus 'Far be it from thy path' opens with entries for solo voices, drawn from members of the choir. It is not hard to see why the unfortunate soprano started her phrase on a D rather than an E, for the transition from the previous number can lead an unwary singer to pitch the first note too low.

[7] Marshall Claxton (1813–81), historical, biblical, and portrait painter. He had spent some time in Rome in 1837.

[8] Probably Jakob Henle (1809–85), anatomist, who was a demonstrator for Johannes Müller in Berlin, before becoming Professor of Anatomy in Zürich in 1840.

came down the staircase, pale and bewildered; Rosen had died in his arms, while the jubilation was go-ing on in the hall. Coley, one of Rosen's friends, came at midnight to make enquiries of him in passing. He had heard that Rosen was not well. He could not believe the news. Klingemann and I walked home slowly and in silence through the empty streets. I really felt that it was a day in my life which I shall never forget.

Wednesday, 13 September

I received a lovely long letter from Felix. I then went to see Aunt Schlegel, who was unwell, and round the town with Mother. In the afternoon went for a drive with Theodor and Julie, worked, and did some writing.

Wednesday, 13 September

Off early to the Birmingham coach.[1] Left London at ten past eight, through Coventry at noon, arrived in Birmingham at half past six in the evening. In the coach my only thoughts were of yesterday's terrible loss, of the day I had experienced. In Birmingham, amid the throng of people, coaches, and chimneys, Moore stood with his servant. He took me to his house, where I was to lodge. There I met Neukomm[2] once more after many years; he is also lodging there. We ate together, and I went to bed early.

Thursday, 14 September

Helped with Julie's fancy-dress costume for tomorrow. Dinner. In the afternoon Louise Colin[3] arrived, to whom I had to show the copy of 'St Paul', as I have already done to many other people. In the evening I went over to see the Bihls,[4] the weather being exceptionally nice, and brought back flowers and fruit.

---

[1] Mendelssohn probably travelled by 'The Tally-Ho' coach, run by S. A. Mountain & Co. and W. Chaplin & Co., which went via St Albans, Stony Stratford, Towcester, and Coventry.

[2] See p. 78 n. 3. Mendelssohn had of course in fact already met him briefly that year on board the steamer.

[3] Louise Colin (1796–1881), a second cousin of Cécile (on the Souchay side), who lived in Hanau.

[4] Johann August von Bihl (1771–1851), a Frankfurt cloth merchant, married Augustine Caroline Wilhelmine Textor (1796–1827), a near relative of Goethe in 1815. Cécile's brother, Carl, was to marry their daughter Johanna Auguste von Bihl (1818–99) in 1839. Although the Bihls' town address was in An der Allee, like many prosperous Frankfurters they evidently also had property with a garden across the river in Sachsenhausen.

To the town hall[1] in the morning—a magnificent room. Letter to Cécile. Visit to Knyvett,[2] the Festival's conductor. Told him that I had to leave on Friday at half past eleven in the morning. He created difficulties. Conferred with Moore about it and gave him a hellishly hot time. Played the piano on an instrument which Broadwoods[3] had sent, with the intention that I should play it at the concert, and as such it has already been advertised in the papers. O England! O publicity! O misery! I wrote to Erard and left it in his hands now not to send the piano I had ordered. Then wrote to Klingemann for whom I had booked lodgings for the Musical Festival. At eight o'clock in the evening I played the most excellent organ for the first time.[4]

Friday, 15 September

Wrote to Felix early in the morning, went out and had a lesson with Rad'l. In the afternoon made garlands for Julie. In the evening a big gathering at the Heyders,[5] where there was a silly surprise in honour of the engaged couple and then dancing. I did round dances with Sophie Hauck and the many partnerless girls, and was happy when I got to bed.

Friday, 15 September

Letter to Mr Clarke[6] in London, in answer to his. Visit to Turle, the organist, and discussion about the organ part of my 'St Paul'. I was presented to the local worthies of Birmingham including Mr

---

[1] The new Town Hall, modelled on a Greek temple, was designed by Joseph Aloysius Hansom and Edward Welch, and opened in 1834, though not at that time quite complete.

[2] William Knyvett (1779–1856), English singer, composer, and conductor. As an alto he was a Gentleman of the Chapel Royal, a lay clerk at Westminster Abbey, and specialized in glee-singing. Principal conductor of the Birmingham Festivals from 1834 to 1843.

[3] English firm of piano makers, established by John Broadwood (1732–1812).

[4] A four-manual organ was installed in 1834 by William Hill. Paid for by the Birmingham Hospital Musical Festival Committee, it was the second largest organ in the country at the time, complete with 32 foot pedal stops, and provided the precedent for the building of organs in town halls throughout the country. In 1837 it was moved backwards into a recess, but was still controlled from a console some 18 feet in front of the organ, connected by very long mechanism, which made the action exceptionally heavy. Mendelssohn makes no comment on this here, and indeed played the organ again at the 1840 Festival. But on this latter occasion he appears to have had trouble with the instrument, judging by a report in the *Musical World* (1 Oct. 1840, p. 220) and when he was invited by Joseph Moore to play the organ at the 1846 Festival, he declined to do so just because of the heaviness of the pedal action (letter to Moore of 25 Mar. 1845—see F. G. Edwards, *The History of Mendelssohn's Oratorio 'Elijah'* (London, 1896), 32). Despite its size, the organ was by no means a total success in its initial state, and it took many alterations over the following decades before it became a really satisfactory instrument.

[5] Johann Georg von Heÿder (1812–88), a Frankfurt banker, married Susanne Elisabeth Ida Saint-George (1815–96) on 19 Sept. 1837.

[6] Charles Cowden Clarke (1787–1877), author and lecturer. He married Mary Novello, eldest daughter of Vincent, and was in partnership with Alfred Novello.

Barker,[1] *who had invited me to dinner, and where I found a fine house, a beautiful garden with "orcadia plants" (orchids?), and fairly pleasant company. Germany was, they thought, a dreadful country. I disagreed. Mr Barker was on board the first steamer which sailed from England up the Rhine.*[2] *They had taken a cook and food with them because they could not eat the German stuff. The house stands in open country a fair way out of Birmingham. Genuine solitude.*

Saturday, 16 September

I wrote to Felix. Theodor Schunck departed. Fritz Schlemmer and Uncle Pietsch[3] arrived. Spent the afternoon downstairs. Aunt Helene[4] came in the evening, and later on Karl, whom we had been expecting for a couple of days.

Saturday, 16 September

To another local worthy, Mr Walker,[5] *for dinner. Rehearsal in the evening, the hall illuminated*[6] *and splendid. The orchestra was still almost entirely absent. Turle accompanied on the organ, and only a few strings were present. I did not understand it at all, as the first day of the Festival is on Tuesday. Häser's oratorio,*[7] *and one movement from the Bach Passion*[8] *was rehearsed, but nothing else.*

[1] George Barker (1776–1845), solicitor, scientist, and benefactor. Deputy chairman of the Birmingham Festival Committee. He lived at a house called Springfield, whose site is now occupied by Springfield Street. He was well known as an orchid grower, and had plants specially sought out for him in Central America.

[2] Barker evidently made the journey in Oct. 1817 on the *Caledonia*, which had been purchased and refitted by James Watt junior in April of that year. It travelled from Margate to Holland and then up the Rhine as far as Koblenz. Barker was an acquaintance of Watt, and in September had asked him to procure a passport for the journey. Although they believed this to be the first such journey by steamer, exactly the same journey had already been done in May/June 1816 by the *Defiance* under its Scottish captain and owner, William Wager.

[3] Jacob Pietsch. He married Fritz Schlemmer's sister, Caroline in 1815 (see p. 114 n. 8).

[4] Helene Souchay, wife of Eduard (see p. 41 n. 9).

[5] Joseph Walker (1780?–1846), Birmingham businessman, perhaps the proprietor of Joseph Walker & Co., factors, St Paul's Square. He was a Visitor of the General Hospital and on the Musical Festival Committee. He lived in the Crescent, about five minutes walk from the Town Hall.

[6] The Town Hall was lit by gas.

[7] August Ferdinand Häser (1779–1844), German composer. His oratorio *Die Kraft des Glaubens* was translated by Willam Ball as *The Triumph of Faith* and given at the 1837 Birmingham Festival on the Friday morning.

[8] The excerpt from the *St Matthew Passion*, performed on the Friday morning, was the Duet and Chorus 'Behold my Saviour now is taken' leading to 'Let lightnings and thunders'. The programme book describes it as 'from the celebrated *Passione*'—this was just 8 years after Mendelssohn's famous revival of the work in Berlin in 1829.

Karl came in the morning and brought us pretty presents from Vienna. Much visiting after church. I wrote to Felix for the last time, and received a lovely letter from him, over which two people rejoiced. Spent much time with poor sick Uncle. In the afternoon went for a walk with Karl to the windmill,[1] and since I was not in the least tired, on to Gogel's estate,[2] where we found Sophie and her husband, and were delighted at the change in him. Ate the first grapes. Glorious sunset. Return journey. Evening.

Sunday, 17 September

Neukomm goes his own way, pays court to the ladies, seeks out old acquaintances. Yet his quiet intelligent manner pleases me this time again afresh, and commands my respect. Moore informed me that the Committee had decided to comply with my wishes, and to allow me to play the organ at the beginning of the concert on Friday, so that I can leave immediately afterwards. He showed me a printed slip, which would consequently be stuck into the programme books, and on which the public is requested to pardon the alteration, because my "engagements in Leipzig" made it necessary for me to depart straight after playing. I was happy to have prevailed in this, and events later showed how necessary it was. Stroll with Moore and Ayrton in the vicinity of Birmingham, where it was very green but also very deserted. Ayrton declared he would guarantee me 1,000 guineas if I would return to England with a new oratorio. Big dinner at Walker's with all the principal musicians and singers. At table the canon 'Non nobis Domine'[3] was most solemnly intoned by all the good voices, whereupon the master of the house was moved to floods of tears. Neukomm tugged at me and said that that was now the third time he had witnessed the same scene, which occurs at every Musical Festival. Then I left the others to chat over the wine, and sat or lay in the comfortable armchair by the fireside, stretched myself out, and reflected on how very far I was from home. Neukomm said that I should take Cécile such an armchair, and her health was drunk, and I expressed my thanks and thought again how far I was from home.

---

[1] The windmill was probably in the present Windmühlstrasse between the railway station and the Main, then just to the west of the built-up area of the town.

[2] See p. 42 n. 8.

[3] A popular anonymous three-part canon dating from the early part of the 17th cent., and which was often erroneously attributed to William Byrd from the 18th cent. century onwards.

Monday, 18 September

Made various purchases with Karl at the fair; wrote to Mother.[1] Worked down below in the afternoon and went for a walk. In the evening there were an awful lot of people downstairs, and I did not feel too well.

Monday, 18 September

Rehearsal day. For all four festival days, all seven performances, just one day of rehearsal. That is how calves are led to the slaughterhouse, and it also leads to just such a feeling of misery and misfortune. It started at eleven with the rehearsal of Neukomm's oratorio.[2] Everything was gone through quickly, one thing after another without stopping. Only if something was just too wrong and falling apart, then perhaps it was started again, but whenever that happened people were disgruntled and grumbled amongst each other. Consequently nothing that ought to be done delicately went well, but the straightforward things and the massive choruses were almost always admirable. Neukomm's music is, like his other works, nicely and neatly put together, but a little thinly and drably conceived, and this time it will not please the musicians, who formerly made much of him. It was over at half past one, but the beautiful fair-skinned Grisi[3] was already standing there, ready to practise her two Handel arias[4] (the rest go unrehearsed). A splendid woman and a splendid voice. My 'St Paul' began immediately afterwards at two o'clock. The musicians received me with a great deal of noise and delight. We rehearsed solidly until half past five, and then the practice and 'St Paul' was over. I did not mince my words and had them repeat anything that I did not consider good enough, spared no one, and swore indiscriminately in English, French, and German. I had never in my life felt as exhausted as after this rehearsal. I thought my last day had come. Neukomm stood behind me and threw a cloak round me. Back home I dropped onto the bed and slept until ten. Then there was a second rehearsal, when I was to rehearse my new concerto that I had composed in Bingen. But half the musicians were in the theatre rehearsing 'Semiramide'[5] and the other half were reduced by sleep and desertion to an eighth. The wind instruments

---

[1] No letter to Lea of this date has been preserved.

[2] The oratorio *The Ascension* (*Christi Himmelfahrt*), composed in 1830, but not published until 1842. The original German text was by Klopstock. Following preliminary rehearsal of this and of Häser's oratorio at the Hanover Square Rooms in London on 13 July, the *Musical World* condemned Neukomm's work as mediocre in the extreme, so that its frosty reception at Birmingham was not unexpected.

[3] Giulia Grisi (1811–69), Italian soprano, one of the leading singers of her generation. She made her London début at the King's Theatre in 1834, and returned almost every summer for the next 12 years.

[4] At the Tuesday morning concert Grisi sang 'Let the bright seraphim' from *Samson*, and 'But bright Cecilia'/'As from the pow'r of sacred lays' from the *Ode for St Cecilia's Day*.

[5] Rossini's opera was given at the Theatre Royal on the Wednesday evening, followed by a 'Miscellaneous Selection' of works.

were almost all missing. I declared that I would not play my concerto without rehearsal, and went away to sleep again, and fortunately slept off the effects of the rehearsal.

Tuesday, 19 September

At eleven went to the St George's wedding. Just in at one door and out of the other. Then to Aunt Elise.[1] Lunch with numerous company. Sad parting of Uncle[2] from his son. Fritz's departure. Spent the evening at a gathering at Victoire's. Fine weather.

Tuesday, 19 September

First performance at eleven o'clock. The hall was not full. Neukomm's oratorio had a terribly frosty reception; not a hand stirred when he appeared, nor during the music, and hardly any applause at the end. It disgusted me to see the complete and groundless change in a public, who, six, and again only three years ago, preferred the same man to all other composers in the world, held him dear, and had generally called him "the king of Birmingham". His composure and equanimity in the face of such unfair behaviour doubled my esteem for him. After his work came another part, with several Handel choruses, which went splendidly and created a brilliant effect especially with the big organ; also arias from Grisi, Tamburini,[3] etc. I went home and wrote to Cécile, the last letter from England, thank goodness. Then back to the hall, where the first performance had just finished. The orchestra was detained for the rehearsal of my concerto. Many of the audience stayed behind. I rehearsed after the three-hour concert on a little dulcimer-like piano. The people just about fell over themselves with pleasure after the first solo passage of the last movement—an unbelievable noise. Mori[4] yelled out at the end: "I want to speak to you". Novello was standing next to me and said softly: "Have you sold this already?" 'Just you wait, you rascal', I thought to myself. Mori came over, took me by the arm, and wanted to have it. I said it would cost him £30; he wanted to haggle; I broke off the conversation. He wanted to think the matter

[1] Elise Schunck (see p. 41 n. 3).

[2] Heinrich Schunck (b. 1782), third son of Johann Carl and Wilhelmine Christine Schunck. His brother-in-law, Cornelius Carl Souchay, made him one of the founders of the London branch of Schunck, Mylius & Co. He married Elise Harnier, retired with a fortune in 1832, and went to live in Frankfurt.

[3] Antonio Tamburini (1800–76), Italian baritone. He appeared regularly in England from 1832 onwards.

[4] Nicholas Mori (1796/7–1839), English violinist and London music publisher. He led the King's Theatre orchestra, and was one of the leaders of the Philharmonic Society's concerts. As a partner with his wife in the music publishing firm of Mori & Lavenu, he was the English publisher of several Mendelssohn works in the 1830s.

over for two days. I promised him to keep it available for that long. Novello came over. I said that I could only give him a decision the day after tomorrow. To the Souchays,[1] whose first party had arrived from Manchester, and for whom I had rented a house near me.

At eight o'clock in the evening the second performance, when I had to improvise on the organ immediately after a Cavatina by Mercadante,[2] which was encored. That put me a little out of humour. I began with the bottom D on the pedal, and as I sounded it, so much applause broke out that I had to leave the organ bench and come forward into the orchestra and first acknowledge it for a little while. I then climbed back and took up the bottom D again, and now had to improvise. I wasn't really in the mood; nevertheless the audience seemed very happy with it. The second part opened with my 'Overture to a Midsummer Night's Dream', which I conducted without rehearsal, on account of which it too went in a rather peculiar fashion. We were obliged to play it again, and then it went better. On the way home I made a further call on the Souchays, since the old gentleman,[3] as I knew, had arrived in the meantime. But it was about eleven and everyone was already asleep. In the hall the concert lasted right up to midnight.

Wednesday, 20 September

In the morning I received a letter from Felix in Birmingham with sad contents. I sewed a good deal and painted a little. In the evening I went to a gathering and was bored.

Wednesday, 20 September

Second day, third performance. My 'St Paul' at eleven. An hour beforehand Klingemann arrived from London, when we were still sitting at breakfast. The performance went just as it did in the rehearsal; what went well then did so again, what did not was no different despite the repetition. The choruses were energetic and splendid. Novello sang 'Jerusalem' quite atrociously. Moreover Turle, who through absent-mindedness did not remember soon enough that the pedal entry at the end of the G minor aria was to be pianissimo, groped around on full organ, and created a devilish noise;[4] likewise again in the

---

[1] Cécile's uncle, Carl Isaac Souchay (1799–1872) and his wife Adelheid, née Dethmar (1809–90). Carl, second son of Cornelius Carl Souchay, was a partner in the Manchester branch of Schunck, Souchay & Co.

[2] 'Vanne se alberghi in petto' from *Andronico*, sung by Grisi and Albertazzi.

[3] Cornelius Carl Souchay (see Introduction, p. xiii).

[4] This refers to the entry on the G minor chord in bar 39 of 'Jerusalem'. The account in *Aris's Birmingham Gazette* merely notes on this point 'The organ pedal pipe introduced on a fundamental note, was perhaps risking the balance of sound'.

last ritornello, because he had forgotten the manual coupler. Shaw sang her aria exquisitely and had to repeat it. Phillips also sang his very well; Machin 'For know ye not' in the second part quite wretchedly, and the tenor aria with cello very indifferently. All the choruses were good. Despite the prohibition on applause at the morning performances, the audience nevertheless received me with a great noise, continued in that way during the performance, demanded several numbers to be encored, and yet was less frantic than that in Exeter Hall. At the end of the oratorio another tremendous outburst. I walked into the Green Room tired out, and found Bennett[1] there, who had just arrived. Upstairs I could still hear various sounds of Grisi's aria, and the 'Hailstone Chorus'[2] of Handel, which they demanded to be repeated, and of Albertazzi's aria,[3] on account of which my 'St Paul' had been shortened.[4] I demonstrated to Bennett his London frostiness by my Birmingham frostiness. He seemed bewildered. I lunched at the Souchays, where I found everyone assembled: Jean and Thekla,[5] whom I met for the first time, and for whom I formed a liking, Carl and Adelheid, the Benecke brothers and Emmeline,[6] Mme Thode and old Herr Souchay. Before the meal I had a wash and brush-up in Benecke's bedroom, and he lent me his hairbrush, which appeared to me uncommonly good. Towards evening we went for a walk to the railroad,[7] Carl Souchay, Klingemann, and myself, to recover Souchay's baggage, which through an accident he had lost on the journey from Manchester. Early to bed, and thus missed and slept through the fourth performance, that of 'Semiramide' in the theatre, which started at eight o'clock in the evening.

Thursday, 21 September

Wrote to Mother in Berlin,[8] and painted. In the afternoon drove out to R. Scharf[9] to show her the copy of 'St Paul'. In the evening Julie had a gathering of young ladies into which Karl crept.

---

[1] William Sterndale Bennett (see p. 53 n. 5).   [2] The vivid chorus 'He gave them hailstones' from *Israel in Egypt*.

[3] Emma Albertazzi, née Howson (1814?–47), English contralto, pupil of Costa. After some years on the Continent in the early 1830s, she reappeared in London in 1837 in Rossini's *La Cenerentola*.

[4] It appears from an annotated programme book in the Bodleian Library that Nos. 41–4 towards the end of the work were omitted.

[5] Cécile's uncle, Jean Daniel Souchay (1798–1871), who married his cousin Thekla Schunck (1809–76). Like his brother, Carl Isaac, he was a partner in Schunck, Souchay & Co. in Manchester.

[6] Friedrich Wilhelm and Victor Benecke, with Victor's wife, Emmeline (see p. 87 n. 1 and p. 58 n. 5).

[7] Carl and Adelheid Souchay evidently arrived from Manchester by rail. The Grand Junction Railway had just opened on 4 July from Birmingham to Warrington, where at Newton Junction it connected with the Liverpool and Manchester Railway which had opened in 1830.

[8] See p. 192.

[9] Probably a relative (daughter?) of Gottfried Scharff (1782–1855), a merchant and several times mayor of Frankfurt, who was married to Victoria Maria Auguste Wagner.

Third day, fifth performance. 'Messiah' at eleven o'clock. Only heard part of it, since I busied myself with packing and preparations for my departure the following day. Moore accompanied me to a cutler's in order to choose a case for Cécile and suchlike things. I received a letter from Chappell,[1] who wants to commission an opera from me, and wishes to speak with me about it. I sent the answer that he could speak to me tomorrow between eleven and midnight in London, or not at all. I gave the same answer to the committee of the Exeter Hall society, who had invited me to the "meeting". Novello asked for the fourth time about the concerto, which Mr Anderson[2] would also like for his wife. As Mori's two days were up, and I knew him well—that he just wanted to wait for the effect it produced at the performance, which was just what I didn't want—I gave it to Novello for £40,[3] which he must pay me immediately. He agreed to everything, he who a fortnight ago appeared to find the same sum too high for the three works. I heard some of the numbers from 'Messiah' which went splendidly as always; Shaw in particular sang in a quite unique manner. On the way home I met Bennett, who walked with me. We encountered Thomson,[4] who introduced a pair of Scottish musicians, who wanted to have me for a music festival in Edinburgh. At my front door Bennett began to ask why I now received him so coldly, and I told him the whole blunt truth straight from my heart, so that floods of tears came into his eyes. He promised me that he would change his awkward gentlemanly English ways, and a better kept promise than this I have in truth not experienced, as it has since proved.[5] We shook hands and separated. Took my leave of Neukomm, whom I have come to like more than ever. Evening at eight o'clock, sixth performance. A miscellaneous concert. I played my concerto on an Erard, for the latter, following my letter saying that there was already a Broadwood here, had answered that I should and would never be allowed to play instruments other than his own through any fault of his, and he would therefore send one so as not to leave me in want. Since I really did prefer his instrument to the other, there the matter thus rested.

---

[1] William Chappell (1809–88), English music publisher and antiquarian. Partner in the family firm of Chappell & Co., until 1843. Founder member of the Musical Antiquarian Society, and best known for his 2-volume work *Popular Music of the Olden Time* (1855–9).

[2] George Frederick Anderson (see p. 102 n. 2). In the end Anderson lent Novello £30 interest free to help finance the purchase of the work, in return for his wife, Lucy, having exclusive rights to perform it in England for six months prior to publication. He was eventually repaid out of the profits from sales. Lucy Anderson first played the work at the Philharmonic Society concert in the Hanover Square Rooms on 5 Mar. 1838, with Sir George Smart conducting.

[3] In fact the sum was 40 guineas (£42), as the contract formerly in the Novello archives testifies.

[4] John Thomson (1805–41), Scottish musician. He first met Mendelssohn in Edinburgh in 1829, and later studied in Leipzig with Schnyder von Wartensee. He had Mendelssohn's recommendation when he successfully applied to become the first Reid Professor of Music at Edinburgh in 1839.

[5] The music publisher Charles Coventry, in a letter to Mendelssohn of 18 May 1838, notes about Bennett that 'you will be pleased to hear the lecture you gave him last year in Birmingham did him much good, he has been extremely attentive to me ever since, nor does he smoke so much, in fact he has been everything you could wish him . . .' (GB VII, 147).

Before my concerto a performer taking his place in the orchestra at the same time as me, said to another: "I won't miss this piece for twopence", which flattered me more than almost anything else. They demanded the last movement to be repeated, but I was too tired and lay down on the sofa in the Green Room, and missed in the meantime the Polacca from 'I Puritani'[1] sung by Grisi, who then also came down exhausted, and with whom I exchanged a few pleasant remarks and invited her to Leipzig.[2] Mori now wanted to have the concerto; I told him it was disposed of. He created the devil of a row—it was a breach of faith—today was the second day. I replied that the deadline was at eleven, and that I had not wished to wait any longer. He summoned Phillips as arbitrator, who found in favour of me. Mori swore, raved, and was furious, and Phillips laughed and kept saying: "I told you Mori was wrong". Robertson,[3] an enthusiastic musician from Dublin, wanted to perform my 'St Paul' there, and to have me there for it. I returned to the Souchays and Klingemann in the hall, and listened with them to one item of the second part, then left. Klingemann set off for London and I for bed.

Friday, 22 September

Final lesson with old Rad'l, then went visiting. Herr Perret's[4] clumsiness. Packing. Went to Aunt Schlegel's in the evening after a stroll.

Saturday, 23 September

Wrote letters in the morning and packed a good many cases. Lunch with old Pastor Dettmar[5] and Frau Hildebrand.[6] Afterwards drove to Bonames in bitter wind and rough weather with Auntie and her little Helene,[7] not returning until late. Aunt Pietsch[8] had come back from Mainz. I finished off a little piece of work for Mother.

[1] 'Son vergin vezzosa' from the Finale to Act 1.   [2] Grisi apparently did not go to Leipzig.

[3] Joseph Robinson (1816–98), Irish singer and conductor. In 1837 he became conductor of the Dublin University Choral Society, and enthusiastically promoted Mendelssohn's music with them.

[4] François Perret (see p. 44 n. 5).

[5] Friedrich Wilhelm Dethmar, Reformed Church pastor, and owner of an educational establishment in Hanover. His daughter, Adelheid, married Carl Souchay in 1827.

[6] Possibly Anna Maria Hiltebrandt, née Garkoch, widow of the Frankfurt merchant Johann Daniel Jakob Hiltebrandt.

[7] Helene Souchay, Eduard's wife, with her daughter, also Helene (1833–8).

[8] Caroline ('Line') Pietsch, née Schlemmer (1796–1878), sister of Fritz Schlemmer. She married Jacob Pietsch. Although referred to by Cécile as 'Tante Pietsch', she was actually a first cousin once removed.

Sunday, 24 September

Went to church in the morning. Sermon on the subject of morality, which a couple of months ago I could not have understood. Visits afterwards. Breakfast at Sophie Hauck's. Lunch at Gogel's estate. Visits in Bockenheim.[1] The weather was so nasty that I got a heavy cold as a result of it.

Friday, 22 September

At eleven o'clock I started off the fourth day and the seventh performance with Sebastian Bach's Prelude and Fugue in E flat[2] on full organ of the large instrument. At the end they waved their handkerchiefs and flourished their hats. A plump old gentleman in the audience waved his yellow handkerchief incessantly and cried out "Goodbye! Goodbye!" The hired carriage was at the door; Moore with his servant in attendance helped me inside. Gauntlett,[3] Thomson, and many others shook my hand once again. At exactly half past eleven I was at the coach office. There had been a delay on the railway, and the coach waited until half past twelve, so that I had time to exchange my black dress-coat for my overcoat, which I kept on until Frankfurt. Inside the coach with me were Thekla Souchay, Emmeline Benecke, and old Souchay—outside sat the two other Beneckes. Thus we left Birmingham; Bennett, Walmisley,[4] and Novello stood at the door of the coach and saluted and waved. We bought some gooseberries, which old Souchay let fall out of the basket into the carriage, and which became terribly crushed. We ate lunch hurriedly on the way, and at half past eleven at night we arrived in London. As the coach began to rush through the London suburbs, old Souchay calmly gave me some verbal instructions and greetings for Frankfurt. Klingemann was at the coach office and took me to a nearby hotel, where I found the Exeter Hall committee assembled. The president[5] gave me the beautiful silver box, showed me the kind inscription, and said as a tobacconist he had filled it with his best wares. Bewildered and flustered I thanked them, and would love to have eaten some of the many fine kinds of ham and sausage which lay on

---

[1] Then a village about 4 km. north-west of Frankfurt.

[2] BWV 552. In view of Mendelssohn's later comments on the heaviness of the action (see p. 106 n. 4) he must have found this work exceptionally taxing.

[3] Henry John Gauntlett (1807–76), English organist and composer. Organist at St Olave's, Southwark, and evening organist at Christ Church, Newgate Street. Mendelssohn esteemed his many talents highly, and he played the organ for the première of *Elijah* in 1846. He wrote about Mendelssohn's playing at St Paul's Cathedral and Christ Church in 'Mendelssohn as an organist', *Musical World*, 15 Sept. 1837.

[4] Either Thomas Forbes Walmisley (1783–1866), English composer and organist of St Martin-in-the-Fields, London, 1814–54, or his eldest son Thomas Attwood Walmisley (1814–56), who had already been appointed Professor of Music at Cambridge in 1836, while still an undergraduate.

[5] John Newman Harrison, who was a tobacconist at 81 St James's St.

the table, but I could not since the coach on which I had to travel to Dover left at midnight. I therefore hurriedly took my leave. Klingemann accompanied me to the coach and gave me a whole packet of letters, amongst which was one from Cécile, which I just could not open in the dark—we shook hands— off we went. During the first moments I noticed that my splendid travelling cap, which I had bought specially for myself in Birmingham in order to be able to sleep properly in the coach, had fallen out of my overcoat during the repacking and was lost; no matter, I was able to sleep bare-headed as well. The sun rose on Saturday, 23 September just before we reached Canterbury. As soon as it was light enough I immediately read Cécile's lovely letter, then the many others; about nine in the morning we were in Dover. The mailboat was only waiting for us, and lay tossing about a fair way out to sea. In our hurry we had to take a boat, were terribly cheated by the sailors, and arrived on board the mail, which bobbed up and down so much that I was seasick even before it sailed. I remained lying on the deck, but the waves finally broke so heavily over my head, that I dragged myself below. There lay two Germans, who vomited and swore blasphemously. It took from half past nine to half past one before we came to calmer water, and instead of reaching Calais we had been driven off course by the storm to Boulogne, where we landed at two o'clock. I took to a bed for an hour until it was time to eat, and read through my letters once more. Then I had a bath and pondered on heaven and hell. Then polished off everything at the table d'hôte, and bought a French beret and two vaudevilles to read in the diligence. Finally off in the diligence at nine o'clock in the evening, slowly and rattling along abominably. The horses in front were like elephants, every other minute they pulled up for any old reason. Inside the window-panes rattled, while outside the horses' bells jangled; nevertheless I slept until Sunday, 24 September. In Lille at one o'clock in the afternoon. I looked for a hotel, stuck my head in at the door and saw a nice family ensconced there, and so retreated, but the woman came after me and urged me inside to their round table, which really and truly was a table d'hôte, at which only the landlord with his wife and children sat. The latter were kept in order and received reprimands. The man and his wife carved for me, and made agreeable conversation. I had little to pay, and at four o'clock I was sitting once more in the mail coach and we rattled on further. After all the commotion and unending business of the previous weeks, sitting quietly without saying a word and having darkness already descend about half past five, offered a double contrast. I grew very restive and time hung heavy on my hands. About seven o'clock, before we came to Tournai, I devised for myself out of boredom a two-part canon[1] in the darkness:

---

[1] Writing canons was a favourite form of intellectual musical relaxation for Mendelssohn throughout his lifetime. This canon was originally notated in a little pocket diary (Bodleian Library, MS MDM g. 4, fo. 40v). It was one Mendelssohn was to copy out several times over the next decade as album leaves for friends. A modern transcription will be found on p. 205.

Then the rattling continued on through the night.

Monday, 25 September

Made various outings, wrote letters, did some sewing, and had letters from Berlin and Leipzig. Received visits in the afternoon. Spent the evening at Aunt Helene's. Final letter from my Felix, which I continued to study for a long time in bed.

Monday, 25 September

In Brussels at five o'clock in the morning. To the Hôtel de Bellevue[1] and had breakfast in the dining-room, which was still untidy from the previous evening and showed traces of supper. On the way again at half past seven. A young married couple had the two corner seats of the coupé, and I noted with apprehension that I had got the middle seat. The husband, however, also noted it with apprehension, because I would be sitting next to his wife. He asked me to change places, which I did most gladly. In Liège at seven in the evening. The ordinary mail coach was to remain there for six hours, so I immediately ordered a special mail coach and a good "beafsteak" [sic], ate the latter, took my seat in the former, and drove once more up the hill into the night. In Battice at half past ten, and in Aachen at two o'clock in the morning. Trouble with the passport. A cold night.

Tuesday, 26 September

In the morning drove across the Main to see Frau Bernay,[2] the Bihls, etc. Went visiting. Brought back flowers for the joint birthday.[3] Grandmother presented me with pretty things for

---

[1] The leading hotel in Brussels, in the Place Royale.   [2] See p. 101 n. 4.
[3] Elisabeth Jeanrenaud's birthday was on 23 Sept., Julie Jeanrenaud's the next day.

my little darling. While working in the afternoon and evening I was already on the look-out all the time for Felix, but he did not come. I went off to sleep after eleven. The last night without my husband, I hope!

Tuesday, 26 September

In Cologne at ten. I was annoyed at having missed the steamer, on which I could have slept. I drove to the Kaiserlicher Hof, ordered breakfast, and discovered that the so-called night boat was not due to leave until eleven, and would arrive in Mainz the next morning. I had breakfast in a hurry and fortunately arrived at the boat in time. On the bank stood Steifensand[1] from Düsseldorf, whose sister had just got married, and with her husband was starting her honeymoon on the steamer. Several other acquaintances shook my hand. Pleasant feeling about once more being able to stretch myself out. Milder weather. In the evening in the vicinity of Remagen I went up on deck and chatted with the newly-weds. They were likewise planning to travel overnight on the steamer—I advised them strongly against it— they would do far better to spend the night in Koblenz, where one can be very comfortable. A night on the steamer would be very tiring and unpleasant. They followed my advice, and so I had done one more good deed. Then I lay down in the cabin and slept sweetly. In my sleep I heard the bell sounding the arrival in Koblenz and the departure at midnight.

Wednesday, 27 September

I have been sitting here waiting since I woke up, and pay attention to every noise in the house, and have already often been deceived. It is half past eleven and Felix is still not here!

Wednesday, 27 September

I woke, however, suddenly at half past two, because it seemed to me that I felt no movement. In fact the steamer was at a standstill and lay by the river bank. I discovered that thick fog had descended, that we would have to remain at anchor overnight, and would arrive in Mainz about six o'clock in the evening at the earliest, rather than in the morning. That permitted no idling around. In reply to my question

---

[1] Either Xaver Steifensand (1809–76), an artist specializing in engraving, or his brother Wilhelm Steifensand (1812–82), a pianist.

as to where we were, the waiter said at a village by the name of Pfaffendorf.[1] *It was strange for me to have spent several hours so close to Uncle in such well-known surroundings without knowing it. I had to loosen my purse strings. I engaged two sailors to carry my cases and took the well-known footpath along the Rhine to Ehrenbreitstein. As I crossed the bridge, where two months before I had so often strolled with Cécile, three o'clock sounded from the Castorkirche.*[2] *I hired a special mail coach, and leaving the steamer behind me reached Boppard just half an hour later. My impatience to get to Cécile in Frankfurt grew with every moment and with every place that I saw again where so recently I had been with her. In Boppard I saw the post-house where we had eaten. In St Goar at five the landlord came to meet me, and told me about Cécile's and Mother's return journey. In Bacharach—at the Mäuseturm— everywhere so many memories. About eight o'clock opposite the Niederwald the fog parted, and I travelled into Bingen in sunshine. By the coach in the courtyard of the post office stood the schoolmaster, who two months ago had wanted to loan me his piano, and he asked whether it had been pleasant in England. I just had time to answer when we moved off again; behind me the thick fog lying quite solidly, in front of me the most beautiful sunny weather. With all my wits about me I was thus in Mainz about midday,*[3] *and at half past two I beheld Frankfurt, drove through the familiar streets; my journey and the separation were at an end, and I joyfully embraced my dearest Cécile once again.*

[1] The village between Ehrenbreitstein and Horchheim. [2] Romanesque church in Koblenz.
[3] A postal coach left Mainz for Frankfurt daily at noon.

Letters of Felix and
Cécile Mendelssohn Bartholdy
to their Families

March to October 1837

Felix Mendelssohn Bartholdy to Lea Mendelssohn Bartholdy[1]

Frankfurt, 24 March 1837

Dear Mother,

In just a few very hasty words I must tell you of our safe arrival here. You know that my wedding is due to take place next Tuesday, so you can imagine how there are no end of things still to be settled and taken care of at this time. Until yesterday the papers were still not in order, since the Frankfurt authorities appear to be even greater creators of obstacles than elsewhere, but a letter came from Schleinitz[2] yesterday, which promised all the necessary testimonials for today, 'that I am not already married, that I am no vagabond' and suchlike rubbish, and so, God willing, it is now arranged for Tuesday. We will be married at 11, and in the afternoon are planning to leave for Mainz, and then go slowly up the Rhine via Speyer, Worms, etc. to Strasbourg, a stretch which I do not yet know at all. We have not yet made a proper travel plan; there is still snow and ice around, and so we will stop mostly in the towns; when spring arrives, then our travel plan will emerge too. I expect to be back here towards the end of May, and to stay for some time, but that too not yet settled. From now on my address for the whole summer will be here c/o M. I. Herz.[3]

I had hoped to find here some news of your safe arrival waiting for me, but in vain. I imagine, however, that you are all safe and well, and that nothing untoward has prevented you from writing, and I look forward daily to seeing your cherished handwriting.

Now adieu, dear Mother, and regards to my sisters. I do not imagine that I will be writing to you again as an unmarried man. God willing, our relationship is unchanged and will always remain so. Think of me on Tuesday, and farewell.

Your
Felix MB

---

1 NYPL, No. 316.
2 Heinrich Konrad Schleinitz (1802–81), Leipzig lawyer and member of the Board of Directors of the Gewandhaus.
3 Frankfurt banking house of Moses Isaac Herz (d. 1848).

Felix and Cécile Mendelssohn Bartholdy to Elisabeth Jeanrenaud[1]

Worms, 30 March 1837

Dear Mama,

I just have to write to you after two days, whether or not you care to read it. I must tell you how happy these days have been, how blissful the whole of our time since leaving Frankfurt, how at this very moment I want to thank you once more afresh for having given me your Cécile, my beloved Cécile, who is renewing my whole life and the joy therein, to whom I owe everything, all life's happiness. O dearest Mama, I cannot describe to you these two blissful days; I will try and do so in person when we meet again, for it is impossible to do it in writing. Everything, however, has come together to render these days perfect; how glorious the weather was on our journey to Mainz, and during our stay there yesterday. Today we have had plenty of spring rain on our way here. In Mainz we had the most elegant and comfortable pair of rooms that one could wish for, with a view of the Rhine; then the lovely countryside between Mainz and here. Today we also visited the Yellow House[2] as you had recommended, and were shown the room you had occupied, which Cécile still recognized. Yesterday we were also pretty hard-working. Cécile did some drawing, while I completed a long postponed musical task and sent it off; then we went for a walk on the ramparts, and could see as far as the Feldberg[3] and Wiesbaden; then we strolled back and forth on the bridge of boats.

A wicked elf must have wanted to spoil the previous day for me, for it was certainly his fault that, at either lunch or breakfast, I ate something that disagreed with me, with the result that I felt really ill in the afternoon, just like that time after the Harkort salad[4] of painful memory. Towards evening, however, it passed over, as did a little toothache from which Cécile was again suffering, and how kind she was to me then, how she took care of me, how happy even did that very thing make me, which otherwise would have so upset me. And today, when we both had the most enjoyable morning in Mainz, then drove here in comfort—and here in the gloomy old town, and in a gloomy old inn, when we ourselves

---

[1] Bodleian Library, MS MDM d. 18, fos. 29–30.

[2] The inn 'Zum gelben Haus' was at Sironabad near Nierstein on the Mainz–Worms road, and situated at a flying bridge crossing of the Rhine. It attracted guests from a wide area.

[3] The highest peak of the Taunus hills (880 m.)

[4] Auguste Harkort née Anders (1794–1857) ran one of the principal salons in Leipzig. She was formerly a singer, and married Karl Friedrich Harkort (1788–1856), a Leipzig merchant who, with his brother Gustav, founded in 1820 the 'Handels- und Exporthaus Carl und Gustav Harkort'. Auguste in 1843 was to become godmother to the Mendelssohn's fourth child, Felix August Eduard. According to Felix's engagement diary for 1837 (see Introduction, p. xii), while Lea was still in Leipzig, they went to the Harkorts on 12 Mar., where there was a 'dreadful soirée with poisoned salad'.

felt neither gloomy nor old, I cannot yet properly write and describe it. I will only say thank you, dear Mama, for all the immense happiness which you have given me, and will remain grateful to you all my life.

Tomorrow we will set out for Speyer. Whether we go on from there to Strasbourg, or back to Mannheim, the weather will decide, which today is itself still undecided. For the time being address letters simply to Speyer poste restante. Hopefully, however, we will receive your news there the day after tomorrow, which will tell us that you are feeling better again, that you are thinking of us, and that you are still my dear Mama, who also loves me a little. Do let me hope so, dear Mama, and farewell for the present

  Your
   Felix

Dear Mama,

Here we are in the same place that I was with you, Julie, and Charles two years ago, in this dreadful town of Worms, where there is nothing but old houses and old churches. Everything reminds me of that time, so happy and so carefree, which causes me to like this town despite its ugliness. It really does seem that I cannot be other than happy and content here in the Rhineland, for I cannot describe just how much I am in precisely that state at present. Felix could not be more lovable, so easy to please, so kind, so considerate, in short just as you know him from our travels, but yet even more charming. Everywhere delights us; besides we had good reason to be pleased in Mainz—the best accommodation in the world, two superb rooms looking out over the Rhine, complete with a balcony of which I became passionately fond, and with all one's wishes promptly executed, in complete contrast to here. Despite the rain and dirt we visited the cathedral this morning, which greatly pleased Felix, and where I grew more and more angry with the stupid people who have daubed and patched up the interior of this church. We spent nearly an hour seeking out the finest doors and the most intricate decoration to the great astonishment of our guide, who then considered much more pleasing the horrible paintings of that church where there is the picture of Luther, which you will recall.

If it had been fine as it was in Mainz, I would certainly have sketched something here to send to you, but it was impossible, and my little view of Mainz, which Felix has helped me with, is by no means finished. For the rest I cannot be as hard-working as you had urged me to be, because, despite all my searching, I have been unable to find my work-box, which you had arranged so well for me and with such great care. It is most disagreeable not being able to resew a shoe fastener if it tears. I would therefore ask you, dear kind Mama, to send it to me in Speyer, where we are going today in our delightful carriage, and will perhaps stay for a few days. I thank you in advance for the trouble I am giving you, as I have to thank you for so many other things you have done for me.

I found the pretty cap on unpacking in Mainz—it is charming. Give my regards and thank everyone at home—Grandmama, Grandpapa, Julie, Charles, Bury, Mlle F[ischbach].[1] When you are as happy as I am, it is impossible to thank God and people enough. Farewell my dear mother, keep well, and think about your devoted daughter Cécile.

NB. This is <u>not</u> the secret letter requested to be sent after <u>four days</u>; that will follow as ordered from Speyer, and neither of us must read that of the other, which we are greatly amused by, but it will be strictly adhered to, since that is what you wish. Please reply to these soon! F.

═══════

Felix and Cécile Mendelssohn Bartholdy to Julie Jeanrenaud[2]

Worms, 30 March 1837

My dear Julie,

I am writing these few hasty lines today just to keep my promise, and just to say quickly what you already know, how the two of us have thought of you so often, even hourly, how I am so grateful to you for all your kindness to me, for all the affection shown during my last stay in Frankfurt, and so it will always remain. Continue to be as kind and good to me as you were then, my dear Julie. Believe me, I now realize completely that in the beginning you could not feel kindly towards me at all, because the thought of a separation from Cécile must indeed have been most painful for you; that I only now perceive so clearly, when her nearness makes me so overjoyed, when, in these couple of days, I have experienced through her more happiness and more joy than in all the other days of my life put together, and when I cannot bear the thought of leaving her for an hour and not seeing her. But that is really the only justification that I can provide for myself, namely that I certainly feel it all and realize it as no one else could ever have done so, and therefore you too should no longer be angry with me. All that, however,

---

[1] The housekeeper. [2] Bodleian Library, MS MDM c. 31, fos. 14–15.

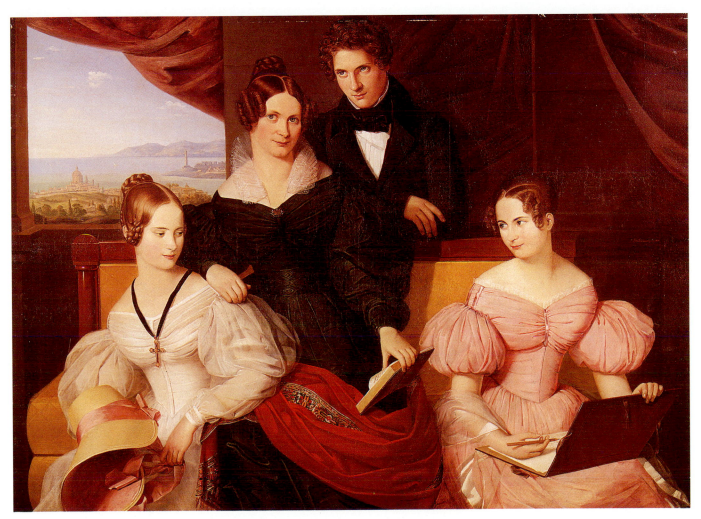

1. Portrait of Elisabeth Jeanrenaud and her family by Bernhard Schlösser, 1835. Cécile is on the right.
(Historisches Museum, Frankfurt am Main)

2. The inn at Höllsteig near Freiburg. (MS. MDM c.21, fo. 127)

3. Felix's drawing of the Fahrtor in Frankfurt from the Jeanrenaud house. (MS. MDM d.11, fo. 2)

4. The entry for the Mendelssohns' marriage in the Frankfurt city register. The subsequent addition of the dates of death was customary. (Stadtarchiv, Frankfurt am Main)

5. A page of Felix's English lessons for Cécile.
(MS. MDM c.29, fo. 3)

6. The Rheinischer Hof at Mainz, the Mendelssohns' wedding night hotel.
(Stadtarchiv, Mainz)

7. Cécile's drawing of Mainz.
(Staatsbibliothek zu Berlin)

8. Felix's drawing of a gnarled root
('Knörzerchen', Carl Jeanrenaud's
pet name for Cécile). (MS.
MDM c.21, fo. 185)

9. Felix's drawing of Todtnau in a
letter to Eduard Devrient.
(Devrient: *Meine Erinnerungen an
Felix Mendelssohn Bartholdy und
dessen Briefe an mich*, Leipzig,
1869)

10. Specimen pages of the
diary for 25–6
August, Cécile's entries
being written at the
top, with Felix's entries
and drawing added in
later. (MS. MDM e.6,
fos. 63ᵛ–64)

11. Burg Rheinfels, St Goar. (Private collection)

12. The Schweizertal near St Goarshausen. (MS. MDM c.21, fo. 130)

amounts to nothing at all; you are of course no longer angry with me, and, what I ask of you, you have already granted on my last visit; accept my thanks for it then, my dear Julie.

I must, however, tell you how splendid our journey here was; the coach runs so smoothly that one could write in it, and when the waiters stand around in the courtyard and admire it, we are both pleased. In Mainz, where we spent the whole day yesterday, we lived in the most elegant style, despite English travellers; we had a sitting-room with a balcony overlooking the Rhine, and paraded on it in the sunshine (wearing our slippers in full view of Mainz, Cécile in those from Ida Becher,[1] I in those given me by Cécile at Christmas). Then we bought a tedious guidebook to the whole Rhine, which I am studying like a Philistine and wish to see all the noteworthy things. Cécile makes fun of me, but I won't let myself be dissuaded, and with her have already looked at Mainz Cathedral and the one here with great pleasure. If only the weather would improve; this evening it looks very uncertain. I must finish so that Cécile can write a couple of words; forgive these few lines; they are naturally not to be reckoned as a proper letter (that should come from Speyer when we have greater peace) but only as a sign of life, a promise kept, and a request for your kind remembrance, dear Julie

>   *Your Felix*

Dear Julie, really only a couple of words to say how very much I love you and how fortunate and happy I am; how also I am looking forward to the whole summer, when I shall have so much joy in seeing you all again. I pray you, remain faithful to me from afar and think of me often, how we were so happy together and loved each other so much. Greetings from me to all the girls and whoever you see—many thanks.

———

Cécile Mendelssohn Bartholdy to Elisabeth Jeanrenaud[2]

Speyer, 2 April [1837]

Dear Mama,

I have been separated from you for four days, and I would very much like to know what is happening now at home. Here I have gathered through some lines of Julie's that you were well

---

[1] Ida Becher (1804–88), daughter of Cécile's great-aunt Caroline Becher. She lived in Heidelberg, and married the historian Dr Georg Weber (1808–88) in 1839.
[2] Bodleian Library, MS MDM d. 18, fo. 31.

at the time and in good spirits, which gave me great pleasure, since I was fairly anxious about your health when I left. As for me, I am very well, very happy, very content. I have not a single wish that Felix does not fulfil; I have but to say the word, for everything to be arranged according to my fancy. Toothache has again troubled me a little, but all that is forgotten at present. We still have the best possible weather and Speyer now pleases me even more; Felix too is quite enchanted by it and amuses himself by using a perspective glass to look at the far-off places that can be seen from here. Yesterday up on the gallery which surrounds the cathedral I too wanted to see the church of Heidelberg which he claimed to be able to discern, but I was trembling so much and was so scared for the first time in my life, that I returned quickly to the interior of the church, and I thought of Julie on Milan cathedral. That is how I have profited from marrying—I have become a child again instead of becoming wise and rational. Felix, however, finds me very amiable and perfectly brought up, on which point he will, I think, pay you a compliment. Since I dare not read his letter, I do not know what he is telling you, but if he speaks badly of me, I pray you let me know. Do please greet everyone for me, especially Grandpapa, Grandmama, Bury, Carl, and Julie.

I would still like to sketch the garden of the church before it gets dark, and therefore I will finish for today. Do you want me to send Mainz in a letter, or should I bring you the drawing?—it is rather big for a letter. My little work-box has arrived in good condition, thanks to your kindness. I am, and always will be, dear Mama, your totally devoted daughter Cécile.

Felix Mendelssohn Bartholdy to Elisabeth Jeanrenaud[1]

Speyer, 2 April 1837

Now, dear Mama, it is the fourth day—and Cécile must read nothing of what I write, and I nothing of what she writes; but what can I then write to you about apart from thanks? And that I have already tried to do in my previous letter, and unsuccessfully. With every passing hour of these four happy, happy days, I have learnt to know my dear Cécile better and to love her more; I thought that was not possible, and yet I feel now so calm and happy, have such a blissful feeling as I had hitherto never thought

[1] Bodleian Library, MS MDM d. 18, fos. 32–3.

possible. But she is really just too kind, kind to a fault. How often I have thought again of Krontal[1] and of my complaints there—only now I frankly admit it, it is the best thing in the world that I love my Cécile with all my heart. As the days fly by, as the individual hours pass so quickly, I do not know how to describe it. Yesterday Cécile again had a severe attack of toothache, and was in such agony with it; it upset her so much, that I became quite anxious; but today all that is once more completely forgotten, and you would be delighted if you saw her. I had already suggested driving over to Mannheim so that she could have the hollow tooth (for that seems to be what is causing her all the pain) extracted, but since it has passed over today, thank goodness, we have abandoned that unpleasant plan again, and will stay here quietly for another few days. We are in a very nice simple and comfortable inn; next to us lives only a young dog, who while he certainly howls pitifully at times, otherwise disturbs us far less than do other travellers. In addition we know not a soul here apart from the cathedral and a sunny bench in front of it, from where Heidelberg, the Bergstrasse, and the Rhine are to be seen, and we sit there in the middle of the day, or go for a walk and chat. On returning home I read to Cécile in the evening or we do a little work (for the little box has arrived safely and is already being put into service). We are <u>both</u> (not just me) eating an enormous amount and praise the landlord and his cooking, and I give lectures on Berlin cakes. We constantly intend to draw, and don't get on with it; I constantly want to compose, and don't get on with it. We intend to stay here for several more days because it really is so comfortable here; we are just so happy; I think I may say we.

I received Julie's kind lines yesterday,[2] and would ask you to give her my best thanks in advance, until I can do it in writing myself. I have not yet been able to do it today, and even this letter I can only write in haste, because I also had to write home today, in addition to dealing with several business letters which have followed me here to Speyer. The weather is glorious; yesterday and today we have had the brightest sunshine, and the buds are bursting out everywhere. That is the sort of springtime which I like to encounter. And now farewell, dear Mama, and give my kindest regards (I forgot them recently) to Herr and Mme Souchay[3] and to Carl and your brothers.[4] Until a speedy, happy return to the Fahrtor in Frankfurt

    Yours as ever
      Felix MB

[1] The village where they became engaged on 9 Sept. 1836 (see Introduction, p. xviii).
[2] Julie's letter is not amongst Mendelssohn's incoming correspondence in the Bodleian Library's 'Green Books'.
[3] Cécile's grandparents, Cornelius Carl and Helene Elisabeth Souchay (see Introduction, p. xiii).
[4] Elisabeth Jeanrenaud had three brothers, Carl Isaac, Jean Daniel, and Eduard Franz Souchay (see p. 41 n. 9, p. 111 n. 1 and p. 112 n. 5). Which of them were in Frankfurt at this time is not known.

PS. Hopefully tomorrow we will receive news from you, perhaps even a reply to our letter from Worms, and hopefully you are once more completely recovered and cheerful, and are no longer angry with me (I still fancy that you were a little so inclined in the final days), and feel just as restored as we hope you are. Julie did at least tell us that you were in good health.

━━━━━━

Felix and Cécile Mendelssohn Bartholdy to Lea Mendelssohn Bartholdy[1]

Speyer, 2 April 1837

Dear Mother and dear sisters,

It is four days now since my marriage—I have not so far been able to write to you—they have flown by all too quickly—but today I really must do it and tell you just how happy I am, and say that you should think of me at this time as a totally overjoyed man. How I feel, being with my beloved Cécile the whole time, how I love her more and more with every hour, how much good these few days have already done for my spirit, so that I feel so calm, cheerful, and refreshed—all that you could imagine yourself, but not how kind and charming Cécile is. I ought to describe everything really carefully; forgive me if I can't yet do so; it has never been possible for me to write about an experience that I am in the middle of. I know, however, that I will never lose this experience, that it is the greatest blessing in my life, that you too are aware of it and will rejoice with me over it, now or in the future.

If I just simply tell you how we have spent the past days, and what plans we have for the next ones, that will be sufficient. Tuesday was our wedding day; we received your kind lines, which Aunt Schlegel gave me in the church after the wedding ceremony; accept my thanks and above all write again soon, and tell me how you all are and what you are up to, my dear sisters; and we do not yet know anything about your return journey from Leipzig, dear Mother. Well now, at half past five in the evening Cécile and I rode in a very attractive and very comfortable carriage, which I had purchased, along my favourite road to Mainz in the most glorious weather, and from Hochheim[2] saw the illuminated bridge and the lights of Mainz, and felt rather cheerful. I will write nothing about Herr Appia's sermon, the singing

---

[1] NYPL, No. 317.   [2] Village 4 km. from the bridge of boats crossing to Mainz.

by the Cäcilienverein,[1] *and all the presents, for you will doubtless have heard about it all from my mother-in-law or Aunt Schlegel; but how nice our accommodation in Mainz was, no one knows but ourselves, so we must write about that—with its balcony overlooking the Rhine, upon which we went for a walk in slippers, and provided with all possible comforts. We stayed in Mainz on the Wednesday, and on Thursday drove to Worms through the lovely fertile countryside in spring-like weather; we passed through Lauberheim, Oppenheim, Bodenheim, and Nierstein—all of them places which just the mere sound of cheers up somebody like me who has lived on the Rhine; and now here I am riding through them with Cécile, and making stops everywhere, drinking wine, viewing the old churches and the door of the cathedral at Worms, where the Nibelungs play. And yesterday we arrived here, where again the most magnificent church along the Rhine is to be found, and were in the garden, which is turning green, from where we can see the Bergstrasse, Heidelberg, Mannheim, and Landau lying before us in the sunshine. What can I do other than to thank God, who sends me so many blessings and so much happiness, and who lets me enjoy so joyfully and completely in reality all the wonderful things which would have seemed almost too much even in a dream.*

We will now stay here quietly for a few days, then travel to Strasbourg, then to Freiburg, and then, if the weather allows, we will visit those places which Hebel writes about, and which I have been so curious about all my life, travel up the Wiesental, into the Höllental and back that way. But all that is still only a vague plan; for the whole summer address things to M. I. Herz in Frankfurt, who is forwarding everything to me. And now I will finish and if you find this a confused letter, forgive me; but be kind to me, dear Mother and sisters, and write soon, just as I will do so again soon; and hearty greetings to Paul, and think often of your happy Felix

Dear Mother,

I would so like to be able to describe how happy and cheerful I feel, for that would indeed give you pleasure, and reward you for the great happiness which I am indebted to you for; for even if I said 'Thank you' for the whole of my life, it would still not be sufficient. All my fondest hopes and thoughts about marriage have been far exceeded, and I would never have thought that one could have so much enjoyment in life. Felix is far too kind and good to me; he does all too much to please me and I can only offer him my good intentions in return. We have the most beautiful spring weather for our journey, and I am glad to see how pleased Felix is with this area, which I have always liked so much. The summer plans are still as undecided as they were in

[1] See Introduction, p. xxii.

Leipzig, but I hope to see you soon and to find you in really good health. Please remember me to the dear sisters and thank them for their kind lines on the wedding day. Give my best regards also to Louise Hensel,[1] and to you, dear Mother, an affectionate adieu from your devoted daughter

Cécile Mendelssohn Bartholdy

Cécile Mendelssohn Bartholdy to Elisabeth Jeanrenaud[2]

Speyer, 5 April [1837]

Dear Mama,

This morning, having relieved my feelings a little in complaints against you, and having begun a sermon addressed to Julie, Felix had the good idea of going once more to make enquiries at the post office, and actually came back with your letter to me, which gave us great pleasure and amused us very much. We examined it in part in the street as we wended our way towards the pretty garden which surrounds the old church, and having arrived at our favourite little spot near the Rhine, Felix gave me all the details in it. I was very pleased to know that you are so well and happy, and make a thousand wishes that you will always be so. You are quite right to think of us as being happy people; in truth I could think of nothing that we lack. Felix too is enjoying himself immensely in Speyer, and doesn't want to move from it. It must be admitted that heaven is favouring us, for we have only had two days of rain in all this time, which has also contributed to the pleasure of the walks by letting the trees open out, so that they now already have a greenish complexion. Despite all the pleasure we have in seeing spring advancing in the garden, despite Felix's zeal for composition and all the agreeable hours that we spend here together peacefully and uninterrupted, we must soon set off for Strasbourg, so as not to lose too much time and return to Frankfurt too late. I would therefore ask you to address future letters to Strasbourg poste restante, and Julie too if she would like to do me the kindness of writing. You have spared her my reproaches this morning; without that I would have tormented her

---

[1] Luise Hensel (1798–1876), sister of Wilhelm Hensel.   [2] Bodleian Library, MS MDM d. 18, fo. 34.

a little. Tell her that I have accompanied Felix today to the church where he played the organ, as she did Fritz. This morning we wanted to perform a sort of student prank, and to go and see the latter and our relations in Heidelberg, which is only a few leagues from here, but in the end we abandoned this heroic idea again. I have discovered here a little man able to deal with my teeth, Mama, a delightful man who immediately cured the problem by filling my bad tooth with a substance like that of Julie's, but more easily applied. Felix drank his health and is quite delighted by him. But I must finish this hotel scrawl and say farewell to you my very dear Mama, asking you to greet everybody from me, for which there is no space for me, since Felix wants to say a couple of words to you, which will be difficult for him as it is. Think of me as a child who loves you very much.

> Your
> > Cécile

Another word or two, since I still have this space left, dear Mama, please let me know in your next letter what the presents from my aunts in Manchester[1] were, so that I don't write anything inappropriate to them, not being able to remember at all that pile of beautiful things that they sent me.

Felix Mendelssohn Bartholdy to Elisabeth Jeanrenaud[2]

Speyer, 6 April 1837

Dear Mama,

Because Cécile wanted to confine me to far too small a space, I am therefore having my revenge and taking my own sheet, and at the same time teasing her as much as I can, for she has still forgotten to give you our <u>exact</u> address, and so I am making up for it here. For we would ask you to write us a couple of words to Strasbourg poste restante <u>one</u>, or at the latest two days after receiving these lines, to give us news of you and your family's good health, for which Cécile greatly longs, and indeed I too, as you

[1] Adelheid, wife of Carl Souchay, and Thekla, wife of Jean Souchay (see p. 111 n. 1 and p. 112 n. 5).
[2] Bodleian Library, MS MDM d. 18, fo. 35.

know. Anything, however, that you want to send more than two days after the arrival of this letter, we ask you to address to Freiburg im Breisgau poste restante until further notice. We have it in mind to travel from here to Strasbourg in three or four days time, and to stay there for three or four days, then straight on to Freiburg, and thus to be in the latter place in six or seven days time. If you yourself are prevented from writing to us in Strasbourg, then it would make us happy if Julie did so; the best thing would be if you both wrote, and so I want to have asked you for this most cordially. How happy these days are—that they are the best in my life you knew well, but the fact that Cécile also counts them among her happy ones, and is content with me, that fills me with all the more joy. I will really never forget the small town, the spring of 1837, and our convivial inn here. Now farewell dear Mama, cordial and kind regards to Julie and Carl, and remain ever true to your

Felix MB

———

Felix and Cécile Mendelssohn Bartholdy to Lea Mendelssohn Bartholdy[1]

Strasbourg, 9 April 1837

Dear Mother,

I am writing to you in real alarm at the complete lack of news from you and my sisters; apart from the kind note which we received on our wedding day, we have had no news of you since your departure from Leipzig, and in those lines there was no word of your state of health or that of my sisters. I hoped then to be able to assume that you were well, but as I have since been enquiring daily in vain after letters from home in Speyer, where we spent over a week, and where we received every possible sort apart from the wished-for one, I am therefore becoming concerned and ask you to write as soon as possible via the address of M. I. Herz and tell me what all this long silence is about. I am doubly anxious just because my sisters have been so often unwell recently, and I have been extremely concerned. Please relieve me soon.

[1] NYPL, No. 318.

For that is indeed the only drawback of the past all too happy, all too delightful weeks. You cannot imagine just how well I feel, and how sweet life with my dear Cécile is. We are, however, truly enjoying it to the full, and the days fly by one after another, without any specific plan, except that of being happy, and that we carry out. It is ages since I idled away my days as happily as now. We will be back in Frankfurt at the beginning of May—that much we know—but nothing else.

Much depends on the weather, which has now become so bitterly cold and wintry again that all the peach and other blossom here in the area has been destroyed by frost, and we did not set out on our journey here the day before yesterday because it snowed for the whole day, and even yesterday we had to drive here from Speyer in thick snow. If it becomes warm and spring-like again then we will go to Freiburg on the first fine day and stay there for a week or longer; if not, then we will soon make the return journey. Yet how glorious yesterday's journey in the heavy snowstorm was; the countryside looks wonderful and above all I was especially amused when, at the frontier, France immediately arrived on the scene with its different traditions and people with French speech, food, and manners. Such courteous customs offiers, and postilions with their pigtails and boots, who row with their arms as they drive and crack their whips as they go through a village, and French signboards with large wide letters, and yellow placards that can be read at a hundred paces, and 50 sous de guide—all that begins right at the border, and everything made me so unaccountably and vividly recall Father and his favourite country, so that I constantly started talking to Cécile about him again and again, and thinking about him.

This morning I hurried to the Minster, and it made an impression on me such as I have not hitherto experienced with architecture in my life. It is the most magnificent I have seen, and I am still completely satiated and enchanted by just strolling to and fro, around and within it, for I first wanted just to look round in a superficial way, and will gradually make myself really familiar with it. The day after tomorrow I will write to Becky; then I will give her a proper account of all our movements and activities in Speyer and here. This afternoon, however, I must go to the Minster again, this evening to the theatre with Cécile, and on top of that I am once more besieged by letters which have to be answered. Forgive me then if I finish; I would like to write at greater length and more often. Tell Fanny that in the Minster, opposite the lovely stained-glass windows there is a Silbermann organ with 32-foot pipes, which even from below commands my respect, and does not look bad at all—I will make its closer acquaintance tomorrow. Tell her also, that amongst other things I have composed three organ preludes in Speyer, which will be published shortly, and I hope that one or possibly two of them will particularly please her.

But above all reassure me soon about your well-being, for even in writing all this I become anxious again, and I am just waiting to see your or my sisters' handwriting on the address of a letter. I would hope that everything is unchanged and well, and look forward to a happy reunion.

> *Your*
>> *Felix*

Dear Mother,

    With these few words, today I too will just beg you to delight Felix and myself with some news; we are very concerned about our dear sisters. Please, please, dear Mother, grant us this wish, and forgive my haste—the dinner bell is ringing. I remain your ever-loving daughter Cécile

---

Felix Mendelssohn Bartholdy to Rebecka Dirichlet[1]

Strasbourg, 11 April 1837

My dear Becky,

    Today I want to wish you good luck,[2] good luck and joy and all the good things that I can conceive and ask for you. I am doubly sorry today that I have had no news from you for so long; I become anxious all over again when I quite naturally want to think about you, and then do not know at the time whether you are all well, and whether I can think of you as happy and cheerful today. God grant it, and I will keep my nasty thoughts well at bay, so that I can write to you about something else. As for my happy life, you cannot imagine just how blissful and content it is, and if, the day after tomorrow in Freiburg, where we are probably heading, we were to find letters from you, then everything really would be well. The letters which are addressed to Freiburg really are the main magnet which draws me thither; for at present travelling for pleasure is an impossibility. I have not felt so frozen the whole winter as I was yesterday and today in the churches, where I played the Silbermann organs with blue hands and admired them with chattering teeth, and it is beginning to snow again and is freezing so as to produce thick ice, and I don't know when it will all end. If it stays like this tomorrow, then I will have the letters forwarded to Heidelberg, and we will travel north again the day after tomorrow; if not

---

[1] NYPL, No. 319.   [2] It was Rebecka's birthday.

and it rains, then to the south. Is that not real student life? If I said that Strasbourg had made a pleasant impression on me, I would be lying. The weather is responsible for much of it; the countryside appears to be glorious, but it can't be seen for the fog, and the Black Forest looks worse than Mont Blanc. It is so bitterly cold in the Minster that one is forced to leave, just when one wants to remain inside more than ever, and we have not even been able to go up the tower yet. Even the exterior, which is so overpoweringly splendid, we have only been able to gaze in wonder at in passing, and know only this about it, that it is the finest in the world. You should see its magnificence, Becky. Especially the open-work tower; it looks like lace, and the light blue sky peeps everywhere through the dark brown of the whole building. And then the stained-glass windows inside, and the delicate, slender pillars and the countless statues, and in short the multitude of art amassed in the building, one doesn't know where to look first. But the people and the whole French show (don't tell Dirichlet) don't please us very much; Cécile especially is quite indignant about her compatriots, the French, who peep beneath her hat on the street and make rude remarks if she goes out on her own occasionally, who sing at meals and hold indecent conversations, and who indeed in their 1830s free-and-easy ways behave almost as if they are still stuck in their years of indiscretion and wanted to disown the old courteous sort of Frenchmen for ever. But it will not do, and the mixture is unedifying. I am already looking forward to the German border again. Oh Becky, you should have spent a couple of days with us in Speyer; a true connoisseur of the science of drinking such as yourself would also have found it enjoyable there. There was such a convivial inn, downright patriarchal, and without many people in it, but everybody friendly and respectable, and a wonderful old Lombardic-style cathedral, which stands on a terrace in the middle of the garden near the Rhine with a Roman ruin[1] near by. And there we sat in the sunshine every morning and afternoon looking at the Bergstrasse, the spires of Heidelberg, the Rhine and Mannheim in front of us, and the bushes turning green; and back at the inn I composed diligently, then did some drawing, ate endlessly and in the evening ordered rice-milk and read Lamartine, whom we disliked, and Hebel's poems, which once again enchanted us. And we knew not a single person in the whole of Speyer; no one could pay us a visit or expect one—that was not the least agreeable thing about it—and yet one evening the waiter brought a visiting card, on which one read the name Arendt with all his titles—he subsequently came in person, and could have almost caused me to regard the palms of Speyer as odious,[2] so little did his

---

[1] Felix is probably referring to the medieval Heidentürmchen.

[2] A private Mendelssohn family joke. The reference is to Gotthold Ephraim Lessing's play *Nathan the Wise*, Act 1, scene 6, where the Templar, wanting to be left alone, rebukes Daja: 'Woman, make not the palms odious to me, beneath which I'm otherwise so content to roam' (*Weib, macht mir die Palmen nicht verhaßt, worunter ich so gern sonst wandle*). This work had a very special significance for the Mendelssohns, since Lessing and Felix's grandfather, Moses, were friends, and the character of Nathan is thought to have been influenced by that of Moses. Furthermore the family owned Lessing's autograph manuscript.

manner appeal to me. Cécile also found him most disagreeable, especially when it turned out afterwards that, of everything he related to us, nothing at all proved to be true. He is just a completely dissolute fellow, and wishes particularly to be remembered to you. Amongst other priceless matters, he talked us into visiting the crypt of the cathedral (so to Cécile's horror he called the subterranean chapel—I hope thereby you hear Arendt speaking)—'There are the splendid old tombs of the kings, there you can hear the baptismal stream gurgling under the ground, which was used to baptize Henry IV's sons—and it is open the whole day to all visitors.' In the first place it was closed, and we could only have it opened up with some difficulty; then the graves turned out to have been destroyed since 1689, and there was not the slightest trace of a stream or a spring.[1] And then he described to us the road to Strasbourg; that was the last straw. I shall have to imitate it for you in person. Now farewell, my Becky, and remain true to me. If only we just had some news! There again you have the prelude and the epilogue of my letters, about which you always tease me. But this time it is meant in earnest, as I greatly long for it. Regards to Mother, to whom I wrote a few days ago, and to Fanny, to whom I intend to write in a few days, and to Dirichlet, from whom you should conceal my patriotism, and to Walter, my dear boy, and above all stay healthy and happy, and that applies to you all, and think of me

    Your

      Felix

———

Felix and Cécile Mendelssohn Bartholdy to Fanny Hensel[2]

Freiburg im Breisgau, 14 April 1837

Dear Fanny,

    When I fetched the letters this morning I found the one from Becky and Mother[3] with the news of the unpleasant accident which has befallen you. How very disagreeable it is, and how it has upset me

---

[1] Only some of the royal graves were ransacked in 1689; others remained, their exact position unknown until work on the crypt area took place at the beginning of the 20th cent. Despite Mendelssohn's remarks on the absence of the spring, it is noted in contemporary guidebooks, and was supposed to cure deafness.

[2] Staatsbibliothek zu Berlin, MA Depos. Berlin 3,20.   [3] Letter of 7 Apr. (Bodleian Library, GB VI 30).

at what is otherwise such a happy time. Both of them, praise God, write that you are well and cheerful, but the letter is already a week old and so we still long very much for confirmation of this news of your good health. If only it would come soon; if only you can soon walk about again and breathe fresh air; the sickroom, with its stuffy air, is so much associated with the memory of the sad accident; with returning strength and health the thought hopefully will desert you again, and hopefully it will already be very much the case by the time these lines arrive, and I shouldn't really be causing you to think of it again; but that is just the fault of the cruel distance. And yet I must tell you how it so upsets me that my disquieting premonitions of the past week have been confirmed by the first letter from home. If only I could send some mountain air as we breathe it here, and sunshine and greenery and mild weather as we have had since yesterday, for you and your time of convalescence. In fact it was the letters which I was longing for that have principally drawn me here; but now I am so enchanted by the journey here and by this area that today I would most gladly have given over the whole day just to showing it to you, so as to comfort and divert you; it would have done you more good than any medicine.

You will doubtless still remember how on the last occasion we ran into the cathedral in the rain,[1] and admired it with its dark stained-glass windows, but then we could see nothing at all of the situation of the town, and anything more beautiful I have never come across, nor can I imagine it; so peaceful and fertile, and on all sides many lovely valleys, and on all sides mountains, near and far, and villages as far as the eye can see, and good-looking neatly clothed people everywhere, rushing mountain streams in all directions. On top of that, all round the valley the first signs of spring, and on the mountains the last of the snow—you can imagine how beneficial it all is, and when I now go for a leisurely walk with my Cécile for the whole of this afternoon in the warm sunshine, keep stopping everywhere and gazing around, and talk with her about the future and the past, then I can indeed say with gratitude what a fortunate man I am. Only the uncertainty over your health bothered us over and over again, and so, as previously, I long once more for letters which might bring me the desired news and reassurance; would to God it comes to pass.

I intend to be very industrious. I would like to bring to light various new things and am making real progress; for this, however, it seems to me necessary first of all to continue working on all the accumulated old things, and so I will do that over the summer, will carry out many old projects, and those which are not realized by the winter, those I will then put away and they will have to be left alone. I have composed three organ preludes in Speyer, which I hope will be to your liking; a volume of Lieder ohne Worte is also almost ready for the press, but I am not thinking of publishing more of these so

---

[1] Probably on the return journey from the family holiday in Switzerland in 1822.

quickly again, and prefer to write larger-scale things. I have almost finished a string quartet[1] and then want to begin a second; work is now progressing just so well and happily.

We are thinking of staying here for at least another week, and of making excursions into the surrounding area, then probably back to Frankfurt via Heidelberg. If during this time I see the snow peaks of Switzerland, those old friends, then it will be difficult for me to turn back northwards, and yet on this occasion there is really nothing else that can be done. Cécile wants to be left some room, so I will finish. Hopefully I will soon hear what I wish and beg, and we will then soon write again. We wrote to Becky three days ago, and to Mother five or six days ago; now farewell, dear, dear Fanny, keep well and many kindest regards to your family

> *Your*
>> *Felix*

I too, my dear kind sister, must say a few words today to show you how very glad I am that you are at least well and cheerful after the distressing days you have experienced. I would, however, much prefer to be able to be with you now, so as to help pass away the time for you as far as possible. I could tell you much of all the lovely things that I am now enjoying through Felix, of everything to be seen here in the glorious surroundings and with the magnificent spring sky. If only the weather were also as nice in the north, then you would certainly be completely recovered very soon, and experience pleasant hours again in the beautiful garden. But my mother has already written from Frankfurt to say that it was miserably cold there, not to mention what it might have been like in Berlin, while we were breathing quite warm air in Speyer. How much we now long for really good news of you can well be imagined, and how hard for us the thought of the great distance and the lengthy journey of letters is becoming.

I wish you all the very best that could be wished, and remain with deepest love

> your devoted sister Cécile M.B.

---

[1] Op. 44 No. 2, in E minor. The autograph is dated at the end 'Frankfurt a/M den 18 Juni 1837', but it then underwent much further revision before publication in 1838. The next of the Op. 44 quartets to be written was No. 3 in E flat, and Mendelssohn announced to Hiller on 13 July that it was almost complete in his head; he did not start to write it down, however, until the autumn and the autograph is dated at the end 'Leipzig d. 6ten Februar 1838' (F. Krummacher, *Mendelssohn—der Komponist* (Munich, 1978), 91–2).

Felix and Cécile Mendelssohn Bartholdy to Elisabeth Jeanrenaud[1]

Freiburg im Breisgau, 15 April 1837

Dear Mama,

Cécile wants me to start off this letter to you, because I am always complaining about not finding enough space at the end. However, so that the same does not happen to her, I only want to say a few words to you about how safely we have arrived here and in good health, how enchanted we are by the beautiful countryside and the more obliging weather, and (what is best) how cheerful and happy we are in our own hearts and with each other. Unfortunately, however, I found here unpleasant news from home; my eldest sister has had a miscarriage,[2] and although the letter talks of her total good health and even of her cheerfulness, yet such an accident is always terribly disagreeable and has greatly spoilt the joy of the previous day. I now very much long for a second letter which at least might confirm her continuing recovery, and hope to God to receive one in the coming days. Since the surroundings here are so lovely, we will stay here for at least another week in order to make all possible excursions. We would therefore ask you to write to us here until further notice, and you know well just how glad we are of letters from you and Julie. Cécile will be angry, if I am not immediately

> Your
>> Felix

Dear Mama,

Having thanked you for your last kind letter, which I received in Strasbourg, as well as Julie for hers written at the same time, but which did not reach me until yesterday, I would ask you to tell the latter that, to my great sorrow, I cannot obtain the desired balm for her teeth. First of all, since the letter found us no longer in Speyer, I could not suspect that she needed it, and even if I did write now to my little liberator, it is probable, even certain, that it would be in vain, for he was then already on the point of departure for Munich, where he spends the greater part of the year. Nevertheless I still have a little of this medicine, and I do hope that Julie will not have need of it before our return when I could give her all of it, having decided to have my bad tooth removed, especially as Mr Brach has told me that I would still have four [sic] teeth.

You have no idea, dear Mama, how lovely it is here, first because of the delightful weather— for it seems that the season is still very late arriving in Frankfurt—then as a result of the superb

---

[1] Bodleian Library, MS MDM d. 18, fo. 38.   [2] Fanny's miscarriage evidently occurred about the end of March.

scenery, which we only caught a glimpse of during our return from Switzerland. I do not know if you still remember the hill situated behind the town. It is from there that yesterday we admired one of the finest views; the whole countryside lies in front of you like a panorama where every moment one discovers something new. I have cultivated my former talent for doing a little walking, for after dinner too we went for quite a long walk towards a chapel called St Loretto. I will tell you another time in greater detail of all this beauty; for today I lack time and paper and I can only say farewell, asking you to give my greetings to everybody, and to trust in the affection of your daughter Cécile M.B.

As well as giving my kind regards, I would ask you to tell Julie that I am writing today to Speyer to procure if possible Dr Brach's tooth cement for her, which, however, I cannot promise, as he[1] was intending to travel to Munich within a few days.

──────

Cécile Mendelssohn Bartholdy to Elisabeth Jeanrenaud[2]

Freiburg, 26 April [1837]

My dear Mama,

Having this morning received your dear letter, which was read and reread again this evening, I would like to be able to reply with something which would give you real pleasure, and which would remove, as with a puff of air, all the melancholic ideas of which I am the cause, but here indignation still makes itself felt most strongly, and what would be perfectly settled by a few words if we were now with you, will perhaps fill up this letter in vain. Indeed, dear Mama, if you could see us, happy and content as we are, in very good health, and living only for our own pleasure, I know that all the fine tales that have been told you about us, would worry you much less. I think that Dr Passavant[3] could make far better use of his talent for eloquence than to cause you anxiety and fear; and then you also could put a little less faith in everything that he pronounces; has it not already been seen that he allows himself to be guided too much by his

---

[1] In the German Felix plays on the ambiguity of the pronoun 'er' adding "(not the cement, but the man!)"
[2] Bodleian Library, MS MDM d. 18, fos. 39–40.
[3] Probably Johann Karl Passavant (1790–1857), a well-known Frankfurt doctor.

imagination? As for the jests of Herr Fallenstein,[1] if that is what they are, I find them rather out of place, and hardly know how he was able to succeed in making you unhappy by such feeble means, you who, in the past, would pay no heed to his talk at all, and who, on the contrary, would consider white anything he called black. All that, my dear Mama, causes me to contend that the gloomy mood in which you found yourself at the time of our departure, and often in the evening in your little chair, has still not completely passed, as I hoped and believed after your first letters, and that the same speeches that I went on repeating then, I must make again —I hope with more success. But one thing, dear Mama, which you never said to me then, and which causes me distress, is that you appear to doubt my love for you; you know quite well that you do me wrong to think so, and that I do not consider I have merited that reproach. They are matters which one can never prove, nor assert, otherwise I would not spare words to let you know how much I love you, but even if I were to repeat it to you all my life, you would never know just how grateful I am for all your kindness towards me. But as to Felix, I can tell you how much he loves you and how often we talk about you, and of all you have done for us and how he often says that he owes all his happiness to you, since if you had not constantly picked him out and encouraged him, he would never have had the courage to come that particular Thursday to speak to you about me. That is what he often says to me, and I can indeed assure you that he has not changed nor ever will change his feelings towards you. Why then, my good Mama, do you prefer to believe people who do not know us at all, like Herr Fallenstein, and through them cause the image of the happiness of your children to be disturbed? You tell me that Felix intimidated you in Leipzig during his mother's stay,[2] but for my part I believe rather that it was a residue of the influenza which gave you such a strong fear of this new acquaintance, and if her eyes looked at you in such a penetrating way, remember how often the same remark has been made about you, without you having had the least intention of doing so. O, how I wished that you could see us, how happy I am with Felix's love, and how I would wish to be able to thank you for having foreseen it then, and for having prepared so much happiness for me. We are so well accommodated here in Freiburg in the same hotel where we spent a night on the return from Switzerland—I think in the room of the slightly mad lady—that we cannot tear ourselves away from this pretty town, especially since at any moment we expect to witness the spring, which we would like to see beautify once more the delightful little valleys and hills of Freiburg. Today it is raining again and it is impossible to go out, but we have so many things to amuse us in our room. We draw—you should see the progress I have made with

---

[1] Presumably Friedrich Fallenstein (see p. 47 n. 5).   [2] See Introduction, p. xx.

Felix's advice—then he has begun to give me English lessons and is thoroughly pleased with me. I am keeping a diary, in which we combine together the most ridiculous drawings, with the result that time flies by without us knowing how. I hope, dear Mama, that you will not carry out the promise you made at the end of your letter, and that, on the contrary, you will write to me often and at length; I cannot tell you how you delight me by devoting a fragment of your time to me. As for Julie, I don't know how to praise her, and Charles remains faithful to those former principles, but I ask you to embrace them for me and to give greetings to everyone at home.

I would also ask you to act as my agent for the wedding presents you mention. For Mlle Seufferheld[1] do whatever you think best, but for Sophie[2] I want you to send her something really pretty from me; I found nothing in the Strasbourg shops which was worth the trouble of sending, so I am relying completely on your good taste—the price is up to you. If the wedding is soon, give her my greetings on the day; I thought I would still be able to witness it. Farewell, my dear Mama, I must finish

> ever your completely devoted
> Cécile

In only the greatest haste can I again express to Julie my most heartfelt (that is the word) heartfelt greetings, and request the letters always to be addressed here poste restante until we direct otherwise. I do not understand the letter with the gingerbread; the former I would ask to be sent to me here, the latter I would ask Julie to make use of at her discretion (eat it up?). But the post is about to go. Farewell. F.

———

Felix Mendelssohn Bartholdy to Elisabeth Jeanrenaud[3]

Freiburg im Breisgau, 27 April 1837

Dear Mama,

Your kind letter of yesterday has really disturbed me a great deal, because I see from it or think I see, that you are alarmed about us and are very anxious, that you think Cécile to be unwell and me to be

---

[1] Louise Seufferheld (1817–93), daughter of the Frankfurt merchant Marquard Georg Seufferheld, and his wife Louise Susanne, née Plazmann. She married Georg Friedrich Bernard Belli on 2 May 1837.

[2] Sophie Gogel married Georg Adolf Heinrich Hauck on 20 May (see p. 42 n. 8 and p. 43).

[3] Bodleian Library, MS MDM d. 18, fos. 41–2.

inconsiderate, and that you are afraid I might not be taking enough care of her. If only I could free you from all these concerns at one go, if you would just believe me <u>how</u> well and vigorous Cécile is, and how there is no trace of illness or weakness in her entire being. You are indeed correct in supposing that I do not know enough about what should be done in cases of illness like that, that I am very inexperienced and stupid in such matters, but that makes me all the more anxious rather than the opposite, and sometimes Cécile laughs at me because of it. The walk which she wrote to you about was the only one so far when we have done anything out of the ordinary, and even that was only one hour there and one back, so there was really no excessive exertion. Nevertheless I have decided to take your advice not to go on such long walks in future, and it will certainly not happen again. The fact, however, that we generally go walking when the weather is fine and are out in the air a good deal, you also will certainly find right and proper, since it can only be beneficial, and as I have said, I will take care to avoid overdoing things with Cécile. If only I could hope by means of these words to calm you and also thereby save you the concern and anxiety which you have on account of Cécile, when she is so healthy and cheerful, and if only you would think of us as quite happy and peaceful, just as the two of us think of you every day with renewed love and gratitude.

You want to know of our further plans, but we do not yet know them exactly ourselves. On no account do I think we shall be going into Switzerland, but hopefully you will not mind that I would like to wait for a few fine days here before we set out northwards again. Yesterday was the first perfect spring day; today it is raining forcefully, though the rain is warm, so I hope to see things turn green in a few days, and up to now we have had to spend so much time sitting in our room that we would dearly like at long last to be properly out of doors on our honeymoon, and so would prefer to stay here for a while yet. Cécile is doing a lot of drawing and that most beautifully; in particular she has completed a picture of Mainz for you, which you will certainly like. Then she is keeping a kind of diary with drawings, portraits, and all sorts of other additions (including the work of my paw), with which we amuse ourselves in a quite childish way, and we have already spent many a rainy afternoon on it. Then I see a pair of brightly coloured slippers grow and blossom before my eyes, and just how much my wardrobe here has already been restored by Cécile, how many buttons and seams owe their complete repair to her, that I would rather keep secret. And as for me, I have a piano up in my room and am composing fairly diligently, so we make good use of the rainy days as well as the fine ones. We reckon to be in Frankfurt again by the middle of next month and to stay until July, if you are willing to have us for so long. Furthermore I have now firmly accepted the invitation to the English music festival, and am giving Cécile an English lesson every evening,[1] when I am astonished how quickly she learns and what an

---

[1] Felix's exercises for Cécile are preserved in Bodleian Library MS MDM c. 29, fos. 1–4 (see Pl. 5).

excellent memory she has. To sum up, dear Mama—you complain to me that you no longer have her with you—I would probably never have been able to sympathize more than now, when I realize afresh day by day what happiness her proximity brings. I do not know what more to say to you, other than the old thing, that I will certainly try to be really worthy of this happiness, although I know that I will hardly be so just by expressing my gratitude. But besides that, dear Mama, you must really not forget that, God willing, we will never spend a long period of time without seeing one another; that you have promised to visit us there, that when we are free to travel, we will probably come through Frankfurt every summer, then you back to us, and that we will really be closer to one another, although further in distance, than I am to my own family, whom I can certainly reach in one day, but from whom I am always separated by my usual travel route to the Rhine and the South. I would like to tell you so much more, but then I remember that this letter will only reach you after so many days, when hopefully your mood is less gloomy, and that it may in the end distress you again rather than calm you, by reminding you of everything once more. In that case do not on any account read it through again, but just think lovingly of your children, and also of your

Felix MB

Cécile and Felix Mendelssohn Bartholdy to Lea Mendelssohn Bartholdy[1]

Freiburg, 28 April 1837

Dear Mother,

   You will be surprised to receive yet more news of us from the same place,[2] one that has probably never been portrayed to you as especially exciting or noteworthy, when, however, it has delighted us so much that we cannot make up our minds to leave it, particularly as it will be the southernmost point of our journey, and spring here is just now beginning to turn the many trees and meadows green and into flower. The continuing good news from you and your dearest contributes greatly to our pleasure, and if Felix returns from the post office in the morning with a

---

[1] NYPL, No. 320.

[2] Earlier letters to Lea from Freiburg have apparently not been preserved. Cécile may be thinking of the letter of 14 Apr. to Fanny.

letter, that day is even happier than the others. Today we received Becky's lovely note,[1] in which she scolds me a little for my anti-French attitude. I note that in this matter I will have many opponents; even you, dear Mother, appear from your last letter to prefer them greatly at all times, and I must complain of Felix that he has supported me so little and allows me to forfeit your goodwill right at the start. I could have kept my tongue, or rather my pen, in check very easily, as I have to do with my own mother, who permits no criticism of a Frenchman, and still speaks with enthusiasm of the time she spent in France, and where I, the little rebel, was born.

To give you news, however, of our doings, I will tell you how we spend our days here, which, despite the already considerable increase of daylight, slip by far too quickly. In the morning, if it is fine, we usually go for a good long walk. In the neighbourhood there are so many attractive paths, it is only necessary to choose mountain or valley. Just behind the town lies the Schlossberg, from which a marvellous view is to be had towards the Vosges and the Rhine, the Bergstrasse as far as Offenburg, into the Höllental, and in front of one the fertile valley and town of Freiburg. Then there lies on a hill half an hour from the town, beneath large nut trees, a small chapel called St Loretto. That is our favourite pilgrimage. From there too one can take in the whole surroundings, and in a dark narrow valley also see an old convent,[2] to which I have asked Felix to send me, when he can stand me no more, as a final kind deed; oh, it is just too pretty. Now when we return home from such walks then hunger and tiredness set in; but this does not prevent us recommencing our walks after dinner. When it rains, this nomadic life is obviously brought to a complete halt, and we are confined to our room, which, however, does have its advantages. Our very pleasant hosts have sent a piano up for Felix, which he says is similar to the small one that you want to send him in Leipzig, and he plays on it a great deal and composes even now as I write. He is also giving me English lessons, which amuse me very much because he is so enormously earnest about it, and does not like it at all if I plague him to give me a kiss. We do a lot of drawing together, and you should see how much progress I have made under Felix's tuition. I have, however, indeed never met anyone with as much talent as Felix for everything he takes on. Our honeymoon is now already over, and we are an old married couple. Our return journey to Frankfurt will probably be within a week or two. We would so much like to enjoy a little of the splendour of spring in this beautiful area, to go into the Höllental and to Hebel's

[1] Letter of 21 Apr., Bodleian Library, GB VI 34.
[2] The Günterstal, whose village of the same name was dominated by a Cistercian convent. Closed down in 1806, the buildings were eventually taken over by the Herrmann brothers from Waldshut, who started a cotton weaving factory in it. Following a severe fire in 1829, a brewery was added to the weaving activities.

Wiesental, before migrating north again. Felix has recently written to England and firmly accepted the invitation to the music festival, so that after staying in Frankfurt for a while, we will doubtless set out for there. Since Felix has acquaintances he wants to visit almost all along the Rhine, our outward journey will proceed very slowly, and we will need at least a couple of weeks for it. To my regret I now see the hope of still visiting you this summer gradually disappearing, although I realize very well the impossibility of combining these two journeys. I have to console myself with the proximity of Berlin and Leipzig, which will hopefully bring us together more often.

Farewell now, dear Mother, give my warmest greetings to Fanny, Rebecka, their husbands and the dear children, and to Fräulein Hensel, and remember kindly your daughter

Cécile Mendelssohn Bartholdy

Dear Mother, this time it is I who write the PS, but I really want to thank you myself for your kind letters,[1] and to ask you to remember us from time to time and to send us all the detailed news that you always do when I see your dear handwriting on the cover. I am being quite industrious here, and amongst other things have begun a new psalm, which is due to be published with two other older pieces,[2] and whose large-scale first chorus will be finished tomorrow; also a new book of Lieder ohne Worte has been sent off to Simrock[3] and will shortly have the honour of appearing, so I hope that you will praise me, although I don't quite venture to apply Walter Scott's charming words[4] completely to myself. A few days ago I definitely agreed to the Birmingham journey, persuaded for various reasons, but unfortunately I will not now be able to come to Berlin in the summer, as I must be in London for some time beforehand, and will have to set off for England at the beginning of July. As soon as I know something more specific about all this and about the music festival, I will write to you; in any case I hope that we will meet in Berlin before the end of the year. If only there was music to be made there apart from the Singakademie and Spontini, both of which are "out of the question" as far as I am

---

[1] Presumably of 7 and 16 Apr., Bodleian Library, GB VI 30 and 37.

[2] Mendelssohn here seems to be confusing two works. The new psalm with the large-scale first chorus is evidently Psalm 42, Op. 42 (cf. diary entry for 29 Apr.), but this was published on its own in 1838. Twice in the same month, however, he wrote to the publisher Simrock that he was working on completing the *Drei Motetten für weibliche Stimmen*, Op. 39, Nos. 1 and 3 of which date back to Dec. 1830, when he was in Italy. No. 2, 'Laudate pueri', was not actually finished until 14 Aug. 1837, although an earlier undated draft exists (in private hands, as is the dated autograph of the final version), and the set was published in 1838. (See Mendelssohn, *Briefe an deutsche Verleger*, 209 ff.)

[3] Op. 38, published in the summer of 1837.

[4] In her letter of 16 Apr. (Bodleian Library, GB VI 37) Lea astutely quotes (in English) Richard the Lionheart's words to Blondel in Scott's *The Talisman*: 'above all, hast thou thyself been busy? But I need not ask thee—thou can'st not be idle if thou would'st—thy noble qualities are like a fire burning within, and compel thee to pour thyself out in music and song.'

concerned.[1] *Meanwhile I will certainly come during my first break at Leipzig, God willing, but for now farewell, dear Mother, give my regards to Fanny and thank her very much for her kind letter, and regards to Becky and thank her for today's letter, and think of us, as we do of you daily and hourly at this happy time.*

Your Felix

━━━━

Cécile Mendelssohn Bartholdy to Elisabeth Jeanrenaud[2]

Freiburg, 5 May [1837]

Dear Mama,

I would have written to you sooner so as not to cause you fresh anxiety, if a little expedition which we made into the surrounding area had not been prolonged more than we had intended. Returning here after dinner, Felix immediately went to the post office and brought back no fewer than seven letters all at the same time, which we read with great pleasure. I thank you ever so much for yours, and beg you to say the same to Grandma on my behalf.

We are now on the eve of our departure from here. Tomorrow we intend to go to Karlsruhe, and the day after to Heidelberg, where we will stay for a few days, weather permitting. Yesterday and the day before we had really bad weather for travelling, especially in a nasty small coach such as we had hired in order to spare our own on account of the high mountains and stony roads. The first two days, however, were superb. Mme Bernay[3] was indeed right in finding hell beautiful. I wished you could have seen it with us. Further on is a landscape just like that of La Chaux-de-Fond,[4] and a small town called Lenzkirch, which has also been completely newly rebuilt and where we spent the night with the owner of a factory producing Italian-style straw hats. He has frequently spent a lot of time in Italy, and I will relay to you the account he gave us, which will make you laugh as it did me. Generally speaking up there almost all the

---

[1] The Mendelssohn family had largely broken their links with the Singakademie after Felix's failure to be elected director in 1832, although he was to be made an honorary member in 1842. Gaspare Spontini (1774–1851) dominated the Berlin operatic scene, and his jealousy of other composers lay behind the many intrigues surrounding the one and only performance of Mendelssohn's opera *Die Hochzeit des Camacho* in 1827.

[2] Bodleian Library, MS MDM d. 18, fos. 43–4.

[3] Probably Marie Charlotte Bernay, wife of the spice merchant Joseph Anton Bernay (1767–1844).

[4] La Chaux-de-Fond, a small town in north-western Switzerland near Neuchâtel, the area from where the Jeanrenaud family came.

languages are spoken, a state of affairs which contrasts greatly with the coarse and rather dazed appearance of the villagers. I will also tell you the details of our charming little excursion, which took us to within a league of Basle. On the way back we would have dearly loved to see Baden-weiler as well, which Carl talks about so much, but it was pouring down, with the result that we only glimpsed it from afar. I do not expect to meet Sophie Gogel, since we will not go to Baden, having already been travelling quite long enough. However, I am sorry to learn that she is unhappy, when I thought her, all things considered, rather pleasure-loving.

Moreover it appears that the social gatherings are not tailing off at all in Frankfurt, as they usually do in the spring. Now it is because of Mme Mylius,[1] now because of Mlle Seufferheld etc. God preserve me from the dinners when I return, for I am less used to them than ever. We always dine in our room, where one is finished quite quickly when there are only the two of you. Is Herr Gansland[2] still just as enraptured by Julie's fine words? The poetry and all that appear rather suspect to me. Tell her that I congratulate her on knowing how to please such a difficult man. I am going to stop and take up my pen again in Heidelberg.

Goodbye, dear Mama, see you ere long,
your devoted daughter
Cécile MB

Remember me to everybody and don't leave anyone out. I am very surprised that I won't find Grandpapa in Frankfurt. Wish him bon voyage and August[3] also.

Just to add my greetings and my good wishes and thanks for your kind letters. Everything else soon by word of mouth. Farewell dear Mama

Your

Felix

If you would like to write to us, address the letter to Heidelberg, poste restante.

———

[1] Wife of Carl Mylius (see p. 50 n. 5). [2] Röttger Ganslandt (see p. 97 n. 4).
[3] Cornelius Carl Souchay's servant.

Felix Mendelssohn Bartholdy to Julie Jeanrenaud[1]

Freiburg im Breisgau, 5 May 1837

My dear Julie,

Yesterday evening, when we returned here from a four-day trip in the mountains I found your very kind letter, and although I now hope to thank you soon in person for it, I must still first do so in writing, since it delighted me just so much. I think it is the loveliest of all your letters to me, particularly the end, and the fact that you tell me that we 'will build on it', for that is spoken as if straight from my own heart, and I am so happy that you too feel things in the same way, and generally about the letter as a whole, which sounds just as if we were talking with one another. You say nothing about your trip to England; instead you say we will discuss the plans for the summer together, and yet Grandfather writes that he would be leaving on the 11th, so that we shall not meet him again in Frankfurt. So it seems to me certain that you are not travelling with him, or rather I hope it is certain. The main motive may well be a selfish one, for you cannot imagine how sorry I would be if, on our return, you were absent, and that we would have only the uncertain prospect of seeing you again in England; and in addition I think these very summer plans could become so splendid if we all worked together on them and took part in them; we could then spend such happy months with one another. I would ask you to think up provisionally a few nice ventures suitable for May and June; we will carry them out in due course, and I will bring along humour in abundance to every possible sort of entertainment. Except that the weather must be more favourable to us than on our present tour, when we had first two glorious days and then two dreadful ones. In particular, a thunderstorm over the Black Forest engaged our attention in a most inconvenient manner, and the heavens were so yellow and murky that one might well have become alarmed. On top of that the weather was so malicious as to desist from raining so long as we were in the inn; during breakfast or lunch the sun shone, only for it to start pouring down a quarter of an hour after our departure. I must, however, testify that we made light of it, and that Cécile only occasionally said that it was a good job that Julie wasn't here, for she would have been scared. This was particularly the case with certain mountain carriages and their brake-shoes, and since I cannot stand these contraptions either, we thought about you with every brake-shoe, as well as on other occasions—

---

[1] Bodleian Library, MS MDM c. 31, fos. 16–17.

that is every ten minutes with the curious Black Forest vehicles. How lovely, though, the fine days were. I would prefer to tell you in person on the familiar sofa, and in addition produce our drawing books. Of the Wiesental and our passion for it you know nothing at all as yet—all that by word of mouth. Many thanks, however, for writing about my 'St Paul' so generously and for saying that it has made a favourable impression on you.[1] That gives me very great pleasure; for just as it is difficult to remain completely devoted to a friend if his wife is not to your liking, so it is with this, and it is indeed always something of an impediment if some close associate or relative creates works which displease one; each becomes uncomfortable with the other. So I am doubly pleased; first, that that was not the case, and then that my music has pleased you, who certainly doesn't pay much attention to double counterpoint and voice leading, of which the pedants continually talk, but to the substance, which is best, and who knows and needs nothing of all the supporting structure. Of course much corruption comes into play, just because of the intimacy—but it's all the same to me. If it has only given you a couple of pleasant hours, then that is the nicest thing for me to hear about it. We are thinking of leaving here tomorrow morning, and being in Heidelberg by Sunday or Monday; there we want to linger for a few days, since I am an old admirer of the broken-apart tower, and would like to do all the excursions once again, and at the same time we want to appear in society as a married couple, and to exhibit ourselves. It is hard at the beginning, with so many unknown relatives and aunts, but Cécile will steer me through nicely, and turn my stubborn countenance rose-coloured. And I will also behave myself; I would so like to shine on my first début, for I don't count the waiter or the coachman, and apart from them, not a cat has yet seen us. Please give your mother and grandfather my best thanks for their kind letters, and ask the former to forgive me that I cannot send an answer today as I would like, but I am once again embroiled in my correspondence. And remember me to Grandmother, and thank her for all the kind things which she has relayed to me through Cécile. And the most important thing is left till last; the gingerbread. You are right to proceed in such a delicate matter only with the greatest caution, and to obtain my repeated legal assurance of the donation of it, but I confirm the same. 'And just as the gingerbread can only say, here I am, so that friends take delicate pleasure in it, so too I can only say, accept it.' But save me a piece, one inch square, so I can see it and can express my thanks in writing from Frankfurt, which the donor will again not understand, since he writes to me in Dutch, which I don't understand. He calls the gingerbread 'eenen Deventer Koch', which made Cécile laugh a great deal, but we have not been able to make sense of anything else in it. May it not taste unintelligible! It is now up to you to

---

[1] See p. 159 n. 2.

report on that. And now farewell, dear dear Julie, remain true to me till our happy reunion and always

Your Felix

━━━━━━━

Cécile Mendelssohn Bartholdy to Elisabeth Jeanrenaud[1]

Heidelberg, Wednesday [10 May 1837]

Dear Mama,

We have been here for two days, and it is pouring with rain. It is very unpleasant, and upsets all the splendid plans we had made on our first evening here up at the castle amid a fine sunset. Since Grandma has left together with almost everybody else, we were thinking that you would perhaps have the time to come and meet us here, and everything would be arranged to receive you. Aunt Becher is all on her own, and it is so beautiful in the vicinity of Heidelberg in springtime. Everything is in flower at Weinheim. The weather, however, doesn't even let us open the window without getting wet, and one cannot go out without getting dirty. I think we won't stay long in such circumstances, and will only wait for a short dry period before setting out for Frankfurt.

I have paid and received visits from the Pickfords; we took tea there, and at Aunt Becher's. Mme Benecke wasn't at home when we went there, and hasn't found me either. Moreover she appears to have recovered fairly well, for she had company the other evening.[2] Mme Nies, Aunt Becher, and Fritz Schlemmer were invited. This last-named does the honours and shows us round Heidelberg perfectly; he spends nearly the whole day with us both on walks and at home; he brings flowers, perfume, music paper, organ fugues, and all sorts of gossip. We are very well accommodated at the Prinz Karl, but with this sort of weather one is only comfortable at home. I dearly want to see you again, you, Bury and Julie, and I think that, given your solitude, you

---

[1] Bodleian Library, MS MDM d. 18, fos. 45–6.
[2] Louise Benecke's husband, Wilhelm, had died in Heidelberg on 8 Mar. 1837.

won't be displeased to see us arrive. You will see me a little dishevelled in matters of my wardrobe, for it was not at all resplendent when I left, and I have not had the time to maintain it greatly. My hat is almost worn out, without my having been able to purchase another straw one, in view of the awful weather and the poor selection of the shops here. Perhaps I will be able to have another go tomorrow in Mannheim, where Fritz wants to take us to the theatre. Each of my dresses is worse than the next, except for the green surtout, which I have only worn a couple of times in Strasbourg, where there are delightful shops, from which I will be bringing you a few samples. I am writing in a confused way today, but it isn't my fault, since going on in front of me is a prattling of music and compositions, and so many things that I cannot connect my ideas together. I would just say that I love you very much and look forward to seeing you again. If in a few days the weather returns to being fine it would be very nice if you could come and surprise us here with Bury and Julie; Aunt Becher invites you, as we do ourselves. Or preferably, don't take us by surprise, but write and let us know which day, so that we can come and meet you in Darmstadt. In any case I will write again to tell you the day of our departure from here. Everyone sends you their greetings, Felix first of all, as well as to Julie and Bury, Mlle Fischbach and all the servants. Farewell, dear Mama, forgive this hotch-potch, and remember your devoted daughter C.M.B.

Cécile Mendelssohn Bartholdy to Elisabeth Jeanrenaud[1]

Heidelberg, 12 [May 1837]

Just a couple of words, dear Mama, to tell you that we will leave here tomorrow morning. I do not know what can have made you think after my last letter that we wanted to stay for the music festival, which has no attraction at all for Felix; the idea seems to have troubled you greatly, to judge by the tone of your letter. I cannot tell you the exact time of our arrival, since

[1] Bodleian Library, MS MDM d. 18, fos. 47–8.

it is possible that we will stop en route if it is fine like today, perhaps at Weinheim, where I would like to show Felix the lovely valleys.

I hope to find you in good health, and will reserve all the details for my return.

Farewell, dear Mama, keep well
Your daughter Cécile

―――――

Felix Mendelssohn Bartholdy to Lea Mendelsssohn Bartholdy[1]

Frankfurt, 15 May [1837]

Dear Mother,

I will now tell you about the successful conclusion of our honeymoon journey; we arrived here in the evening of the day before yesterday happy, refreshed and freezing, for unfortunately right up to the last moment we had literally to struggle with the bad weather; all our coats, muffs, and umbrellas proved insufficient help. So we had to drive from Freiburg along the wonderful Bergstrasse of the Black Forest, its orchards in full blossom, with the windows shut. We could not go either to Badenweiler or to Baden, although we caught sight of both towns, and in Heidelberg as well as here we have found ourselves very content next to the warm stove. It is just too much for the south and for the middle of May. Here we have found everyone well and cheerful, and will certainly stay here for at least six weeks, much to my delight. I have a pleasant small study with a piano in it, and intend to make use of both. Yesterday we received your kind letter with the lovely poem of Walter Scott,[2] and I thank you for both very much. Cécile is leaving it to me for the time being to say thanks on her behalf as well, until she writes to you herself; please forgive her that she can't do it today or for the next few days, but you can imagine how all her relatives and acquaintances here lay claim to her, and her friends want to see her again for the first time as a married woman. In the meantime then I sit peacefully in my little back room, and compose my psalm,[3] and let the storm of visitors pass by. Cécile wishes to say that I am fully

[1] NYPL, No. 322.   [2] This letter is not extant.   [3] Psalm 42.

supplied with linen and at present need no more either for England or any other country; so I thank you for your offer to send some here, and request instead that it be sent to Leipzig in due course, and at the same time I thank you for the enormous excellent laundry list, the sight of which quite braced me up.

I was annoyed, however, to hear that Fanny says the new school of piano-playing has left her behind (you say that she has written to me about it, but I have recently had only the letter about her recovery,[1] otherwise nothing from her), but there is absolutely nothing to that. She really plays all of the little fellows such as Döhler[2] into the ground; they can manage a couple of variations and party tricks nicely and then everything becomes terribly boring, and that never happens when Fanny plays the piano. Then there is something other than party tricks. Thalberg[3] and Henselt[4] are a rather different matter, for they are supposed to be true virtuosi in the manner of Liszt (who outclasses them all); and yet it all amounts to nothing more than a Kalkbrenner[5] in his heyday, and blows over during their lifetime if there is not some spirit and life in it, and something better than mere dexterity. That, however, Fanny has, and thus need not fear any of them, any more than Kalkbrenner previously, about which these days I have to laugh. For my part I believe that Chopin is by far the most inspired of them all, although Liszt's fingers are yet more amazing and supple than his. The latest news is that Neukomm is coming here, and will probably conduct the Cäcilienverein for a year (on trial); Hiller leaves for Italy in a few months, and if Neukomm stays then it would certainly be a great piece of good luck for the Frankfurters; he would be the best man for the job, and would perhaps in addition succeed in reconciling the Bundestag with the cause of decent music.[6] I saw Aunt Schlegel yesterday; she is well and sends many greetings to you all. Forgive me, dear Mother, this disorganized chatty letter, but I am writing it in a hurry, between the torrent of visits which sometimes drives me to distraction. At the next opportunity I will send Becky my new book of songs,[7] which has such an exceedingly finely engraved title-page that I tremble at the sight of it myself, and I will send Fanny my six Preludes and Fugues;[8] I found both of them waiting here. O Lord, would that I could get on with composing a piano concerto! I must close with this sigh, for I am just being called again, and the time for the post is approaching. Farewell, dear dear Mother, and you my dear roguish girls; keep well and happy and think often of

Your Felix

[1] Letter of 13 Apr., Bodleian Library, GB VI 32.   [2] Theodor Döhler (1814–56), Austrian piano virtuoso.
[3] See p. 101 n. 2.   [4] Adolf Henselt (1814–89), German pianist and composer.
[5] Frédéric Kalkbrenner (1785–1849), French pianist and composer of German extraction.
[6] The Bundestag at this time had its seat in Frankfurt, and was not generally held in high regard.
[7] *Sechs Gesänge*, Op. 34.   [8] For piano, Op. 35.

Cécile wishes to send you her special regards, and to my sisters and to Paul and Albertine, whom we thought of so often on our journey through the snow, especially . . . [remainder of letter missing]

━━━━━━

Cécile Mendelssohn Bartholdy to Lea Mendelssohn Bartholdy[1]

Frankfurt, 28 May [1837]

Dear Mother,

It is now already over a week since we arrived back here, and I still have not thanked you for the lovely letter which I found here.[2] I will, however, do so today cordially and beg you to half forgive me this delay, which is brought about through the many little tasks that a return home brings with it, the many drives and walks for which the fine weather is to blame, the many conversations with my mother and sister caused by the long absence, and the considerable number of visits. We were doubly pleased over the good news which you gave me and Felix, because during our stay in Heidelberg we had to go without letters for some time. Now Felix has even received your last one, which makes him very happy, and which he reckons to be the loveliest of all those you have written to him. I have rarely seen Felix as cheerful as in these past few days and you really notice it in his face; everybody says he looks thoroughly prosperous and well, and Aunt Schlegel maintains that she has never seen him like it in her whole life. She said that to me recently when we were together with Herr Mendelssohn and his lovely daughters[3] in a pleasure garden near here. This unexpected visit delighted us greatly, and we only regretted that they had allowed so few hours for their stay in Frankfurt, which had to be divided amongst so many relatives. Felix, Mother, and I, however, also had the pleasure of accompanying them for a good distance on their way out and to talk with them in greater peace. The two girls have altered so much since last year; they have become so big and strong and pretty. Mother is very angry with me that I have become so sunburnt on the journey, and have not taken enough care of myself. That very much refutes the charge of musk perfumes which you make against me, and really, dear Mother, I do not know how I come to deserve it. There is truly no one who hates this scent

---

[1] NYPL, No. 324.   [2] Letter of 6 May, Bodleian Library, MS MDM d. 21, fos. 7–8.
[3] Alexander Mendelssohn with Marie and Margarethe (see diary entry for 19 May).

as much as I do, and I cannot imagine at all where the unfortunate letter may have suggested it. In truth you could suspect the postman sooner than me; in any case, dear Mother, if you have not done it already, burn it immediately, so that I am not the cause of headaches and unpleasant feeling. The big list of Felix's linen has greatly amused my domestic sense, and allayed the sorrows which I experienced at the first sight of his wardrobe—the wonderful handkerchiefs of which there were once six and which are now reduced to two or three in number, and all the erratic number of shirts, socks, etc. Yet Felix maintains that, with a few repairs, everything will still be quite fit for the English journey, and as he does not look in the least untidy, but always looks like the finest "gentleman", you need not take the trouble to send the things here; I will then receive everything in Leipzig with double delight, when the need will be greatest.

My paper is coming to an end, and I must finish, dear Mother, with kindest regards from my mother and Julie, whom I found here again in very good health, and with many kisses for my dear sisters and their children. Farewell, dear, kind Mother, and remember lovingly your daughter Cécile M.B.

All your relations here, headed by Frau von Schlegel, are very well; yesterday we saw the old aunt yet again looking so sprightly and cheerful that it was a joy to see her. Herr Veit has just painted a picture, which has delighted all who have seen it, Felix included. It represents the two Marys at the tomb of Jesus,[1] and is said to be really delightful. Adieu again, dear Mother, excuse the closely written letter which may perhaps be tiring for your eyes.

———

Felix Mendelssohn Bartholdy to Lea Mendelssohn Bartholdy[2]

Frankfurt am Main, 29 May 1837

Dear Mother,

Your kind letter which I received the day before yesterday[3] has so greatly delighted me that I must thank you for it wholeheartedly. Please write often, just as much, and just as pleasantly and cheerfully. You must surely know how it continues to refresh your distant family for a long time afterwards, and disseminates the same long-lasting, cheerful frame of mind amongst them. The fact that you are all fit

---

[1] See p. 45 n. 4.   [2] NYPL, No. 323.   [3] Letter of 19 May, Bodleian Library, MS MDM c. 34, fos. 52–4.

and well was told me by Alexander and his daughters, who passed through here several days ago and had seen you shortly before their departure; they also told me, however, that my sisters are angry with me because I cannot come to Berlin in the summer, and their long silence really has led me to fear something like that. I will write to them both today on that account, but I must thank you all the more, dear Mother, that you have not stopped writing to me, and writing such loving letters; and I think also that perhaps my sisters are not really that angry, but only too lazy to correspond. Paul has still not written to me at all since my wedding, nor answered our letter from Freiburg.[1] I fret, fret, fret!—but I am hardly any better myself when I have as much to experience as at present, and it is already nearly a fortnight since my last letter to you.

How that time has flown by, so merrily and enjoyably, I need hardly tell you. I really could not have imagined that I would ever be so completely happy in my life, and now I am. It is such a blissful time for my life and my art that I never know how to thank God enough for it, with musical thoughts and work in abundance for new pieces, while the old ones are making all the impression I could wish for. My 'St Paul' has been performed here twice in a week to full houses, and now they are even talking of a third performance after only four weeks;[2] and I may hope that one of these days I will write something that will approach what I would always so dearly like to express, and only so rarely can—and at the same time I have these happy days with my wife, whom I now love far more than I ever believed possible, whom I find increasingly lovable with every passing day, and with all the pleasant cheerful people here—it might almost seem like too much happiness, and I know that most people are afraid of expressing such a feeling; but just because I do it in full thankfulness, so I may do it also truly without fear, and I know that it pleases you.

I was very interested in what you write about Henselt's playing, and from other sides too I hear your opinion of his recital in Berlin confirmed. That is just what I meant in my last letter, that all the dexterity and exploitation of dexterity no longer easily dazzles even the public; it must be inspired if it is to carry everyone along, and thus I might perhaps prefer to hear Döhler play for an hour than Fanny for an hour, but after a week boredom means I can no longer listen to him, and only then do I begin to really appreciate the other sort of playing, and that is a good thing. I am sorry to hear what you tell me about the apartment, that it is still unlet, because it seems to be worrying you, but for some reason I can't share this concern, and still think that a beautiful apartment in a beautiful house cannot remain empty for long.[3] It may well be the case for a while—but over a long period, I think, certainly

---

[1] Letter of 20 Apr., NYPL, No. 542.

[2] There were performances by the Cäcilienverein on 24 and 28 Apr. conducted by Hiller. The third performance was presumably that of the choruses only, which Felix describes in the diary entry of 31 May.

[3] Parts of the Leipzigerstrasse 3 house in Berlin were let out.

not, and I am at the moment not at all concerned about having to live off the capital. Perhaps the most respectable tenant has already looked at the place as I write this, and you no longer have it on your mind. Special thanks too for your stories about the Princess of Mecklenburg;[1] they are of great interest, because here, as with you, there has been much talk about her in the last few days. But I belong more to the Dirichlet camp than ever, and nothing that I read in the newspaper can change my views, and just as Father used to, I insist that a princess can have neither a headache nor toothache, an opinion with which I create a great stir here at home. Now farewell, dear Mother, write to me again really soon and at great length. I am staying here until July in order to finish off my concerto and other things I am working on, and I hope that you will often give me the pleasure of reading about you and hearing of your and everybody's well-being. Farewell

    Your Felix

    If you have the opportunity to find out, let me know if a letter from me to E. Devrient has duly arrived.[2] And please ask Paul if old Schlesinger has paid up;[3] if not then I would very much like <u>to have my manuscripts back again</u> and let him get away with the 10 Louis. He has to pay five; God won't help him get out of that. Enclosed is a letter from Cécile—many greetings from her mother.

————

Felix Mendelssohn Bartholdy to Fanny Hensel[4]

Frankfurt am Main, 29 May 1837

. . . This is a measly time for musicians—take the Cäcilienverein[5]—experienced singers, respectable pleasant people, obliging directors, no requirements other than a little piano-playing, and a little inclination for good music, and a little knowledge, neither genius, nor energy, nor politics, nor anything out

---

[1] Helene, Princess of Mecklenburg-Schwerin (1818–58) married Ferdinand, Duke of Orléans, on 30 May 1837.

[2] Letter begun on 3 May and finished on 15 May, printed in E. Devrient, *My Recollections*, 198–203, but without the drawings, which are only printed in the German edition (*Meine Erinnerungen*, 193–8).

[3] Presumably for the *Drei zweistimmige Volkslieder*, which Schlesinger published separately between 1836 and 1838.

[4] Part of letter only, as printed in *Briefe aus den Jahren 1833 bis 1847*, ed. Paul and Carl Mendelssohn Bartholdy (Leipzig, 1863), newly translated and supplemented by the end of the letter from the reproduction in Sotheby's catalogue of 18 May 1995 (lot 195). The letter is now in private ownership, and the beginning was not available for this edition.

[5] Seeking a permanent successor to Schelble.

of the ordinary—I would have expected 50 people to have applied and for them then to have had their choice, but there are hardly two who could possibly be considered, and not one who is able to carry it on in the right, true, and noble spirit in which it was begun—that is, in plain speech, not one who concedes that Handel and Bach and such people stand above anything that they themselves can do or say. Neukomm, in whom I would have had most confidence, took part in negotiations, had firmly accepted the position, and has now suddenly equally firmly declined it. So there will be no one to take over the thing apart from Ries, who will probably do it, but who unfortunately lacks the necessary respect for great works of art, which is and will remain the main thing as far as I am concerned. It is a pity on account of all the trouble and untold work that it cost Schelble to establish something which is in the end to fall apart again. Everyone here is extremely content with Hiller's direction, no matter how hard they might have made it for him at the start; but he is going to Italy in two months' time and doesn't want to remain, and who knows, whether that is not also a reason why they all now so regret his departure—that is the dreadful thing about the world.

It occurs to me that if in the course of the next few months you want to have something to sing again, then get hold of 'Theodora' by Handel and have a look at it. It will in any case give you pleasure, as there are quite glorious choruses and arias in it, and perhaps you could have a German translation made (which clearly needs to be greatly improved, for the original text is quite ridiculously absurd) and perform it at home with your small choir. Unfortunately it is not suited to a larger-scale performance, but bits of it, for example the final chorus, are as lovely as anything one can hear in Handel. Veit has now almost finished a small picture which is giving immense pleasure here, and seems to me certainly one of his best oil-paintings. For a start the subject is very well chosen: the two Marys seated at the tomb early in the morning, who gaze so longingly at the tomb and desire so much for it to open up. What I have seen of the Düsseldorfers who are now painting here, was, however, nothing special. Everything still savours completely of old pictures by Lessing and Schirmer, and contains nothing individual. And then in Mannheim I saw an exhibition of the Darmstadt Art Association; it was quite atrocious, especially a large idealization of Goethe in oils—it was the nadir of awfulness, painted by Fasel in Karlsruhe.[1] Alexander and his family[2] are bringing you my six Preludes and Fugues for piano with them; I just hope they please you! I would particularly want the one in B flat to do so, because it is my favourite. Write to me about them and about the six songs which I am sending Becky. Six Lieder ohne Worte of mine will also appear shortly and probably the Psalm, which I have recently completed and

---

[1] Georg Wilhelm Fasel, artist active in Karlsruhe 1829–48: the Goethe painting dates from 1836.
[2] Alexander Mendelssohnn and his daughters (see p. 43 n. 4).

which I am very pleased with. Now farewell, dear sister, my kindest regards to Hensel and Sebastian, and remain true to me

Your Felix

———

Felix Mendelssohn Bartholdy to Rebecka Dirichlet[1]

Frankfurt a/M, 29 May 1837

Dear Becky,

How sorry I was to learn through Alexander and his daughters that you are angry with me, and that I had to explain your long silence towards me in this way. I have now indeed to believe it, and I am writing to you today really only to beg you to be my friend again, and to tell me soon that that is what you are once more. I have written today to Fanny at length about the journey to England, and ask you to learn about it from her, so that I need not repeat the same thing; but believe me, there is no alternative, and I could not have declined the invitation without doing a very wrong thing. In all such cases it comes to my mind again how sorry I am that I cannot just lead my life with you in Berlin; but then I have always to testify to myself that I have certainly done my part to bring it about, but that it was made quite impossible through the circumstances, and that no one is thus really to blame for it—things were probably meant to be as they are. And yet I often come back to the tiresome 'if' and 'had I only'. Especially when I am alone with Cécile and she looks so lovable and kind-hearted, then it occurs to me all too often that you should get to know her, and then I would gladly relegate Birmingham to Never-Never-Land. But as I said, I could and should not decline it, and must even be very glad that it has thus come about. All my connections with England appear thereby to be more firmly established again; few weeks pass by in London when something of my music is not given; recently my Piano Concerto and my A major Symphony were performed in the same Philharmonic concert;[2] all that makes me happy, because I am already working on a pile of new things and for all these reasons I know that am right to go there once again. Apart from the Beneckes and Klingemann, who have offered us accommodation with them, my publisher, Novello, also wants to have us at his home, and in a nice letter has promised me every comfort and "snugness"; and yet I think that I will remain faithful to the

---

[1] NYPL, No. 325.   [2] On 15 May.

ironmonger.[1] But all that is still undecided, since we are not planning to leave here until four weeks hence, and to arrive in London towards the end of July. We have had summer weather for the past two days, so spring is at an end. But you have no idea how lovely it is here; in the forest beyond Sachsenhausen (you will remember it well) there are such a vast number of flowers beneath the most glorious beech trees in the world, that the whole ground appears alternately light blue and then light yellow, and so we always bring Cécile's parasol back home completely full of forget-me-nots or great bunches of woodruffs out of which we make May-punch in the evening. Recently we wanted very much to get the Senator[2] drunk on it, but he held his drink well, and became only a little merry. We also sometimes meet Aunt Schlegel in the forest; she is very well and sprightly, and only yesterday we found her sitting there in the open air with her whole family and friends. O God, if only the young artists in the house would say just <u>one</u> word, be it as silly as it may! I would prefer that to this dreadful silence about everything in the world. I recently paid one of them a compliment about a picture of his which I had seen at the exhibition in Mannheim, a Saint Cecilia—but all to no avail, he remained dumb and yet is called Brentano.[3] This is usually not a fault for which they are known. Only a few days ago I met Mme Savigny,[4] who overwhelmed me with all conceivable Berlin enthusiasm and Berlin disdain; one thing was divine and another beneath contempt, just too awful etc. etc. Lessing[5] has fallen from his horse and broken his arm, which, as people say, is a great piece of luck, as otherwise he would be dead. He is now working on his painting of Huss before the Council. Have I already told you that Schirmer presented me with such a lovely picture for my wedding?[6] It is quite large and represents Lake Lucerne with its snow peaks at the moment when the moon is rising and the sun has not yet lost its strength, that is the half-light. In the foreground is a large farmhouse with a light inside; it is just so pretty. I know nothing at all of the Woringens and the other Düsseldorfers; do you have anything further? But now farewell, Becky, and write soon. Stay in good health and cheerful; regards to Dirichlet and Walter,[7] and remain ever true to your

 Felix

---

[1] Friedrich Heinke (see p. 89 n. 2). [2] Eduard Souchay, Cécile's uncle (cf. diary entries for 26 and 27 May).

[3] Franz Brentano (1801–41), portrait and religious painter, and a distant relative of the Frankfurt senator of the same name; he was a pupil of Philipp Veit at the Städelsches Kunstinstitut, 1832–6.

[4] Kunigunde (Gunda) von Savigny, née Brentano (1780–1863), wife of Friedrich Karl von Savigny (1779–1861), and sister of Clemens and Bettina Brentano.

[5] Carl Friedrich Lessing (see p. 80 n. 9). The painting on which he was working, *Johann Hus im Verhör zu Konstanz*, was not completed until 1842, and is now in the Städelsches Kunstinstitut, Frankfurt.

[6] See p. 48 n. 3. [7] Walter Dirichlet (1833–87), son of Lejeune and Rebecka.

Felix Mendelssohn Bartholdy to Lea Mendelssohn Bartholdy[1]

Frankfurt, 8 June 1837

Dear Mother,

I am writing to you today to give you a piece of news which I am sure will delight you, because I know how interested you are in everything that concerns my life and my happiness. In the last few days I have experienced the greatest joy that can be granted a man, and if I go on to tell you that it has come about through my dear Cécile, then I need write nothing further as to what this joy consists of; you will know it already. For several weeks I have been hoping to be able to pass on this news to you, which is bound to give you so much happiness as well, but Cécile did not want me to, because she still regarded it as uncertain; but now there appears to be no more doubt about it, and so I hasten to tell you, dear Mother, and to ask you to rejoice with me at the hope which has come to us so quickly and so joyfully. Now may God just grant such health and happiness to my dear Cécile as she has enjoyed up to now, and then all our wishes will be fulfilled, positively all that I could have on earth at all, and there remains only the one—for the continuation of what heaven has sent me, for which I desire to thank him daily and do not know how to begin. I really feel strange when I write this to you, dear Mother, but I would like you to know what a fortunate man you have given life to, and to think of him from time to time. In these moments I also feel like thanking you again afresh for everything and for my life, and that also I do not know how to begin to do. You, nevertheless, understand it well, even if I do not actually say so.

I ask you, dear Mother, to give many many regards to my sisters and to Paul and Albertine, and to tell them the news, and also to say that yesterday I received the three letters from my brother and sisters all at the same time.[2] Now I do not know whether I will be able to answer them in the next few days, and yet there is something in the letters of both sisters which demands a swift answer. Fanny expresses it openly and in Becky's letter too it seems to be there: that they both for some reason or other think or thought me to have altered.

If only it could be stated on this occasion between all of us once and for all (and for all possible future times) that we will never ever change with regard to one another. Fanny says that I need only say that she is mistaken, and she would gladly believe it—but is that then a pleasant feeling for me to have to say in the first place that she is mistaken about something, in which I would have to fail to recognize and scorn myself if she were right? And as for the individual points which she writes about, I want to answer her myself, for none of them is really correct. But today I would just like to beseech you all,

---

[1] NYPL, No. 326.

[2] Letters from Rebecka and Fanny, both dated 2 June, are in the Bodleian Library, GB VI 42 and 43; Paul's letter is not present.

stop believing in changes and all such things which embitter life and make it so petty. Especially right now, when my way of life is becoming more far-flung and diverse; then I feel more than ever the necessity of knowing that my family are really mine and will remain so. Formerly I was able to alter my plans, my travels, and my advance decisions whenever I wanted in order to do whatever I preferred myself or what you wished (and they were almost always the same thing), but now I can't do it any more. And just because of this I would like to beg you, don't believe in any change, don't read between the lines of letters, don't listen to people's talk, but trust that I will love you so all my life, that I am so closely connected with you that I cannot do anything else. As I have said, I will answer the individual points as soon as possible, but today I must tell you that. And now my thanks also to Paul for his kind and excellent letter, which pleased me so much and made me feel good inside. And now farewell, dear Mother. It now seems indeed as if I will have to travel to England alone; the idea has been so painful for me over the past few days; however, Mme Jeanrenaud is so determined about it, and the family doctor is also so insistent (on account of the return journey), that I have now given up hope. I do not have a firm travel plan as yet, but I must probably already be over there within six weeks. Farewell, dear Mother, and write soon

> *Your*
> *Felix*

Felix Mendelssohn Bartholdy to Lea Mendelssohn Bartholdy[1]

Frankfurt, 24 June 1837

Dear Mother,

I have to thank you for your two letters,[2] which are as kind and as delightful as any I have ever received from you. The last one has given us both such pleasure, and your sharing in our happiness has again so moved and pleased me, that no word can express how thankful I am. Every word that you write in this letter makes me glad, and so too the fact that you are able to write to me in such a lively and vivid manner as happens in both letters (this and the delightful long earlier one), for that is the nicest proof of your good health, and of your untroubled, lively soul. You say that you wrote so much for the reason that I had requested it, so now every one of my letters shall begin with the request to

---

[1] NYPL, No. 327.   [2] 7 June, Bodleian Library, GB VI 44, and 12 June, MS MDM c. 34, fo. 58.

write to me at great length and really often, and with thanks for all the goodness and love I have received. My Cécile is most fortunately as sound as a bell and feeling well, although she must now already be in the third month, as the experts put it. How I have to thank God for her good health, for I cannot rid myself of my fear every time she suffers from headache or tiredness and goes to lie down again early in the evening, and if she were to suffer a lot, then it would keep me away from all work and from all other thoughts to which I can now so eagerly give rein. I cannot, however, begin to describe how happy each new day with Cécile makes me, how her lovable character becomes more and more beneficent and delightful for me; there is just something inexhaustible about such genuine spiritual kindness. She now often torments herself that she cannot do any work properly, when she is occasionally so tired out for a whole day, and then she will not realize at all how little that matters now, and then she often becomes quite downcast and depressed about it—but it seems to me to be more of a physical thing, for when she has had a proper sleep again, she is normally as cheerful and youthfully carefree as she always was before, thank God. You know well, how hard and difficult separation from her would be for me, but we have almost resigned ourselves to it, and will thus even in the very first half-year have to be separated from each other for more than a month. You will not believe how strange it is for me, when I reflect on everything, how one thing after the other changes and shifts so, how I first corresponded about it during my engagement, then accepted it especially on account of Cécile, in order to show her England in such an agreeable way, and now in the end I have to go alone. Perhaps the whole story will now change once more, since we learnt today of the King's death, and I think that a big political upheaval will result from that and render the music festival impossible for the time being. I am now very curious as to what the end result will be. Klingemann, to whom I immediately wrote this morning, will now have to leave London, since Cumberland will be a king in his own right with a kingdom of his own.[1] All that is implied in the short telegraphic dispatch, which merely contained the statement about the death of the old king.

You write to me about Fanny's new pieces,[2] saying that I should encourage her and seek out an opportunity for her to have them published. You praise her new compositions, and that is truly not necessary in order to make me look forward to them cordially, and I consider them lovely and excellent, for I know of course from whom they come. Also on this subject, I hope that it is unnecessary to say that, as soon as she decides to publish something, I will create the opportunity for it, so far as I am able, and so will relieve her of all the trouble that can be avoided. But to <u>encourage</u> her to publish something I cannot do, because it is against my opinion and judgement. We have discussed this a great deal previously, and I am still of the same view. I consider publication as a serious matter (it should at least

---

[1] The Duke of Cumberland, Ernest Augustus (1771–1851), fifth son of George III and brother of William IV, became King of Hanover, since only male heirs could succeed to the Hanoverian throne.

[2] In the letter of 7 June.

be that) and believe that one should only do it if one wants to appear and remain as an author through-out life. Consequently this means a series of works, one after the other; from one or two on their own one can only expect trouble with the general public, or it becomes a so-called 'manuscript' for friends, which I also do not like. And for this type of authorship Fanny, as I know her, has neither inclination nor vocation; for that she is too much a woman, as is proper; she brings up Sebastian[1] and cares for the house, and thinks neither of the public nor of the musical world, nor even of music, except when this primary vocation is fulfilled. The start of publication would only upset her in this regard, and I just cannot reconcile myself to that at all. For that reason I cannot encourage her, forgive me. Show these lines, however, neither to Fanny, nor to Hensel, who would take it amiss or otherwise misunderstand me—better to say nothing about it. If Fanny of her own volition, or in order to please Hensel, decides to do it, I am, as stated, willing to help her just as much as I have the power to do so, but to encour-age something that I do not consider right, that I cannot do.

Please write and tell me also whether these big gatherings which Fanny is holding, and the music-making at them are not putting a great strain on her. I myself have always been quite exhausted by them, and as Fanny especially also often suffers from weak nerves, like me, I therefore think that she ought to take great care over the matter. And then will nothing at all persuade her to go to the seaside resort as well? It is such a splendid cure, so definitely invigorating in effect, that I would find it per-fectly delightful if she were to do so, and if I can now separate myself from Cécile so shortly after our wedding, then she, after several years of marriage, can do so from her family for the short time. You say that it is not a necessity, but it would be well worth the sacrifice if it turned out to be good for her and invigorated and restored her. O please persuade her, dear Mother; I myself will also write her a couple of lines and badger her about it.[2]

Cécile's painting of Amalfi was completed right at the beginning of January.[3] She wanted to write to you herself today, but I doubt whether that will happen, considering the great heat, which is having a stupefying effect on everybody. She thinks it is now certainly ready for varnishing.

It is once again quite ridiculous how my 'St Paul' was performed in Berlin, eleven numbers and in such an order.[4] In that case I would only like to hear the performance at Fanny's, and to see my beloved

---

[1] Sebastian Hensel (1830–98), son of Wilhelm and Fanny.   [2] In the end Fanny did not go to the the seaside.

[3] Felix had made a pencil sketch of Amalfi on 31 May 1831 in one of his Italian drawing books (Bodleian Library, MS MDM d. 3, fo. 16), and made a watercolour version of it in Nov. 1836, which is now in Cécile's album, MS MDM c. 21, fo. 123. This album was given to Cécile by Felix as a Christmas present in 1836. Cécile's Amalfi was probably based on one or other of Felix's drawings.

[4] In the Friedrichswerdersche Kirche on 6 June, where the numbers from *St Paul*, with organ and trombone accompaniment, were intermingled with psalmody by Andreas Romberg and others, as described in Lea's letter of 7 June 1837. Fanny's performance was at her Sunday morning concert in the Gartenhaus of Leipzigerstrasse 3 on 25 June (cf. Fanny's letter to Felix, 19 June 1837, Bodleian Library, GB VI 47).

cantor at the piano; that will certainly sound fuller than many of the noted public performances about which the papers write twaddle. Nothing but stuff and nonsense. If one thinks about it seriously, it's bound to make one angry. They will certainly one day perform my 'St Paul' publicly in its entirety, but by then I will already have something else ready, and will no longer be in need of their appreciation and criticism. As to whether 'St Paul' has been given in Boston, Rellstab[1] will know better than I, for here I read neither literary nor musical nor any other journals, and feel all the better for it. They bring nothing but misery anyway. It occurs to me, have you read 'Servitude et grandeur militaire' by Alfred de Vigny?[2] Please do so, if you don't already know it. You won't regret it; it is first-class and quite interestingly modern.

And now farewell, dear Mother; very many regards to Becky and Walter and Dirichlet. When is Becky due?[3] (You see, I am already measuring time.) And do write to me also, if you know when Uncle Joseph is going to travel to the Rhine. But above all write soon and at length, and farewell. Your

> *Felix*

Felix Mendelssohn Bartholdy to Fanny Hensel[4]

> *Frankfurt, 24 June [1837]*
> *on the day when a freemason drowns*
> *after a midsummer night's dream[5]*

Dear Fanny,

Yesterday I received your Prelude No. 6 in B flat major to my Fugue in B flat,[6] for it really is the same inside and out, and delights me by the neat coincidence. Is it not strange that sometimes musical

---

[1] Ludwig Rellstab (1799–1860), German poet, novelist, and journalist. A selection from *St Paul* was performed at the opening of the organ of the Trinity Church, Boston, Mass., on 14 Mar. According to Felix's letter to Lea of 13 Aug. (p. 184), there was also a second performance, which has not been traced.

[2] Alfred de Vigny (1796–1863); *Servitude et grandeur militaire* was published in Paris in 1835.

[3] Rebecka's child, Felix, was born on 10 Oct. 1837, but died 13 months later on 17 Nov. 1838.

[4] Staatsbibliothek zu Berlin, MA Depos. Berlin 3,31.

[5] This is evidently a private family joke. 24 June is of course Midsummer Day.

[6] Felix here means that Fanny's prelude would be a suitable substitute for his own, which precedes the last fugue of the six Preludes and Fugues for piano, Op. 35, a published copy of which he sent to Fanny after 15 May (see p. 156). The resemblances cited by

ideas seem to fly around in the air and come to earth here and there? Thus in this case it is not merely the same figurative movement and structure which astonishes me, but more especially exact minor details which do not appear to be found at all in the theme, i.e. in the notes, and yet are there, i.e. in the mood, and which are consequently repeated so strikingly by both of us. For example this forte in C minor when it appears in octaves in yours and then goes to D flat, and then especially the 'piano' repeat at the end etc. etc. It is all too comical. Besides it is nice that our thoughts remain so close to one another.

Accept my thanks too for all the consideration which you are showing my 'St Paul' in Berlin. It can doubtless do with it there after the selection which was given in the Werdersche Kirche, which Mother wrote to me about. It will sound well in your hands! But just take care not to over-exert yourself; the heavy accompaniment to the choruses especially is a severe strain as I know from experience. And since I am talking about it I will pester you to go to the seaside resort. Mother writes to me that Albertine is going there, and that you did not want to accompany her, as it would mean leaving Hensel, but I certainly think that you should not let such a welcome opportunity for such vigorous treatment pass by. Last year, when there was nothing in particular the matter with me, but when I was nevertheless in need of some real relaxation, then the seaside resort did me a great deal of good. I am convinced that it would now do the same for you—even just the fresh sea breeze and the thorough cooling effect that you feel when you go to the beach, and the general nature of the air there are so beneficial. So you should do it, and if you are reluctant to part from Hensel, then think of me, who must go on his own to England in a few weeks and leave Cécile here, and I am not yet four months married, and still am forced to do it. And merely in order to go to a music festival—a seaside resort is quite another reason. There will be a real hurly-burly at the music festival; it lasts four days, and so far I have to do nothing less than play the organ on the first day, conduct 'St Paul' on the second, play the piano on the third, and finally to play the organ again on the fourth. In addition there is talk of giving my new psalm 'As the hart pants' and my 'Midsummer Night's Dream'. In addition Neukomm is presenting another big new cantata 'The Ascension'. In addition he is planning to have several movements of the Bach Passion sung, for which he, as they say here, has added many trombones. In addition the Italian singers will sing. In addition the whole of 'Messiah'. In addition a symphony and an overture in every concert. Goodness gracious! And it will last until 22 September and on the 30th I have to take a rehearsal in Leipzig, and on 1 October is the first subscription concert. It is no joke. But perhaps the King of England's death

Felix are between the two preludes, not between Fanny's prelude and Felix's fugue, and are indeed remarkable. Fanny's prelude was composed on 28 Mar. 1837, Felix's wedding day, as we know from Lea's letter to Felix of 7 June 1837 (Bodleian Library, GB VI 44), where the resemblance of the preludes is first mentioned. Felix's copy of it is contained in a privately owned volume, but a copyist's manuscript (headed simply 'Andante con espressione') is in the Staatsbibliothek zu Berlin (MA Ms. 44,12, 71–3).

will put a spoke in the wheels of the whole project. It is an unfortunate occurrence for Klingemann right at this moment, when he was just comfortably settled in.[1] *Now there is again a terrible uproar in England.*[2] *What you write about Henselt strikes a sad note—but what I could write about the musicians here would not exactly be any more cheerful—they are a wretched race, full of arrogance, vanity, and a low-spirited fawning nature. Ries is taking over the Cäcilienverein, and is beginning to boast about it, when he was cursing only a fortnight ago. Aloys Schmitt*[3] *has a nasty illness, which he entertains people with who come to see him. Guhr*[4] *is stirring up the whole theatre personnel and considerable hubbub in the newspapers; Hiller is living far out in the country and plans to go off in a few weeks—O what a profession! Liszt is running off with the Comtesse d'Agoult,*[5] *Henselt with Mme Vogel,*[6] *Thalberg with my cousin,*[7] *Meyerbeer from his wife*[8]*—goodness gracious again! What a mess! At Veit's here it would be quite pleasant, if only more people like Aunt Schlegel were there. Mme Zimmermann*[9] *monopolizes the conversation. Such importunate tiresome vulgarity as this person possesses I have not yet encountered. She could drive me out of town with her low-voiced chatter, which continuously digs further below the surface and whines on.*

Moser[10] *was only here for a day, and brought good news. Yet he could not tell me anything new about Hensel's work, since I knew the main things, and there is just so little one can do to describe a picture. I think he missed seeing the miniatures at Brentano's, and I am sorry about that, for they are extremely interesting. I have finished one string quartet and will start again on a new one;*[11] *I am also considering some larger-scale piano pieces.*[12] *The concerto is proving to be a real pain for me; the Andante*

[1] It looked as if Klingemann, as Secretary of the Hanoverian Chancery, would have to leave London, with the separation of the British and Hanoverian thrones, but in the event he continued on in London at the newly created Hanoverian Legation.

[2] If any rumours of disturbances were circulating in Germany they seem to have been unfounded. As Charles Greville noted in his journal on 25 June 1837, 'The Crown has been transferred to the head of the new Queen with a tranquillity which is curious and edifying'.

[3] Aloys Schmitt (1788–1866), pianist, composer, and teacher, settled in Frankfurt from 1829; conductor of the Instrumentalverein.

[4] Karl W. F. Guhr (1787–1848), Kapellmeister of the theatre in Frankfurt from 1821, and composer of opera and church music.

[5] Liszt first met Countess Marie d'Agoult (1805–76) in 1833 and eloped with her to Switzerland in 1835, a relationship which lasted until 1844.

[6] Perhaps the wife of Adolphe Vogel (1808–92), composer and teacher in Paris.   [7] Unidentified.

[8] Giacomo Meyerbeer's frequent periods of separation from his wife Minna, whom he married in 1826, would seem to be due to her poor health; while Meyerbeer at this time was principally occupied with the Paris Opéra, she resided mainly in Baden-Baden. Meyerbeer's published diaries and letters give no hint of marital problems.

[9] Johanna (Johanne) Zimmermann, widow of the Berlin painter and lithographer Carl Ferdinand Zimmermann (1796–1820). She taught the piano and singing; the novelist Paul Heyse was one of her pupils.

[10] Julius Moser (b. *c.*1808), historical and genre painter. He became a pupil of Wilhelm Hensel in 1831.

[11] See p. 140 n. 1.

[12] The autograph of the Capriccio in E major, published posthumously as Op. 118 in 1874, is dated Bingen, 11 July 1837. Perhaps the Allegro in E minor, Op. 117, also dates from this summer (see p. 184 n. 2).

and last movement are, it is true, almost finished, but the first movement still torments me, because it has to be brilliant, and you know!!

But enough for now; Cécile is sitting next to me, suffering like me from the heat, but is otherwise well and sends all her love and regards to you. Very many regards to Paul and Albertine from us, and farewell. Write soon and at length, kiss Sebastian for me, and regards to Hensel.

> *Your*
>> *Felix*

Cécile Mendelssohn Bartholdy to Lea Mendelssohn Bartholdy[1]

Frankfurt, 25 June [1837]

Dear Mother,

Yesterday Felix quite mercilessly finished off his letters without wanting to wait for my scribble. Admittedly I could not tell you anything new after he had written you a large sheet full, but I too wanted to thank you very much for your sincere interest in our good fortune and for the kind letters which you have written us. So then I am doing it today, although you will perhaps be surprised at hearing from us so often. Felix is sitting by me and painting—a landscape of Lake Como,[2] which he had previously sketched there—and doing it so beautifully that I cannot refrain from watching him and continuously admiring him. He really is able to do anything he sets his mind to, and he has you to thank for all these many talents. Recently he read to us a story by Hoffmann,[3] where the subject is the imprints which children receive from their mother before they are born, and which have an influence on their whole life. This gives me the idea of asking you for the name of the good witch with whom you were in contact before Felix was born, so that I can also consult her, for in truth it often appears to me unnatural how everything flows from his hand; it is at least so very different from my own character. I really now do nothing at all in the world apart from live, eat, drink, go for walks, sleep and wake up again to renewed almost

---

[1] NYPL, No. 328.   [2] The view of Cadenabbia referred to in the diary entry for 23 June (see p. 56 n. 2).

[3] 'Das Fräulein von Scuderi' (cf. p. 44 n. 2), where the murderous goldsmith blames his propensities on an incident during his mother's pregnancy.

animal-like life. And if I begin to occupy myself at some point, to write, draw, or do something else, then I can be certain that within half an hour Mother or Felix will come to me and admonish me about the great exertion of far too much stooping and constant sitting!!

I do not like to say or write anything more at all about the journey to England, for it seems that a special will-o'-the-wisp governs that, and propels one's own opinion now in one direction, now in another. Since your last letter, when you too advised me to remain here, I had submitted most gracefully to the necessity, and had also spoken very little of this sad separation; and just now the king has to go and die and the whole music festival be put in doubt. I think that Felix will soon receive answers to the letters which he immediately wrote to Birmingham following the news, which will then put me back into my former state of resignation, or will give me the joyful hope that we will not be separated within the first six months of our marriage. There is an unbearable amount of building and repair work going on in our house at present; unpleasant dust and dirt is to be found everywhere, so that we will probably shortly all go together for a couple of days into the country or to the nearby spas. Grandmother, who after all has organized everything, now moans terribly about it, and more generally over the great trouble of having one's own house, about which Felix says that you would certainly agree with her. Yesterday, however, during a walk, he told Julie and me so much of the great attractions of your house and garden that I think of it as a heavenly abode. There is only enough space left for me to send you warm greetings from Mother and my family, and to beg for the continuance of your love.

Your Cécile

———

Felix Mendelssohn Bartholdy to Lea Mendelssohn Bartholdy[1]

Bingen, 13 July 1837

Dear Mother,

We have been here for a week, having suddenly set forth from Frankfurt, and as it is now fairly certain that we shall stay here for the next few weeks, I want to write and thank you for your kind, kind

[1] NYPL, No. 329.

letters,[1] and to beg once again for many more long ones. So here we are, and by we I mean my wife, her mother (who sends you the enclosed letter), and Julie. In Frankfurt they were pulling down the whole house about our ears, the dust was enough to kill us, the weather glorious, and so a fortnight ago we went off lock, stock, and barrel into the Taunus hills to Homburg, where we intended to stay— but it was no good staying there, what with a poor inn, unfriendly people, and unpleasant Frankfurt company—in short we drove back to Frankfurt the same evening and stayed in the dust—until I suggested Bingen, whither then once again lock, stock, and barrel a pilgrimage was made. Here things are now better; the view from the windows alone is worth the journey, for our inn lies on the Rhine, facing the Niederwald, to the left the Mäuseturm, to the right the Johannisberg. Today I have finally even obtained the loan of a piano and a bible; both were hard to come by, in the first place because in Bingen they are unmusical and then because they are Catholic, and want nothing to do with pianos and the Luther translation; nevertheless I have procured them in the end, and am now beginning to be very comfortable here. I must work hard, for not a single note of my concerto is yet written down, and yesterday I had news from Birmingham that the music festival will definitely take place, and that they even entertain the hope of seeing Queen Victoria there—that would provide enough good cheer. I will thus go to London in the middle of August, and stay with Klingemann. Apropos the lottery ticket,[2] I will give him your instruction in person if it will then still be in time; I cannot, however, do it in writing because I have recently written to him at length and will doubtless now not do so again before my arrival. I will not have a chance to meet Moscheles, since he is travelling to Hamburg with his family at the beginning of August. I am very sorry to have to miss him; I have always enjoyed myself when I met him again from time to time. Recently old Schadow together with W. Schadow, and both accompanied by their families, were here, and we came across one another in the entrance hall. I wished you had heard the description which the old man gave of Fanny when she accompanied Mme Decker[3] on the piano— he became all full of enthusiasm and tremendously heated about it. And a description of the sessions of the musical section of the Academy,[4] where he has to preside, made a very fitting companion-piece. Apart from Spontini no one speaks or shows any sign of life at it—and that is just and fitting too. But really it is quite serious how Spontini rouses everyone in Berlin against him, debases everything and ruins everything, and yet himself receives only irritation, trouble, and distress from it—as in a bad

[1] Letters of 26 and 29 June, Bodleian Library, GB VI 52 and 53.

[2] Lea had told Felix that she had written twice to Klingemann wanting to know whether he wanted tickets for the current Berlin lottery, but had received no reply (letter of 29 June).

[3] Pauline von Decker, née Schätzel (1812–82), German soprano. After a successful youthful four-year Berlin operatic career up to 1832, she then limited herself to concert appearances.

[4] The Akademie der Künste in Berlin.

marriage, in which both parties are in the wrong when they fight each other. Apropos of which, is Mme Zimmermann in Berlin? She left Frankfurt in despair, would not tell anyone where she was going, and Aunt Schlegel seemed to be greatly distressed about that. Ask Fanny, dear Mother, what she would say if I were to play in Birmingham the Bach organ Prelude in E flat major and the Fugue which is found at the end of the same volume.[1] I think they will grumble at me, but I think I would be right all the same. The prelude especially should be very accessible to the English, I would think, and both in the prelude and in the fugue one can show off the piano, pianissimo, and the whole range of the organ—and it is not a dull piece either in my view! Mme Jeanrenaud is just bringing some fine cotton, because the three ladies decided today at breakfast that I had to have stockings knitted for me—I have a host of woollen ones which I cannot now wear—and so four new pairs are due to be laid at my feet within three days. Music, the Rheingau, gossip, and stockings walk hand in hand in this letter—forgive me, dear Mother—but that is how it is in reality, where everything happens here in a crazy manner. Ask Becky if you will, whether she would like to write to me again soon; I do not quite know whether it is _my_ turn, but things have been going rather topsy-turvy recently, and the letters to you are also certainly intended for my sisters; I hope she will fulfil my wish and write again. I have recently made a firm decision to have a new oratorio ready for the next Düsseldorf music festival—true it is still two years away, but I must keep going on it. I will write about the text as soon as I have a definite one. I have not heard anything from Holtei;[2] in his present entangled position as Director perhaps he too cannot manage it. The text would probably be slipshod, if done at all—and so I must start on the second oratorio, even though I would have so much liked to have had an opera just now. I am lacking an ideal person for many fine ventures; whether he will yet appear or whether I am on the wrong track I do not know, but thus far he cannot be found, and so I must stay quiet and wait.

I am practising my figure-drawing here constantly, but real success eludes me; through lack of practice during the winter I have forgotten what I could do better last summer. All the same yesterday I drew Bishop Hatto as he is about to be eaten by the mice—a splendid subject for all modern painters. In the coming days we will perhaps go and pay Uncle Joseph a visit. Our daily routine goes like this: in the morning everyone does their own work until one o'clock, then we eat at the table d'hôte with unspeakable Philistines, then do some drawing, then a little more work, then a couple of hours going for a walk or sailing on the Rhine; in the evening I read to the ladies, which gives me great pleasure.

---

[1] BWV 552 in Part 3 of the _Clavierübung_.
[2] Karl von Holtei (1797–1880), German dramatist, noted for his light comedies. In 1837 he left Berlin to become theatre director in Riga.

And now I must close this disorganized concoction of a letter; excuse it, dear Mother, and please, please write soon.

Kindest regards and kisses from Cécile for you and my sisters. Farewell to all and remain true to me.

> *Your*
>> *Felix*

Address letters just to poste restante here at Bingen a/R.

――――

Felix Mendelssohn Bartholdy to Lea Mendelssohn Bartholdy[1]

Bingen a/R, 22 July 1837

Dear Mother,

Your letter, just received, and that of my sisters[2] have so delighted us that they must immediately be answered and thanks rendered for them. Cécile wants to write to Becky, and I am writing this family letter to you all. This here is indeed the well-known inn with the two pavilions and the garden by the Rhine in which Fanny and Paul have slept—the Weisses Ross of Soherr's, celebrated in the whole neighbourhood. It is also not possible to stop saying how beautiful it is here. For the past week we have had unsettled weather and even that has its peculiar attraction, since the clouds come here so thick and grey from behind the hills above the Bingerloch and only decide when they are quite near whether they will advance over the Niederwald—then it rains here—or up over the Nahe towards Kreuznach and the Donnersberg—then it stays dry here, but looks quite dreadfully evil and gloomy. The Wisper wind, which comes from Lorch out of the Wispertal, brings fine weather with it, but hasn't blown now for a long time. Yesterday evening I walked up into the Niederwald again for the first time;[3] the weather was too damp and uncertain for the ladies. I first came to the forester's house and shouted 'tuba' on the rock where the echo is, and as previously with Father, the echo answered back quite merrily five or six times. I also very much wanted to see the visitors' book on the Rossel in which Father had written all our names on 24 August, but it was no longer anywhere to be found. On my return in the evening I found

---

[1] NYPL, No. 330.   [2] Lea's letter of 17 July (Bodleian Library, GB VI 57) and Fanny and Rebecka's of *c.* 10 July (GB VI 56).

[3] i.e. since the Mendelssohn family visit in 1820 (see p. 71 n. 3).

a crazy old Englishman who has come from Italy, and who kept on repeating that he had heard my "divine opera" 'St Paul' in Düsseldorf, and that I should just beware of the theatres in England where they wanted to perform 'St Paul', and I should assert "my dignity" and ensure I was very well paid— and that I should drink a "glass of wine" with him in the garden. And in the evening of the day before yesterday Mme Greis from Cologne[1] with her sister were suddenly sitting there. They told us every conceivable thing about our friends in Cologne and that they had entered into a sort of correspondence with you and Fanny. They drove back to Kreuznach and are returning shortly; and thus almost every day brings new faces or old acquaintances as you, dear Mother, rightly suspected. Over in Rüdesheim lives the painter Grabau, brother of our singer, who was the mainstay of the basses in the Singverein at Düsseldorf, and often rescued me from embarrassments during those two years of combative memories. I mulled over the old times with him, and that is a double joy when the present is as wonderful as now. Cécile is just sitting and drawing the view from the window for Becky; she is, thank God, well and cheerful, and lovely enough to eat. Recently she has drawn a large ball in Kreuznach for our diary quite delightfully. The men, who are dancing in frock-coats, and the women, who are doing leap-frogs, and the whole colourful crowd she has captured admirably; it looks just too comical. We are thinking of staying here until the beginning of next month, during which time I want to finish off my piano concerto (see below); then go for a few days to Koblenz, Cologne, and Düsseldorf, and from there I will go on alone about 20 August via Rotterdam to London, while the ladies travel back to Frankfurt in my beloved brown and blue carriage. Were it not for the rushed return journey, Cécile would still have been able to travel with me, but that is the decisive factor, and so I will pick her up again in Frankfurt, and reckon to do the journey there from Birmingham in four days, God willing. If only this awful business were over and I were back together with Cécile; 'there is no getting out of it' as they say in Hanau,[2] if I have to gad about there on my own; you can imagine how I sometimes curse.

And yet everything in the world is so good and fair, and it is unthinkable that I should not be simply full of happiness. My new works, which I played through to myself yesterday and the day before on a wicked piano, please me exceedingly; I only hope that they will please the others too and I should have liked to have played them to you, dear Fanny. The Psalm which you ask me about is for five-part choir and full orchestra:[3] No. 1, a chorus in F major (v. 2 'Like as the hart' etc.); No. 2, a soprano aria in D minor (v. 3); No. 3, a quintet in B flat major for 4 men's voices and soprano (vv. 9 and 10), and

---

[1] Evidently on their way to Bad Kreuznach (see diary entry for 28 July).

[2] Possibly a saying of Cécile's great aunt Wilhelmine Schlemmer, who lived in Hanau.

[3] Psalm 42, Op. 42, begun in April 1837 (see p. 148 n. 2). In the final version, which was completed about the end of the year, Mendelssohn added a further three movements between the existing second and third ones, thus incorporating virtually the whole of the psalm text. He also revised the other movements, including reducing the chorus of the first movement from five to four parts. See

No. 4, final chorus in F major (v. 12). The first chorus and the quintet would certainly please you, that I know, and so I hope also would at least the Scherzo and last movement of my new string quartet in E minor.[1] The concerto, which you ask about, will be nothing very special as a composition, but the last movement creates so much effect as a piece of pianistic pyrotechnics that I often have to laugh when I happen to play it properly. There will be once again three connected movements, the first in D minor, an Adagio in G major, and the last in D major. I also have a new string quartet and a new psalm almost completely in my head, and moreover intend to finish them in part here.[2] Next winter I want to follow your example and also have Sunday morning music-making, and to compose various trios and suchlike things for it. I only have a real desire to do so when it is for a specific occasion and I have to have it ready; then one thing leads to another.

Enclosed is a letter of reminder to Holtei, which I beg you, dear Mother, to convey to him; may it bring about the desired result and the longed-for text, but by now I rather doubt it. Today I am send-ing Rosa Woringen[3] the third book of Lieder ohne Worte which I have dedicated to her; will it still find her in Düsseldorf? O Becky, what have I done that you mutter away that I disregard your recommen-dations? As a punishment I now propose straight away to visit the Ahrtal on the way to Cologne,[4] and to find it quite awful, and if, however, it then turns out to be beautiful, then I will insist I am right all the more resolutely. Seriously now, I will do it, and seriously I would give anything if we could change places for just a day, let alone have you here with us. When then is the mouse coming, of which you write?[5] Let me know, I have already asked several times. Certainly at present it may often be unpleas-ant in the sand,[6] especially when more of such products of genius like the new Hanoverian decree[7] come to light. I can imagine how the whole of Berlin is exhausting itself in talk about it, and it is indeed truly vexing enough. And yet it is not at all bad at Leipziger Strasse No. 3, and I wished often enough that I were there as a fellow grumbler.

Now farewell, farewell dear Mother. If you write again soon then I would still receive the letter here poste restante; from 10 to 20 August please address things to Düsseldorf poste restante, then to London

D. Seaton, *A Study of a Collection of Mendelssohn's Sketches* (diss. Columbia Univ., 1977), 136–9. In the Luther translation of the Psalms (unlike the English and Latin versions) the preliminary description of the psalm is numbered as verse 1, so that the actual text of the psalm begins at verse 2.

[1] Op. 44 No. 2.
[2] The string quartet was Op. 44 No. 3 in E flat (see p. 140 n. 1). The new psalm was 'Laudate pueri' (see p. 184 n. 1).
[3] Daughter of Otto von Woringen.   [4] See p. 76 n. 5.
[5] 'The mouse' is the baby Rebecka was expecting (see p. 168 n. 3). In her letter to Felix and Cécile of *c.*10 July 1837 (Bodleian Library, GB VI 56) she remarked, 'Compared with me my outer covering is only a strip, so that I am curious as to whether this moun-tain will give birth to only *one* mouse'.
[6] A reference to Berlin; Felix always says that the sand around Berlin is to blame for the dryness of its people.
[7] In announcing his accession by letters patent on 5 July, the new King of Hanover, the conservatively minded Ernest Augustus, declared his intention of suspending the recent more liberal constitution of 1833.

at Klingemann, No. 4, Hobart Place, Eaton Square, Pimlico. And if in the meantime a couple of lines were to go to Uncle, then I will call for them too in Horchheim. And now farewell and kind regards to Paul if he is back from the sea, and to Dirichlet, Hensel, Sebastian, and Walter.

Your

Felix

On account of today's beautiful weather Cécile's letter will not be finished until tomorrow, and she therefore begs your pardon, dear Becky.

———

Cécile and Felix Mendelssohn Bartholdy to Fanny Hensel[1]

Bingen, 24 [July 1837]

Dear Fanny,

Many thanks for both your lovely letters[2] and for the sympathy which you showed towards me in the first, and which I hope you are reserving for the time when I will have real need of it, which is slowly approaching. Have you ever been separated from your husband? It seems intolerable to me and my heart always sinks into my boots when I think of the moment. But no more of that—for the time being things with us still look rose-coloured, like the piece of paper which I have taken to tell you about our pleasant life.

So you know the house with the beautiful view and the little garden by the Rhine, and the two pavilions inscribed with names and bits of verse, and will doubtless be so good as to render some sense to my poor drawing for Becky. But do you also know just what a delight it is to sail on the great Rhine in a little boat, past the Binger Loch and all the whirlpools by the rocks, and to look down into the depths without sighting the bottom, and to dabble one's hands in the cool water, and what is for me that greatest of delights, the splashing of oars, the rocking to and fro and bobbing of the boat?—Felix very often gives me this pleasure. Soon we are to sail to Assmannshausen, then walk up the hill behind the village, until I can go no further, and do some drawing at a nice shady spot where the poor folk bring us marvellous strawberries and

---

[1] Staatsbibliothek zu Berlin, MA Ep. 110.

[2] Fanny's letter of 10 July to Cécile, sent together with a slightly later undated joint letter of Fanny and Rebecka to Felix and Cécile (Bodleian Library, GB VI 56).

raspberries. For I get no true enjoyment without eating; I, who formerly was always laughed at and plied with food on account of my sparrow-like appetite, I now stuff myself (forgive the expression) like a werewolf. Our most frequent excursion is to sail up the Rhine to Rüdesheim, from where the loveliest walks can be undertaken. Only yesterday we were up at the Eibingen convent, which lies on a hill just above Rüdesheim, and I cannot describe to you how beautiful it was there. On the way back, however, we encountered many drunks (blessed consequence of it being Sunday), whom Felix introduced into his drawing of the convent, and for whose completion I just now have to sit or rather lie when I am not writing. In Rüdesheim, where we drank tea, we spoke again with the painter Grabau, who, however, feels very bored in such a small place, especially in winter. It also seems to me that this is not at all suitable country for a painter of livestock, for one sees hardly any or only very unattractive animals. He told me recently to my surprise that there was to be an art exhibition in Leipzig in the autumn. I cannot tell you how that pleases me, for in Leipzig there is almost no one who, when it comes to music, does not put in his twopenn'orth, but nothing at all is said about painting, and no one knows anything about it, and one cannot think of a beautiful picture in the whole of Leipzig. But I have hardly enough room to say adieu to you, and am using it to complain about the Leipzigers. I ask you to give many and the kindest of regards, dear Fanny, to the whole family, many kisses to the dear children, and I ask this sheet of paper to tell you how much I love you. Your devoted Cécile.

Do you yet know my 3-part album canon,[1] dear Fanny? I have requested room to set it down for you.

Canone a 3

There is still some room. Do you know the 2-part one?

Can. a 2

If you don't know it, then try to solve it. It is difficult. Don't forget to admire the most wretched melody which the latter contains: that is true erudition.

[1] This canon is first found written down for Carl Kunzel, on 16 Dec. 1835; it became a favourite one for Mendelssohn to write in albums (cf. *The Letters of Fanny Hensel*, ed. M. Citron (Stuyvesant, NY, 1987), 243). No earlier source of the second canon is known.

Adieu. I have to portray a drunk lying in the ditch. That too is difficult. Our departure from here for Koblenz is fixed for 2 August. Please write to us there. Tell Mother also how very much I would like her to do so; regards to your family.

Your F.

Cécile and Felix Mendelssohn Bartholdy to Rebecka Dirichlet[1]

Bingen, 24 July [1837]

Dear Becky,

   I have doodled away at the simple drawing for so long that my letter has to wing its way to you two days later than that of Felix to Mother, in which company and protection it should have

---

[1] NYPL, No. 331. Below the verso of the drawing Felix wrote "Cécile wants to write over the drawing—but I yell out and absolutely forbid it".

travelled, for my letters are in great need of it; they are unworthy, artless creatures. And now I do not yet even know whether you will be able to find your way through this muddle of undergrowth and huts, and whether it can be understood if you are not actually standing at our window and comparing the scene. But you have of course already been to the beautiful Rhine several times and the setting of Bingen will certainly be present in your memory. If you therefore imagine behind the house the Mäuseturm, Felix's favourite spot, round the corner of the hills Schloss Rheinstein, above the ship the Niederwald and the Rossel (which I have not yet reached), further below the ruin of Ehrenfels and still lower in the garden pavilion, Felix, Mother, Julie, and myself, sitting together, then your memory will not often lead you astray.

Ponder also—this will be easy for you—on the joy of the newly married state, on little dreams of motherhood which one really should not yet indulge in, but yet so readily does, and you will soon imagine and sympathize with our blissful state here. O, how I would so like to have you here, so like to be able to see you, but what use is it lamenting; I will look forward to next winter when one day you will visit me in my immobility together with what will certainly be your delightful little child. Apropos the beauty of those to come, I am of the opinion that mine will suffer greatly through our stay here, for I see every day at the table d'hôte such exceedingly ugly people, such peculiar faces, that I am really afraid of looking at them. So afterwards I gaze all the longer at Felix's black eyes, and if it does not catch them, I will no longer pay any attention to predictions or the lack of them, none at all. There I am again in the middle of my favourite theme, and absorbed, like Felix in his music there in front of me. He sits facing me trilling with his fingers, writing, singing, blowing the trumpet and flute, all at the same time; then he walks up and down in the room again with his sheet of music, beating time or playing the double bass with his arm; his piano concerto is costing him all this exertion, but it will also certainly turn out to be very beautiful.

In recent days it has been dreadfully windy here; has it been the same with you, or does it just get particularly caught up in the mountains? The steamship has just sailed past and the smoke was driven right onto the deck and did not even spare the King of Württemberg,[1] who to Felix's annoyance, was on board. He still rails against kings, and not even ten horses could have dragged him to the quay today, where we very often observe the unloading of the ship, taking the greatest pleasure over the tall Englishmen which it disgorges. Our inn is the meeting place of all nations, and sometimes, especially on Sundays, all too lively; we will soon leave it and go down the Rhine; then there are only another three weeks until Felix's departure. O Becky,

---

[1] Wilhelm I (1781–1864), who succeeded to the throne in 1816.

weep greatly for me then! Beg Fanny's pardon that I have left her kind letter unanswered for so long. I would write to her today, but Felix is pestering me to stop, because we still intend to go for an excursion on the water and are already overdue. So farewell, dear Sister, regards to all, especially Mother, and love me

Your Cécile

And since the aforementioned great wind is blowing worse and worse, the water trip (to the Morgenbach) has had to be cancelled, not the letter to Fanny. Today was yet another nice day, dear Becky, and since I should describe it in order that you can share the enjoyment, so you should know that I got up very early today, and first went across the Rhine in a small boat to a small rocky island upon which a crazy Hofrat from Frankfurt had his brain and his heart buried (the stomach according to his will was buried on the Johannisberg;[1]) then I sailed to my highly revered Mäuseturm, where there is a splendid bathing place, and bathed* (*Note to reassure Mother: I should mention that the water there only reaches up as far as my chest and that I am very lazy in my swimming this summer, and only let the water splash me). Thereupon I went up between the vineyards to the ruin of Ehrenfels, about which it is possible to compose several symphonies, and of which Lessing has painted a whole host of pictures—then I came home again and woke Cécile. Then we had breakfast. There appeared a large Bingen cherry cake (regarded as classic amongst the connoisseurs), and a beautiful bunch of flowers bearing elegant verses within, because today is the anniversary of our famous window drawings in Frankfurt;[2] then I finished a considerable piece of the piano concerto; but in order for things not to turn out overly well, our outing to the Morgenbach, which we now wanted to start at five was blown away. Out of spite we are now going for a walk on the Ingelheim road, which is also not at all bad—really life here would be too good and happy, if one felt the wish to be totally thankful every single day. Have you or Dirichlet ever been to the Eibingen convent just above Rüdesheim? Do you know the priest there? Yesterday he spent the whole evening playing the violin, improvised from A flat to A major not at all badly, and we stood on the road and listened as the old priest strolled up and down on his violin. Then up came three drunkards one after another, who made Cécile feel scared; the third tried to take his hat

[1] Johann Nikolaus Vogt (1756–1836), historian and Frankfurt politician. He had close connections with figures of the German Romantic movement, especially Clemens Brentano, and published a collection of *Rheinische Gedichte und Sagen* (Frankfurt, 1817–36). Prince Lothar von Metternich (see p. 70 n. 5) was a friend and former pupil, and Vogt spent much time at Schloss Johannisberg, where his body is buried next to the entrance to the Schlosskirche. His brain and heart were buried on the Mühlstein, part of a reef in the Binger Loch near the ruin of Schloss Ehrenfels, because, according to his will, 'I have passed the best time of my life in these glorious and beautiful surroundings'. An iron cross still marks the spot.

[2] Felix's drawing of the view from the window of the Souchay/Jeanrenaud house, done on 24 July 1836, is in Bodleian Library, MS MDM d. 11, fo. 2 (see Pl. 3). No drawing by Cécile appears to have survived.

off, but from the exertion of it fell over the ditch into the vineyard and knocked down a whole vine trellis. I had sketched the convent, and now yesterday evening I went to the trouble of drawing in the three drunkards as background figures. You can imagine how the one in the ditch looks—as if <u>he</u> were smashed, not the trellis. In this you will recognize me. I really wished that you knew Cécile, who is sitting opposite me; I would give a lot for that. God willing it will happen soon. Regards to your husband and to my friend Walter. Remain true to me, dear Becky. F.

Cécile and Felix Mendelssohn Bartholdy to Lea Mendelssohn Bartholdy[1]

Koblenz, [13 August 1837]

Dear Mother,

So far we have travelled in very good spirits and good health on our excellent and comfortable journey, taking time everywhere to see all that is beautiful; we spent two days over the journey from Bingen to Koblenz, when the steamship covers the whole stretch in a few hours. It would have been a thousand pities had we too, as we had half a mind to do, viewed the Rhine in this speedy way, since my sister and I are admiring it for the first time with proper appreciation, and I cannot remember passing such enjoyable days as these two in respect of our surroundings for a long time. Felix did a lot of drawing in Bacharach, where we stopped at midday, and in St Goar, where we spent the night. I am far too idle for it, for until I have dragged myself to a very beautiful spot, I am really so tired that the first tree trunk or stone or even the bare ground has to serve me as a seat, from which no one can get me off until it is time to leave. In Horchheim Felix found letters from his sisters and from you, dear Mother,[2] which gave us great pleasure. Now you also will have nothing more to complain about concerning loneliness, for it is certain *that you have plenty of visitors, just as we do, who call Cécile away from writing, and create the time for me to do so instead. The day after tomorrow we will move on, and, what is more via*

---

[1] NYPL, No. 336.

[2] Lea's letter of 29 July (Bodleian Library, GB VI 58), Rebecka's of 30 July (GB VI 59), and Fanny's of 31 July (GB VI 60).

the Ahrtal to Bonn and Cologne. All the Horchheimers have promised to accompany us for the first two days of travelling (perhaps the first three), so that we can celebrate Uncle's birthday, the 15th, together in Bonn or somewhere along the Ahr. I have never seen Uncle looking healthier, more cheerful, and more amiable than this time; we meet daily, and visit the nearby and more distant environs of Horchheim; it appears as if my ladies have taken a real delight in the Horchheimers and vice versa. In addition I have completely finished my concerto, as well as a little piece of convent music to go with the two others, so that they can be published,[1] and begun a new piano piece,[2] and now I will soon have to bite into the sour English apple. If Cécile were able to travel with me, then there would be no sweeter one. For I have yet to tell you, dear Mother, that my English publisher passed through Bingen,[3] spent a funny evening with us, but brought along the most agreeable news; it appears that as a result of 'St Paul' my music has got into its stride again there just as much as it ever was at the time of my personal presence. They sing arias from the oratorio at concerts, including St Paul's arias in B minor and B flat major at the Philharmonic,[4] likewise the overture. I was also correctly informed about the performance in Boston; they even performed it twice there, and before my departure for Birmingham I will probably conduct it in London on 12 September, at which my "Englishman" predicts there would be a vast number of listeners, and that would be doubly agreeable, as it could be looked upon as a rehearsal for the music festival, since most of the same orchestral players would be taking part. It is the same society at Exeter Hall which performed it last winter that now wants to do it for me in London. All's fish that comes into my net, but September is already approaching so fast, that I often think of Leipzig, the start of the concert season, and above all of my moving in with Cécile there, and look forward to that more than anything else. Then we will also be nearer to each other again, and I hope that the winter will not pass without us all having seen one another. Much still has to happen before then, but, God willing, it will surely come about, and how I look forward to all this and how thankful I am for all the good fortune that has come my way in this delightful year.

And now it is my turn again and I notice that Felix has not thought to leave me much more room. I would have told you so much, about Horchheim and how greatly I liked it there, and

---

[1] 'Laudate pueri', Op. 39 No. 2, manuscript dated 14 Aug. 1837 (Paris, Bibliothèque Nationale, Conservatoire MS 196). The two others were composed in Italy in Dec. 1830, and the three pieces were published as *Drei Motetten für weibliche Stimmen mit Begleitung der Orgel*, Op. 39 (Bonn, Simrock, [1838]).

[2] Perhaps the Allegro in E minor, first published as *Albumblatt* (London, 1859), and subsequently as Op. 117.

[3] Joseph Alfred Novello.

[4] The B flat aria is 'Jerusalem'; the B minor aria, 'O God have mercy'. Only the latter, however, seems to have been given at the Philharmonic Society's concerts in 1837, on 13 Mar.

how all my new relatives, whom I became acquainted with there, are so friendly and amiable towards me and my family, and how we enjoyed ourselves together, using all the even partly fine days for excursions into the glorious neighbourhood. Above all, however, I wanted to send you a long petition, dear Mother, that during my grass-widowhood you should not completely forget me, and should not deprive me of the pleasure of reading your kind letters, which hitherto I have always enjoyed with Felix. In return I wanted to make the solemn promise to send you Felix's letters from England, and when they are too voluminous, to copy out the most important parts for you in the most punctual and accurate manner, so that you should never lack news. But dear Mother, I beg you very very dearly, let me also hear something from you from time to time. And now I must finish; Felix is waiting to take the letter to the post office; in a moment he will appear on the bridge of boats with Benny's white horse beneath him. So farewell, dear Mother; we send our regards together for the last time, and in a few days think of me as—for a short time—a deserted wife. Kindest regards to all

    Your
        Cécile

Cécile and Felix Mendelssohn Bartholdy to Lea Mendelssohn Bartholdy[1]

Düsseldorf, 24 August [1837]

Dear Mother,

I an writing these few lines to you in the middle of the dual packing and all the visits made to us out of both friendship and courtesy, partly from yearning for news of you, which we have missed for a long time, and partly to say many thanks to Hensel on Felix's behalf for the beautiful leaf in the édition de luxe of 'St Paul'. He would have liked to have done so himself, for the beautiful drawings give him immense pleasure, but the poor fellow is so overwhelmed with acquaintances, shopping, and tasks which really must be finished before the English journey,

[1] NYPL, No. 332.

that I myself have seen him and spoken to him very little these past few days, which by the way is a good thing!

Here next to me is the beautiful book which Herr Rietz handed over within the very first hour with a most flattering epistle. It is very beautifully and elegantly bound, and very nicely printed on large vellum paper. First comes a delightful title-page by the painter Schrötter [Schrödter], representing the muse of Music, just as she is adding Felix's name to other praiseworthy company on a palm-leaf. The palm tree ends in wonderful arabesques, amongst which are the most amusing bits of nonsense, kettledrummers who beat out with their hands and feet, ludicrous double-bass players and the like. Then follow in the appropriate places two drawings by Hübner—Stephen beholding the heavens open, and a weeping figure at the aria 'Jerusalem', which I find quite enchanting. After that a drawing by Mücke[1]—the stoning I believe—and then Paul on the road to Damascus by Steinbrück, most splendidly and, in my opinion, beautifully painted. The volume concludes with Paul and Ananias by a young painter here whom Felix doesn't know, an empty leaf for Bendemann, and my brother-in-law's lovely picture, for the sight of which I too must say thank you. Once we are in Leipzig the whole thing will have to be sent to you; it will certainly please you.

In the meantime we are receiving worrying news here from Berlin about the cholera. Herr Fränkel, whom we met here, is travelling there with all haste, Herr von Woringen confirmed the news, and we have had no letters from you for a long time. Felix, although without fear for his dear ones, greatly hankers after an indication of your good health; O please, dear Mother, let us hear something from you soon. Write first, however, to Felix in England, because the letter otherwise could be delayed by my return journey, and I would very much like him to be reassured about us all in England, where he has to lead such a busy, turbulent life. He sails on the steamship at ten o'clock tomorrow. I won't tell you anything at all about our stay here, reckoning on the eloquence of Herr von Woringen, who is coming straight to you next Saturday. We have spent lovely days here. I will just send you all my kindest regards and will write in greater detail when I receive Felix's first letter. I am, thank God, as well as one can possibly be, and your faithful daughter

    Cécile

---

[1] Heinrich Karl Anton Mücke (1806–91), historical painter. Pupil of Schadow in Berlin from 1824, he followed him to Düsseldorf in 1826.

Dear, dear Mother,

Tomorrow I must set off, and can only write a few words. We have had no news of you here, although we wrote from Koblenz, and there is said to be cholera in Berlin—so I doubly beg you, write soon and reassure me. Address it to Klingemann in London, and do let me hear from home at least once a week.

Are my sisters well? What is Becky up to?

I wanted, dear Hensel, to write you a letter of my own in order to thank you for the wonderful drawing with which you have adorned my score. You have succeeded quite magnificently, and I wanted to write in detail about where all my favourite figures in the fine composition are, and my favourite bits; or really I should have been able to do it in person. Now there remains only a moment to send you most heartfelt thanks. Accept them, nevertheless, cordially.

━━━━━━

Felix Mendelssohn Bartholdy to Lea Mendelssohn Bartholdy[1]

London, 4 Hobart Place, Pimlico
29 August 1837

Dear Mother,

I am writing to announce my safe arrival here, but at the same time to say how very sorry I am, and how it now also begins to worry me, that I have had no news of you for so long. Since I found no letter in Düsseldorf, I was hoping for one here but have been disappointed again, and today your last letter is a month old. Please tell me what is happening—old Woringen[2] had written to Düsseldorf, and according to that everything seemed to be well and lively, nevertheless I am now becoming alarmed once more. Is it true about the cholera? And how is Becky? I arrived here the day before yesterday in the afternoon after a dreadful sea crossing, 30 hours from Rotterdam to the Custom House. Klingemann came up to the steamship on a small boat; I had to manage completely without my things until yesterday, because it was Sunday; however, I wrapped myself up in my "gentlemantality" which had to radiate out of my shabby clothes. We drove to Pimlico; Rosen and the two Beneckes came to dine, and today I am once more quite at home and well known in London. Klingemann lives most delightfully and his home is so comfortably furnished, with such pleasant rooms, ceilings and sofas, such a decent elderly

---

[1] NYPL, No. 333.   [2] Otto von Woringen (1760–1838) (see p. 81 n. 3).

John Bull of a manservant and a cook to go with it, and such a nice grand piano, that it is beyond price for me to live here with him, and as he says, to treat all London as a plaything. Rosen is well, cheerful, as amiable as ever and quite the unaltered old fellow. So too I found all the Horsleys, with whom I spent a very enjoyable evening yesterday, and whose lasting friendship gives me very great pleasure. I like the morning time with Klingemann best, when we prattle, make music, and think about you all a great deal. And yet I need hardly tell you how much I count off the hours until I am back in Germany with my Cécile. We separated in Düsseldorf on Thursday and now I have to stay here for another three weeks. I will probably go to Birmingham on 13 September and stay with Mr Moore, the apple tree jester.[1] The festival begins on the 19th, and on the 22nd after the last concert I will seat myself in the coach, and travel continuously until I am with my Cécile once again. They are giving me enough to do, for on top of everything else I have now entered into a correspondence with the Birmingham people, who will not allow me to conduct my 'St Paul' at the performance here, because I have to belong to them body and soul for the whole time. That really annoys me and I am trying to set myself free, but if they insist on it I will give way in order to avoid a row; this now results in the choicest English letters being written, with which Klingemann is assisting. I will probably get to see the Alexanders for the first time today, and you will be aware that the Moscheles and the Taylors are not here. Please, dear Mother, ask Paul whether I could not equally well pay the money over to Benecke (Schunck, Souchay & Co.) as to Doxat;[2] I would much prefer it, because Benecke is coming to Birmingham and I need not then detain myself in London with this business on the return journey. Please don't forget to let me know his decision on this.

And now farewell for today—this is meant to be a family letter again, and Klingemann wants to finish it off. Reassure me soon, very soon, with news, and good news at that, God willing, and remain the same as ever towards me. Farewell, dear Mother, goodbye for the present. Your

Felix

[Remainder of the letter is by Karl Klingemann.]

▬▬

[1] According to F. G. Edwards (*The History of Mendelssohn's Oratorio Elijah*), Joseph Moore 'had early made the acquaintance of the Mendelssohn family in Berlin'. Presumably there had been an incident with the apple trees in the Mendelssohns' orchard, to which Felix is now alluding.

[2] London merchants, at 13 Bishopsgate Without.

Cécile Mendelssohn Bartholdy to Lea Mendelssohn Bartholdy[1]

Frankfurt, 2 September [1837]

Dear Mother,

Ever since my arrival here I have only been waiting for a letter from England before writing to you. To my great joy it has now arrived and I am hastening to send it on to you this very day, but can only add a few words of thanks for your kind reassuring letter,[2] since it is already so late.

How glad I am that you are all so well and cheerful, and hope and wish that you will continue to remain so. My poor husband has certainly been downright miserable on the sea crossing, and is certainly now greatly plagued with business.

I must also just quickly say many, many thanks for the all too splendid birthday present. You have, to be sure, made me a month older,[3] dear Mother, but I am greatly surprised that you have thought of my unimportant birthday at all.

Today I have already written a long, long letter to Aunt Schunck in Leipzig about the decorating and painting business and about a maidservant, who can only be procured in Leipzig at certain times. It is difficult to negotiate over a dwelling which one does not know at all, but I think I will take care of most things during our stay at the inn. God grant me then the continuance of my present good health!

I must finish; next time I will write in greater detail. My mother and sister give their kind regards and I send best wishes and regards to all.

    Farewell, dear Mother
        Your Cécile M.B.

—————

[1] NYPL, No. 334.

[2] Letter of 28 Aug. 1837 (Bodleian Library, MS MDM d. 21, fos. 12–13).

[3] Cécile's birthday was not until 10 Oct., but Lea in her letter thought it was in September. The birthday present was a knitted bedcover and two pillows, which Lea was arranging to send direct to Leipzig

Cécile Mendelssohn Bartholdy to Lea Mendelssohn Bartholdy[1]

Frankfurt, 8 September [1837]

Dear Mother,

I wrote to you recently in such haste and so sketchily that I must make good the omission. During all the rainy days that we have had since our arrival here, I penned whole journals to Felix, and through my sitting hunched over brought on back pain, which I had previously never suffered from, so that my beloved place at the writing desk had to be avoided as much as possible, and in its place I have been going for walks every day since the arrival of better weather. The glorious weather has also driven all pains away, so that not a single limb aches any more, and I can now write in comfort. I have not much to tell about my very monotonous life, since my grandmother, mother, and sister, and our former governess constitute the entire house personnel, and the summer and the desire for travel have dispersed most of our acquaintances; our days mostly pass very quietly. I spend a lot of time with my friends, whom I want to see as often as possible while I can still do so, and drive sometimes into the country not far from here to see a young lady whom I dearly love and from whom separation will be difficult.[2] She is almost two years younger than me, rather delicate, and is expecting her confinement in the same month as myself; she has neither a father nor mother and only distant relatives. Perhaps you recall having seen her poor, paralysed father and her strikingly beautiful mother.[3] She said that they had visited your house in Berlin, and now she has lost them both within one year; her maiden name was Du Fay; she was the most charming and lively girl in the world, is now very happily married and will soon be a mother of scarcely 18 years. It is a great joy for me that Felix and her husband get on so well, because otherwise our more intimate association would most likely have ceased. Dear Felix is in the meantime completely immersed in work. In his last letter he writes to me that he has sent off a very detailed letter to you, so I am not enclosing mine. You will also know that the Birmingham people have created difficulties for him over the performance in London, which, however, have now all been cleared up and 'St Paul' will be sung next Tuesday by mere amateurs, mostly tailors, shoemakers, and printers. It must be giving him a lot of trouble.[4] In Birmingham it will most probably go better. How I would like to have heard Felix play on the

---

[1] NYPL, No. 335.   [2] Marie Bernus.

[3] Marie's parents were the merchant Alexander Du Fay (1789–1836) and Johanna Carolina, née Thurneyssen (1794–1835).

[4] Cécile seems to have misunderstood Felix's information, for of course he did not conduct the London performance, although he did attend some of the rehearsals.

big organ and to have been able to hear the new piano concerto with all the instruments, which I know only piecemeal from Felix's singing. Patience, however, till next winter!

My grandfather, who is going to the music festival with my uncles and aunts from Manchester,[1] will enjoy it greatly, and will still be talking about it on winter evenings. I won't see him again before my departure, as he always travels via Paris and stops off there for a while. We expect my brother, however, daily, and I am glad that I will still have a couple of weeks with him here. His stay in Vienna was excessively prolonged, so that in the end he was no longer enjoying it so much there, especially as all the families to whom he was recommended were gone into the country, and he had to remain alone with his uncongenial business activities.

In your letter you ask me about our apartment in Leipzig, dear Mother. I know nothing at all about it myself, for when we were in Leipzig, the foundations of it had just been laid. It is not far from my aunt, and judging from all the descriptions is very pleasant. Yet there is still no end of things to be done in it, and we will probably have to live at the inn for some weeks. I have asked my aunt to have the painting done, so that at least the offensive smell will have completely gone when we arrive, and I have also given her various things to take care of, since she most kindly offered me her services. I just wish for really good health next winter, and given that, organizing my new housekeeping can only be a pleasure for me.

I live in the pleasant hope, dear Mother, that you are all quite well, and that the warmer air and sunshine also prevail in Berlin and completely get rid of the dreadful cholera—that at any rate is what the newspapers think will happen. Felix wrote to me in his last letter that he was uneasy at having heard nothing from you for so long, but he has probably received letters by now. I think especially of Rebecka a great deal at this time and give her my best wishes. I need hardly ask you to give kind regards to her and Fanny, and to Paul and Albertine, if they are with you again. Please also remember me to the Von Woringen family, should they not yet have left. I have to give you kind regards from Aunt Schlegel; she recently spent an afternoon here with us in the best of moods. Today I hear that she is a little unwell. If you have time and inclination again, I beg you to think of me and send me some indication of your well-being, even if it should only be a couple of words. And now, farewell, dear Mother, remember now and then your abandoned Cécile M.B.

Many compliments from Mother, Grandmother, and my sister.

---

[1] Carl and Jean Souchay with their wives Adelheid and Thekla.

Cécile Mendelssohn Bartholdy to Lea Mendelssohn Bartholdy[1]

Frankfurt, 21 September [1837]

This will probably be the last time, dear Mother, that I write to you from here. I am expecting Felix next Tuesday, and by then I must be completely ready to travel, in order to accompany him the next day, for you know of course that his orchestra is expecting him on the 30th for the rehearsal of the first concert. We will then be a good deal nearer to you, and perhaps this proximity will bring us the pleasure of your company, once I am in the position to arrange the domestic comforts as well as possible for you. Dear Mother, how greatly I look forward to next winter, with the thought of making my Felix's life in his home really pleasant! The poor fellow's stay in England this time has been greatly soured by the death of his beloved friend Rosen, who died on the day of the performance of 'St Paul' in London. I don't know whether you too knew this excellent man. Felix had told me so much about him, and he had been described to me as such an amiable man by my relatives in England, that I now must doubly regret not having met him. His illness was very short and seems to have been the result of his excessive work and exertion; in his last letter Felix wrote that Rosen was ill with a cold, which was preventing his intended journey to Germany; today I receive the news of his death. Here is a passage from Felix's letter: 'Tuesday, while Rosen was ill, was a day that I will never forget. It was really one of those days in the world, with its mysterious incomprehensible ways. A thousand different people crossed my path and I had to associate with them, and no one was concerned with what was affecting me, and no one cared whether I was sad or happy, and Rosen became worse and worse; no one cared whether he lived or died, and yet they all meant so well. I wrote to you early in the morning, and then went to play the organ. There were I suppose about a thousand people gathered together there, the church packed full. I could hardly push my way through to the organ bench, and there sat a 78-year-old organist, the most famous one here, Wesley, who, though old and weak, had had himself brought there by his daughters, and at my request he sat himself at the organ bench and played, and it was so moving that his daughter burst into the bitterest tears and had to be led down into the sacristy. I played for a very long time, and there was then a sort of uproar, such handshaking and crowding around me as is only to be found in England; hands appear from all sides, and speeches from so many voices that one does not know where to turn. The churchwardens had prepared a sort of breakfast for me, which the

---

[1] NYPL, No. 337.

vicar also shared in, and I could only get away with some difficulty and go to Rosen, whom I found greatly altered and in a very critical state, and the doctors with serious expressions; and yet I would never have believed such a quick end possible. Klingemann stayed with him, while I had to go to the performance of my oratorio, which began at seven, and from which, on account of all the uproar in the papers, I could not absent myself. I heard my oratorio for the first time, and on another day that would in itself have thrilled me, while on this particular day I noticed hardly any of it. The performance went far beyond my expectation, in some movements quite splendidly, only atrociously in the recitatives. Against that there was a truly heavenly sound in the immense hall from the many voices and instruments. The aria 'Jerusalem', the contralto aria,[1] the chorale 'Sleepers, wake', the duet of the two apostles,[2] and the chorus of the Gentiles in A major[3] were all demanded to be encored and so sung. When, just before the start of the second part, I went to take my seat again in the gallery, some of the audience downstairs spotted me, turned round and began to call out my name, and the whole crowd of people turned round at one and the same time and applauded madly, and waved their handkerchiefs and shouted hurrah, so that I became quite tired from bowing; and the same uproar and clamour broke out at the end of the whole work and lasted still longer—it refused to come to an end. Next to me sat Benedict, whom I had known in Naples; friends from the Rhine and a whole family from Rome, whom I would never have suspected of being in London,[4] came and suddenly stood in front of me again. Fanny Horsley brought me a couple of pretty pieces of handiwork which she has made for you, and so it turned eleven o'clock. When I finally got to Rosen, Klingemann came to meet me and told me that we had lost him, and we walked home in deep sorrow. Early the next morning at seven I set out for here and so concluded my London stay for this visit.' Schelble's death had greatly distressed Felix during his journey; now he has all but witnessed this one; in all that the memory of his beloved father is vividly present in his mind every time. The great amount of business, the performances and the resultant uproar, even if they give him pleasure, must still wear him out, and therefore it is with some anxiety that I imagine him returning exhausted after the rushed journey. Let us hope it is unfounded. As for me and my health I can only give you the best of news. I feel the joy of soon seeing my husband again in all my limbs, and it sometimes makes me so frolicsome that I forget all

[1] 'But the Lord is mindful of his own'.   [2] 'Now we are ambassadors'.   [3] 'Lord, thou alone art God'.
[4] See p. 104 n. 7.

consideration that I am responsible for a certain small person. Yet I only suffer for it when I sit for too long bending over; any walking or even leaping about is quite agreeable to it. I look forward eagerly to news of Rebecka, and hope soon to receive another nice letter from you. All is well with Aunt Schlegel, I have just received a note from her; she sends her kind regards, as do my mother, grandmother, Mlle Bury, and Julie.

I must finish with a request to excuse my poor, careless writing. I always rush to leave the writing desk as soon as possible. Farewell, dearest Mother, regards to every one of my dear friends, and think lovingly of your devoted

Cécile M.B.

———

Felix and Cécile Mendelssohn Bartholdy to Lea Mendelssohn Bartholdy[1]

Leipzig, 4 October 1837

Dearest Mother,

It should have been my first task to write to you as soon as I had some degree of peace again after the busy time of the last weeks, and I had to thank you for so many lovely letters to me and Cécile; I wanted also to let you know straight away of our safe arrival here, and yet two days have gone by without it being possible for me to do so. I am making use of first thing in the morning today for it, otherwise people will come again, one after the other, and the posting time will be past, like yesterday and the day before. And today is also virtually my first proper rest day; I was so completely worn out in the past few days that unpacking seemed to me like hard work, and nothing came easily except eating and sleeping, and scarcely even that. Now, however, I feel quite fresh and cheerful again, rejoice over my good health, which probably in the past would hardly have endured such hardships so well, and am

---

[1] NYPL, No. 338.

writing to thank you for the really delightful letter which we found waiting for us here;[1] God grant that we may soon receive the desired happy news of Becky,[2] and that everything is well, as I hope. You have I daresay heard about me constantly through Cécile. Upon my arrival in Birmingham I began a letter to you, which is lying in front of me; I wanted to write to you at length about our dear Rosen, since I could not do so in the same way to Cécile, who had never met him. Then came the days of the music festival, and the terrible crowd of people poured along, so I had enough to do to keep my head above water in the whirlpool, and had to abandon writing. Even now I cannot devote myself to describing it; it would require many sheets of paper, as well as whole evenings when we are once more together again, just to mention superficially the many remarkable things which crowded upon each other during those days. But I must tell you, because I know it will please you, that I have never had such a brilliant success and can indeed never have a more unquestionable one than at the music festival. The applause and the calls for me when I merely put in an appearance refused to come to an end, and at times really caused me to laugh, because, for example when it came to my piano concerto, I could not get to sit at the instrument; and what is better than the approbation, and what guarantees my success, are the offers which were made to me from all sides, and which this time sound different from ever before. They want to give me 1,000 guineas for a couple of performances of a new oratorio, without obliging me to sell the copyright; a large publishing house wants to commission an opera for me from Planché[3] and then to buy it etc. etc. I now intend to go to England in the spring two years hence, and hope by then to have sufficient new things to take along. Then I would also earn some proper money, and I can indeed say that, for I have just now seen how all that will only be granted me because, as far as my work goes, I do not concern myself with what people want and praise and pay, but only with what I consider good, and because I will now let myself be even less led astray from that path. On that account of course I also love this success, and I know all the more certainly that I will never do the slightest thing for it, just as I have never done so up till now. At the same time I also had a real demonstration of what is to be thought of all such things—that is the way in which they received Neukomm this time in Birmingham. You know how previously they had been devoted to him and in truth overrated him, how all his works were in demand and praised there, so that the musicians always called him "King of Brummagem", and this time they have pushed him aside in such an unseemly manner. Only one short piece of his was

[1] Apparently not extant.

[2] Rebecka's son was born on 10 Oct., and Lea sent Felix a letter the same day (Bodleian Library, GB VI 80).

[3] James Robinson Planché (1796–1880), English dramatist and librettist, who had written the libretto for Weber's *Oberon*. Commissioned by Chappell's, in 1838 he submitted an historical libretto, *The Citizens of Calais*, to Mendelssohn, who liked it at first, but subsequently rejected it.

given on the first morning (the worst possible occasion), and even that was received by the audience without the slightest attention, so that it was really a matter of shame on those people who three years ago knew nothing more exalted and better than Neukomm's music. The only thing he is to be reproached with is simply that three years ago he wrote an oratorio for the music festival[1] which was very much calculated for effect—the big organ, the choruses, the solo instruments, all were introduced so as to please the audience, and the audience notices these things, and it does not go down well. That they, however, show their gratitude in treating him thus, is just another sign as to what is to be thought of all their delight, and what one gets in return when one seeks it. I found him this time once again very genial and as kind as before, and he can serve me as an example in a hundred ways; such calm and refinement with, at the same time, the greatest sincerity I have yet to find in any man. And then he truly is a faithful friend, and takes such a great interest in you all, and is also so very fond of Cécile. I am sending you herewith a full schedule of the music festival itself, since in view of the short distance it is perhaps worth the postage. Just think of that enormous quantity of music! And on top of all the colossal amount of music were the many acquaintances who flocked together there during those days; one needed to be as cold-blooded as a fish in order not to explode. There were Carl and John Souchay from Manchester with their wives, old Herr Souchay whom I hadn't seen since my wedding, the Beneckes from Berlin,[2] Benecke from Deptford, Klingemann, Bennett, Thompson from Edinburgh, Neukomm, the Stewarts[3] with whom I had danced so much in Rome, etc. etc. After that, as soon as I had played the last chord on the splendid organ, I then had to get into the Liverpool mail; Bennett, Walmisley, Novello, and Mr Moore accompanied me to it and in their presence I took off my fine frock-coat and waistcoat and put on a cheap one for the coach, and then rode six days and five nights in succession until I was with my Cécile in Frankfurt. The mail coach reached London in ten and a half hours—it is just as far as from here to Berlin; I calculated that on the way and envied the English for it. I arrived in London around midnight; Klingemann met me and took me to the Committee of the Sacred Harmonic Society, who ceremoniously presented me with a big fat silver box with an inscription. At half past twelve I was

[1] The oratorio was *David*. Mendelssohn here seems to be echoing the opinions of William Horsley, as expressed in his letter to Mendelssohn of 17 July 1834 (Bodleian Library, GB III 215).

[2] Victor and Emmeline Benecke.

[3] Probably Andrew Stewart (1771–1838), his wife Margaret (d. 1839), and their sons. Stewart, who first trained and practised as a doctor, was then ordained into the Church of Scotland, and became minister at Bolton in East Lothian. From 1828 to 1830 the Stewarts travelled abroad with their children, and may therefore have met Mendelssohn in Rome at the end of this period. Of their three sons, Robert Walker (1812–87) also entered the ministry, living in Italy from 1845, while Alexander Patrick (1813–83) became a well-known London doctór.

sitting in the mail coach again and was in Dover at nine the next morning, where there was not enough time for breakfast; instead I had to get straight into the boat that took us to the steamer, since it was already low tide, and the steamer could not remain in the harbour. I thus arrived on board the steamer already seasick, had a miserable crossing, and instead of being in Calais in three hours, I was in Boulogne in five, and that much further from Frankfurt. There I sought out the Hotel Meurice,[1] because I remembered that Fanny once stayed there, and recovered as well as possible, ate again at midday, and at nine in the evening set off in the diligence to Lille. Here is the place to interpolate (Dirichlet may well rage against it as much as he likes) that French and Belgian diligences with glass windows on the cobbled roads, with their three large horses in front, whose tails are braided and who do not trot at all but roll along, are the most atrocious, most wretched means of transport in the whole world, and that a German express mail is a hundred times quicker, more pleasant, and better than this most atrocious etc.—see above. The September Days were being celebrated throughout Belgium,[2] and Independence trees were placed in the squares in front of the town halls. I arrived in Cologne at ten in the morning; at eleven a steamer departed, which was to sail through the night; so I settled down on it and was glad to be able to lie down on the fifth night, stretched out and without the clatter of paved roads. I had already gone to sleep at nine, and did not wake up until two in the morning; then I felt that the steamer was at a standstill, and when I asked, it turned out there was such a thick fog (as there had been also already the day before) that they could not continue until six o'clock in the morning at the earliest, and would not be in Mainz before six o'clock in the evening. It was quite close to Horchheim that the ship lay so stationary, so I then engaged two boatmen to carry my things, showed them the well-known footpath along the Rhine, arrived in Koblenz at three o'clock in the morning, took the mail coach, and was in Frankfurt at half past two on Wednesday afternoon. Everything was fine there; Cécile was well, looked in good health and lovely, and I now had only the worry as to how she would survive the journey. We set out at two in the afternoon on the Thursday, and then had such a delightful, pleasant, and cheerful journey that I cannot be thankful enough for it. I am just so fortunate that my dear Cécile is in such good health; I am so very anxious about her, and would certainly have completely lost control of myself on the journey if she had felt unwell. But as I said, she endured all the early rising and late arriving splendidly, and we arrived here on Sunday at two. The Schuncks[3] met us in the most delightful and

[1] In the rule de l'Écu (now rue Victor Hugo). The hotel survived until the bombardment of the town in 1944.
[2] Sept. 1830 saw the uprising against the Dutch for Belgian independence; on 27 Sept. Prince Frederick admitted defeat and left Brussels, and a provisional Belgian government was declared on 4 Oct.
[3] Philipp and Julie Schunck.

comfortably furnished apartment,[1] *where my grand piano stood, my pictures were hanging, and even my Düsseldorf curtains were put to use. The first subscription concert began at six; I had to conduct the Jubel Overture*[2] *and the C minor Symphony,*[3] *and the trombones and timpani exerted themselves so much that I admit I felt somewhat worn out at the end of the concert. It was Schleinitz's birthday, so after it was over I still had to go and see him to congratulate him, and then I finally came home to my Cécile, and have been resting since then. The fourteen such stuffed-full days were indeed as much as a man can possibly take in, but since I had had the whole of the past summer simply for enjoyment and pleasure, then I am glad that just before my return here there was this period of heavy activity as well, which in addition was important for my career. Here it is now just so lovely the way in which my Cécile knows how to organize everything so well and agreeably; I cannot describe to you how nicely she conducts herself as the mistress of my house, how she knows how to talk with the decorator, the carpenter and the mason, and to command respect from the maidservant, all so succinctly and "to the purpose" as nobody else could, and how she spoils and coddles (as she says) me, and how singularly good lunch tasted today, when we ate for the first time all by ourselves at home. The whole day and every hour is now like a festival for me, and whilst in England, despite all the honours and pleasures of life, I did not have a single really happy moment, now every day consists of a round of joy and happiness for me, and I am only properly appreciative of my life again since I have my Cécile. Today she is still too preoccupied with arranging things, making notes and conferring with Mme Schunck to write, but she sends her warmest regards to you all, and will send a letter very soon. We want and hope we shall be able to move into our apartment next door*[4] *(which we like very much) as early as four weeks hence; it is spacious with the finest view that one can have here, and once we are there, then we can invite you all to stay with us with a good conscience, and hope that it would be pleasant and comfortable for you. Cécile will, I admit, still not give up the idea of travelling to Berlin at Christmas, but I believe that it would hardly be wise and am seeking to talk her out of it, because I would like to be as careful as possible. I must now also tell you that on my arrival here I received the diploma of an honorary member of the Gesellschaft der Musikfreunde of the Austrian Empire,*[5] *and I now hope you will withdraw your complaint about me that I do not tell enough about myself, and admit that this time I have been as detailed about myself as if I were an ailing monarch. Cécile is just saying she also would like to write after all, so I must finish; but I just want to ask you not to forget my old piano when you send my things, dear*

---

[1] Rather than the Mendelssohns living at an inn while their new apartment was being finished, as was originally proposed, Julie Schunck had managed to rent an apartment for them below the Schuncks' own.

[2] By Carl Maria von Weber.   [3] Beethoven's Symphony No. 5.   [4] In Lurgensteins Garten.

[5] The diploma is preserved in the Mendelssohn-Archiv, Staatsbibliothek zu Berlin (MA Ep. 484).

Mother. And then my thanks for the beautiful silver gift that you want to make us, and for all the love and kindness of your letter. Give my kindest regards to Fanny and Becky and Paul, and farewell for today.

> *Your*
>> *Felix*

Dear Mother,

In addition to the fat letter I am sending herewith a whole bundle of newspapers articles, which Felix brought back for me from the Misses Alexander. You will understand them for the time being better than I, who cannot make out much, apart from his name and a few eulogistic phrases. Mr Novello, who has also written me a long letter in English, has a clear style and constantly speaks highly of Felix's modesty and good manners when receiving great applause. Felix has filled all the space with writing so that there is simply no room left for me to thank you for . . .

[Continuation missing, probably only a few words.]

Appendix

Allegretto in A major

Felix Mendelssohn Bartholdy

Freyburg den 22sten April 1837

Die Freundin

Goethe
(Marianne von Willemer)

Felix Mendelssohn Bartholdy
(1837)

1. Zart - er Blu — men leicht Ge - win - de Flecht' ich

Dir zum An - ge - bin - de Un - ver-gäng-lich-es zu bie - ten war mir

lei — — der nicht be - schie - den, Un — ver-gäng-lich - es zu

bie - ten war mir lei - der nicht be-schie - den war mir lei - der nicht be-

schie - - den.

2. In den leichten Blumenranken
  Lauschen liebende Gedanken
  Die in leisen Tönen klingen,
  Und dir fromme Wünsche bringen.

3. Und so bringt vom fernen Orte
  Dieses Blatt dir Blumenworte,
  Mögen sie vor deinen Blicken
  Sich mit frischen Farben schmücken.

Canon in B minor

Bibliography

ALBERT, PETER P., and WINGENROTH, MAX, *Freiburger Bürgerhäuser aus vier Jahrhunderten* (Augsburg and Stuttgart, 1923).

ALEXANDER, BOYD, 'Felix Mendelssohn and the Alexanders', *Mendelssohn Studien*, 1 (1972), 81–105.

—— 'Felix Mendelssohn Bartholdy and Young Women', *Mendelssohn Studien*, 2 (1975), 71–102.

Allgemeine deutsche Biographie (Leipzig, 1875–1912).

ANDREE, ROLF, et al., *Die Düsseldorfer Malerschule: [Katalog einer Ausstellung im] Kunstmuseum Düsseldorf [und auf der] Mathildenhöhe Darmstadt*, ed. Wend von Kalnein (Mainz, 1979).

ANGEMÜLLER, RUDOLPH, *Sigismund Neukomm: Werkverzeichnis, Autobiographie, Beziehung zu seinen Zeitgenossen* (Musikwissenschaftliche Schriften, 4; Munich, 1977).

Aris's Birmingham Gazette, 25 Sept. 1837.

[BAD HOMBURG], *Verzeichniß der . . . in Homburg angekommenen Kur- und Bade-Gäste*, 1837.

[BAD KREUZNACH], *Festschrift 150 Jahre Casino-Gesellschaft Bad Kreuznach 1824–1974* (Bad Kreuznach, 1974).

—— *Unterhaltungen*, 26 (30 June 1837).

BADER, JOSEF, *Die Schicksale des ehemaligen Frauenstiftes Güntersthal bei Freiburg im Breisgau* (Freiburger Diocesan-Archiv, 5; Freiburg im Breisgau, 1870).

BAEDEKER, KARL, *A Handbook for Travellers on the Rhine from Switzerland to Holland* (London, [1861]).

BATES, ALAN, *Directory of Stage Coach Services 1836* (Newton Abbot, 1969).

BÄUMER, REMIGIUS, and SCHEFFCZYK, LEO (edd.), *Marienlexikon* (St Ottilien, 1988–94).

Birmingham Musical Festival in aid of the funds of the General Hospital [Programme book] ([Birmingham], 1837).

BLUNT, WILFRID, *On Wings of Song: A Biography of Felix Mendelssohn* (London, 1974).

BOASE, FREDERIC, *Modern British Biography* (Truro, 1892–1921).

BOERINGER, JAMES, *Organa Britannica: Organs in Great Britain 1660–1860* (Lewisburg, Pa., 1983–9).

BOWLEY, ROBERT, *The Sacred Harmonic Society* (London, 1867).

Bradshaw's Illustrated Hand-Book for Travellers in Belgium, on the Rhine, and through Portions of Rhenish Prussia (London, [1853]).

BRUNEL, ISAMBARD, *The Life of Isambard Kingdom Brunel, Civil Engineer* (London, 1870).

Cathédrale de Strasbourg (La) (Strasbourg, 1973).

CLEMEN, PAUL, *Der Dom zu Köln* (Die Kunstdenkmäler der Rheinprovinz, 6/3; Düsseldorf, 1937).

CLUTTON, CECIL, and NILAND, AUSTIN, *The British Organ*, 2nd edn. (London, 1982).

[COLOGNE], *Wallraf-Richartz-Museum Köln: Von Stephan Lochner bis Paul Cézanne, 120 Meisterwerke der Gemäldesammlung* (Cologne, 1986).

CRUM, MARGARET, and WARD JONES, PETER, *Catalogue of the Mendelssohn Papers in the Bodleian Library, Oxford* (Musikbibliographische Arbeiten, 7–9; Tutzing, 1980–9).

DARNTON, JOHN EDWARD, *The Von Schunck Family: A History of the Hanau Branch and Connections* (privately published, 1933).

DEHIO, GEORG, *Handbuch der Deutschen Kunstdenkmäler: Baden-Württemberg I*, ed. Dagmar Zimdars *et al.* (Munich and Berlin, 1982).

—— *Handbuch der Deutschen Kunstdenkmäler: Hessen*, 2nd rev. edn. by Magnus Backes (Munich and Berlin, 1982).

—— *Handbuch der Deutschen Kunstdenkmäler: Rheinland-Pfalz, Saarland*, 2nd rev. and enlarged edn. by Hans Caspary *et al.* (Munich and Berlin, 1984).

Deutsches biographisches Archiv, microfiche edn., ed. Bernhard Fabian (Munich, 1982).

DEVRIENT, EDUARD, *Meine Erinnerungen an Felix Mendelssohn Bartholdy und dessen Briefe an mich* (Leipzig, 1869); Eng. trans., *My Recollections of Felix Mendelssohn-Bartholdy, and his Letters to me* (London, 1869).

Dictionary of National Biography, ed. Leslie Stephen and Sidney Lee (London, 1885–1902).

Dictionnaire historique et biographique de la Suisse (Neuchâtel, 1921–34).

DÖHNER, OTTO, *Das Hugenottengeschlecht Souchay de la Duboissière und seine Nachkommen* (Deutsches Familienarchiv, 19; Neustadt an der Aisch, 1961).

DÖRFFEL, ALFRED, *Geschichte der Gewandhausconzerte zu Leipzig* (Leipzig, 1884).

DRÜLL, DAGMAR, *Heidelberger Gelehrtenlexikon 1803–1932* (Berlin and Heidelberg, 1986).

[DÜSSELDORF, KUNSTMUSEUM], *Die Gemälde des 19. Jahrhunderts*, 2nd edn. (Malerei, vol. 4; Mainz, 1981).

ECKARDT, JULIUS, *Ferdinand David und die Familie Mendelssohn* (Leipzig, 1888).

ECKSTEIN, FRIEDRICH AUGUST, *Nomenclator philologorum* (Leipzig, 1871).

EDWARDS, FREDERICK GEORGE, *The History of Mendelssohn's Oratorio 'Elijah'* (London, 1896).

EISENBARTH, WILLI, *Historische Stätten und Sehenswürdigkeiten in Lahnstein* (Lahnstein, 1993).

ELKIN, ROBERT, *The Old Concert Rooms of London* (London, 1951).

ELVIN, LAURENCE, *Bishop and Son, Organ Builders* (London, 1984).

ESSER, JOHANNES, *Die neue grosse Chororgel der Heiliggeistkirche Heidelberg* (Heidelberg, 1986).

Europäische Stammtafeln—Stammtafeln zur Geschichte der europäischen Staaten, NS vol. xi, ed. Detlev Schwennicke (Marburg, 1986).

Festbuch zur 25. Haupt-Versammlung des Vereins kath. deutscher Lehrerinnen (Koblenz, 1910).

FOSTER, MYLES B., *History of the Philharmonic Society of London, 1813–1912* (London, 1912).

FRANKFURT AM MAIN, STÄDELSCHES KUNSTINSTITUT, *Die Gemälde des 19. Jahrhunderts*, ed. Ernst Holzinger, rev. Hans-Joachim Ziemke (Kataloge der Gemälde im Städelschen Kunstinstitut Frankfurt am Main, 1; Frankfurt am Main, 1972).

Freiburg im Breisgau—Stadtkreis und Landkreis Amtliche Kreisbeschreibung, ii/1: *Die Gemeinden des Landkreises A–K*, ed. Staatliche Archivverwaltung Baden-Württemberg (Freiburg im Breisgau, 1972).

Freiburger Adresskalender aus das Jahr 1837.

GARLAND, HENRY and MARY, *The Oxford Companion to German Literature*, 2nd edn. (Oxford, 1986).

GAUNTLETT, HENRY, 'Mendelssohn as an Organist', *Musical World* (15 Sept. 1837), 8–10.

GOTCH, ROSAMUND BRUNEL (ed.), *Mendelssohn and his Friends in Kensington* (London, 1934).

GREVILLE, CHARLES C. F., *A Journal of the Reign of Queen Victoria from 1837 to 1852*, vol. i (London, 1885).

GWINNER, PHILIPP FRIEDRICH, *Kunst und Künstler in Frankfurt am Main vom dreizehnten Jahrhundert bis zur Eröffnung des Städel'schen Kunstinstituts* (Frankfurt am Main, 1862–7).

HARTMANN, GÜNTER, 'Ein Albumblatt für Eliza Wesley: Fragen zu Mendelssohns Englandaufenthalt 1837— und eine spekulative Antwort', *Neue Zeitschrift für Musik*, 101 (1989), 10–14.

[HEIDELBERG], *Adressbuch der Ruprecht-Karls-Universität zu Heidelberg, Sommer-Halbjahr 1837.*

Heidelberger Wochenblätter, 1837.

HENSEL, FANNY, *The Letters of Fanny Hensel to Felix Mendelssohn*, collected, ed., and trans. with introductory essays and notes by Marcia J. Citron (Stuyvesant, NY, 1987).

HENSEL, SEBASTIAN, *Die Familie Mendelssohn 1729–1847 nach Briefen und Tagebüchern* (Berlin, 1879); Eng. trans., *The Mendelssohn Family (1729–1847) from Letters and Journals* (London, 1881).

HERCHENBACH, W., *Fremdenführer für Düsseldorf und Umgegend* (Düsseldorf, 1869).

HERZOG, BODO, '"The Defiance": Das erste Dampfschiff auf dem Rhein im Jahre 1816', *Technikgeschichte*, 39 (1972), 313–21.

HEYDEN, EDUARD, *Gallerie berühmter u. merkwürdiger Frankfurter* (Frankfurt am Main, 1861).

HILL, JOSEPH, and DENT, ROBERT K., *Memorials of the Old Square* (Birmingham, 1897).

HILLER, FERDINAND, *Felix Mendelssohn Bartholdy: Briefe und Erinnerungen* (Cologne, 1874); Eng. trans., *Mendelssohn: Letters and Recollections* (London, 1874).

HOELLBECK, E. AUGUSTE, *Almanach du commerce, de l'industrie, des sciences, des arts et des métiers de Strasbourg* (Strasbourg, 1836).

HOPPE, REINHARD, *Vor den Mauern Heidelbergs: Stadtteil Schlierbach*, 2nd edn. (Heidelberg, 1984).

HORSLEY, JOHN CALLCOTT, *Recollections of a Royal Academician* (London, 1903).

HOWARTH, T. E. B., *Citizen-King: The Life of Louis-Philippe, King of the French* (London, 1961).

HÜTT, WOLFGANG, *Die Düsseldorfer Malerschule, 1819–1869* (Leipzig, 1984).

JENDERKO-SICHELSCHMIDT, INGRID, *Die Historienbilder Carl Friedrich Lessings* (diss., Cologne, 1973).

Journal des débats (Paris), April 1837.

KAUTZSCH, RUDOLF, *Der Dom zu Worms* (Denkmäler deutscher Kunst; Berlin, 1938).

KLEIN, JOHANN ADAM, *Rheinreise von Strassburg bis Düsseldorf*, 4th rev. edn. (Koblenz, 1843).

KLEIN-EHRMINGER, MADELEINE, *Our Lady of Strasbourg Cathedral Church* (Lyon, 1986).

KLINGEMANN, KARL [jr.] (ed.), *Felix Mendelssohn-Bartholdys Briefwechsel mit Legationsrat Karl Klingemann in London* (Essen, 1909).

[KOBLENZ], *150 Jahre Landgericht Koblenz* (Boppard am Rhein, 1970).

KRUMMACHER, FRIEDHELM, *Mendelssohn—der Komponist* (Munich, 1978).

KUBACH, HANS ERICH, and HAAS, WALTER (edd.), *Der Dom zu Speyer* (Die Kunstdenkmäler von Rheinland-Pfalz, 5; Munich, 1972).

KUTSCH, K. J., and RIEMENS, L., *Großes Sängerlexikon* (Berne, 1987–94).

LAMBOUR, CHRISTIAN, 'Eine Schweizer Reisebrief aus dem Jahr 1822 von Lea und Fanny Mendelssohn Bartholdy an Henriette (Hinni) Mendelssohn, geb. Meyer', *Mendelssohn Studien*, 7 (1990), 171–8.

LEONHARD, CARL CAESAR VON, *Fremdenbuch für Heidelberg und die Umgegend* (Heidelberg, 1834).

LEYS, M. D. R., *Between Two Empires: A History of French Politicians and People between 1814 and 1848* (London, 1955).

LIESSEM, UDO, *Baudenkmäler in Pfaffendorf* (Koblenz, 1988).

LIVET, GEORGES, and RAPP, FRANCIS (edd.), *Histoire de Strasbourg des Origines à nos Jours* (Strasbourg, 1980–1).

[MAINZ], *Gedenkbuch an die festlichen Tage der Inauguration des Gutenbergs-Denkmal zu Mainz am 13., 14., 15. und 16. August 1837* (Mainz, 1837).

[MANNHEIM], *Sehenswürdigkeiten von Mannheim und seiner Umgebung* (Mannheim, 1833).

Mannheimer Adress-Kalender für das Jahr 1837.

MARQUARDT, HERTHA (ed.), *Henry Crabb Robinson und seine deutschen Freunde: Brücke zwischen England und Deutschland im Zeitalter der Romantik. Nach Briefen, Tagebüchern und anderen Aufzeichnungen*, 2 vols. (Palaestra, 237, 249; Göttingen, 1964–7).

MENDELSSOHN BARTHOLDY, FELIX, *Briefe an deutsche Verleger*, ed. Rudolf Elvers (Berlin, 1968).

—— *Briefe an Ignaz und Charlotte Moscheles*, ed. Felix Moscheles (Leipzig, 1888); Eng. trans., *Letters of Felix Mendelssohn to Ignaz and Charlotte Moscheles* (London, 1888).

—— *Briefe aus den Jahren 1833 bis 1847*, ed. Paul and Carl Mendelssohn Bartholdy (Leizpig, 1863); Eng. trans., *Letters of Felix Mendelssohn Bartholdy, from 1833 to 1847* (London, 1863).

—— *Felix Mendelssohn Bartholdy, Briefe aus Leipziger Archiven*, ed. Hans-Joachim Rothe and Reinhard Szeskus (Leipzig, 1972).

Die Mendelssohns in Berlin: Eine Familie und ihre Stadt (Staatsbibliothek Preußischer Kulturbesitz, Ausstellungskataloge, 20; Berlin, 1983).

MUIRHEAD, JAMES PATRICK, *The Life of James Watt* (London, 1858).

MÜLLER, CARL HEINRICH, *Beiträge zur Geschichte des Deutschen Männergesangs: Frankfurt und der deutsche*

Männergesang in der Zeit von den Freiheitskriegen 1813 bis zur Reichsgründen 1871 (Frankfurt am Main, 1925).

—— *Felix Mendelssohn, Frankfurt a.M. und der Cäcilienverein* (Darmstadt, 1925).

MÜLLER, F. MAX, 'From the Memoirs of F. Max Müller', in R. Larry Todd (ed.), *Mendelssohn and his World* (Princeton, 1991), 252–8.

MÜLLER, JOSEF (ed.), *Rheinisches Wörterbuch* (Bonn and Leipzig, 1928–)

MURRAY, JOHN, and SON, *A Hand-Book for Travellers on the Continent* (London, 1836).

MUSCH, HANS, 'Felix Mendelssohn Bartholdy in Freiburg und im Schwarzwald', in Hans Musch (ed.), *Musik am Oberrhein* (Kassel, 1993), 181–213.

MYLIUS, JOHANN CARL, *Geschichte der Familie Mylius* (Buttstädt, 1895).

NAGLER, GEORG KASPAR, *Neues allgemeines Künstler-Lexikon* (Munich, 1835–52).

NASSAUER, SIEGFRIED, *Was die Frankfurter Brunnen erzählen* (Frankfurt am Main, 1921).

NATH-ESSER, MARTINA, *Gartenzauber: Geschichte des Homburger Kurparks, anläßlich des 200. Geburtstags von Peter Joseph Lenné* (Bad Homburg, 1989).

Neue deutsche Biographie, ed. Historische Kommission bei der Bayerischen Akademie der Wissenschaften (Berlin, 1953–).

Neuer Nekrolog der Deutschen (Ilmenau [later Weimar], 1824–54).

The New Grove Dictionary of Music and Musicians, ed. Stanley Sadie (London, 1980).

Nouveau dictionnaire de biographie Alsacienne (Fédération des sociétés d'histoire et d'archéologie d'Alsace; Strasbourg, [1982]–).

Orgues en Alsace, vol. iv: *Inventaire technique des orgues du Bas-Rhin 2*, Ministère de la Culture, Direction de la Musique et de la Danse; Direction du Patrimoine, Conseil régional d'Alsace ([Strasbourg], 1985).

OTTENDORFF-SIMROCK, WALTHER, *Castles on the Rhine*, new edn. (7th) (Bonn, 1989).

PETERSCHMITT, ELIE, *Théophile Stern (1803–1886), organiste chrétien* (Strasbourg, 1992).

PETITPIERRE, JACQUES, *Le Mariage de Mendelssohn* (Lausanne, 1937); Eng. trans., *The Romance of the Mendelssohns* (London, 1947).

PHILLIPS, GORDON, and ALTMAN, LUDWIG (edd.), *Samuel Wesley and Dr Mendelssohn: Three Organ Fugues* (London, 1962).

POLKO, ELISE, *Erinnerungen an Felix Mendelssohn-Bartholdy* (Leipzig, 1868); Eng. trans., *Reminiscences of Felix Mendelssohn-Bartholdy* (London, 1869).

The Post-Office London Directory for 1838.

PRANG, HELMUT, *Friedrich Rückert: Geist und Form der Sprache* (Schweinfurt, 1963).

REICH, NANCY B. (ed.), 'From the Memoirs of Ernst Rudorff', in R. Larry Todd (ed.), *Mendelssohn and his World* (Princeton, 1991), 259–71.

Rhein- und Mosel-Zeitung, 6 Aug. 1837.

RICHEL, ARTHUR, *Katalog der Abteilung Frankfurt, Stadtbibliothek Frankfurt am Main* (Frankfurt am Main, 1914–29).

ROGERS, H. C. B., *Turnpike to Iron Road* (London, 1961).

ROTH, GUENTHER, 'Heidelberg-London-Manchester: Zu Max Webers deutsch-englischer Familiengeschichte', in Hubert Treiber and Karol Sauerland (edd.), *Heidelberg im Schnittpunkt intellektueller Kreise* (Opladen, 1995), 184–209.

—— 'Weber the would-be Englishman: Anglophilia and Family History', in Hartmut Lehmann and Guenther Roth (edd.), *Weber's Protestant Ethic: Origins, Evidence, Contexts* (Washington, DC, and Cambridge, 1993), 83–121.

RÖTTGER, BERNHARD HERMANN (ed.), *Die Kunstdenkmäler der Pfalz, iii: Stadt und Bezirkamt Speyer* (Die Kunstdenkmäler von Bayern. Regierungsbezirk Pfalz, 3; Munich, 1934).

RÜB, OTTO, *Die chorischen Organisationen (Gesangvereine) der bürgerlich Mittel- und Unterschichte im Raum Frankfurt am Main von 1800 bis zur Gegenwart* (diss., Frankfurt am Main, 1964).

SACRED HARMONIC SOCIETY, *Annual Report for 1838* (London, 1838).

SCHAEFER, M., 'Les Anciennes Orgues Silbermann du Temple-Neuf à Strasbourg', in R. Minder (ed.), *La Musique en Alsace hier et aujourd'hui* (Strasbourg, 1970), 95.

SCHLEGEL, KLAUS, *Besselich am Mittelrhein* (Cologne, 1980).

SCHMIDT, HANS, *Musik-Institut Koblenz* (Koblenz, 1983).

SCHREIBER, JOHANN HEINRICH, *Das Münster zu Freiburg im Breisgau* (Karlsruhe and Freiburg, 1826).

—— *Freiburg im Breisgau, mit seinen Umgebungen: Geschichte u. Beschreibung* (Freiburg im Breisgau, 1825; 3rd edn. [1852]).

SCHUMANN, ROBERT, *Tagebücher*, ed. Gerd Nauhaus (Leipzig, 1971–87); Eng. trans. of the joint section of Robert and Clara as *The Marriage Diaries of Robert & Clara Schumann*, trans. Peter Ostwald (London, 1994).

SCOTT, HEW, *Fasti Ecclesiae Scoticanae*, new edn., ed. William S. Crockett and Francis Grant (Edinburgh, 1915–28).

SEATON, DOUGLASS, *A Study of a Collection of Mendelssohn's Sketches and Other Autograph Material, Deutsche Staatsbibliothek Berlin 'Mus. Ms. Autogr. Mendelssohn 19'* (diss. Columbia Univ., 1977).

SEYBOTH, ADOLF, *Das alte Strassburg vom 13. Jahrhundert bis zum Jahre 1870* (Strasbourg, 1890).

—— *Strasbourg historique et pittoresque* (Strasbourg, 1894).

SITZMANN, ÉDOUARD, *Dictionnaire de biographie des hommes célèbres de l'Alsace* (Rixheim, 1909–10).

SOLOMON, MAYNARD, 'Antonie Brentano and Beethoven', *Music and Letters*, 58 (1977), 153–69.

STEPF, JOHANN HEINRICH, *Gallerie aller juridische Autoren* (Leipzig, 1820–2).

STERN, CAROLA, *'Ich möchte mir Flügel wünschen': Das Leben der Dorothea Schlegel* (Reinbek bei Hamburg, 1990).

STRUCK, WOLF-HEINO, *Wiesbaden im Biedermeier* (Geschichte der Stadt Wiesbaden, 5; Wiesbaden, 1981).

—— *Wiesbaden in der Goethezeit* (Geschichte der Stadt Wiesbaden, 4; Wiesbaden, 1979).

SUHR, NORBERT, *Philipp Veit (1793–1877): Leben und Werk eines Nazareners: Monographie und Werkverzeichnis* (Weinheim, 1991).

Summer Tourist's Pocket Companion, or Continental Note-Book (The), No. 1: The Rhine (London, 1838).

THIEBES, BRUNO, *Kleines Dombuch: Einführung in Geschichte, Bau und Bedeutung des Domes zu Speyer*, 7th enlarged edn. (Speyer, 1990).

THIEME, ULRICH, and BECKER, FELIX (edd.), *Allgemeines Lexikon der bildenden Künstler* (Leipzig, 1907–50).

THISTLETHWAITE, NICHOLAS, *Birmingham Town Hall Organ* (Birmingham, 1984).

TOEPKE, GUSTAV (ed.), *Die Matrikel der Universität Heidelberg*, pt. 5 1807–1847 (Heidelberg, 1904).

WALDECK, FLORIAN, *Alte Mannheimer Familien*, vol. i (Mannheim, 1920).

WARD JONES, PETER, 'Mendelssohn and his English Publishers', in R. Larry Todd (ed.), *Mendelssohn Studies* (Cambridge, 1992), 240–55.

WEECH, FRIEDRICH VON, *Badische Biographien* (Heidelberg, 1875–1906).

WEICK, WILDERICH, *Freiburg im Breisgau und seine Umgebungen* (Freiburg, 1838).

WEINDEL, PHILIPP, *Der Dom zu Speyer: Geschichte, Beschreibung*, 6th edn. (Speyer, 1990).

WEIZSÄCKER, HEINRICH, and DESSOFF, ALBERT (edd.), *Kunst und Künstler in Frankfurt im neunzehnten Jahrhundert* (Frankfurt am Main, 1907–9).

WERNER, ERIC, *Mendelssohn: A New Image of the Composer and his Age* (New York, 1963); rev. edn. in German as *Mendelssohn: Leben und Werk in neuer Sicht* (Zurich, 1980).

[WIESBADEN], 'Kurze Chronik des "Hotel Rose"', *Hotel Rose Almanach*, 1959, No. 1 (Wiesbaden, 1959).

WILSON, MARIAN, 'Mendelssohn's Wife: Love, Art and Romantic Biography', *Nineteenth-Century Studies*, 6 (1992), 1–18.

WURZNACH, CONSTANT VON, *Biographisches Lexikon des Kaiserthums Österreich* (Vienna, 1856–91).

Index